The Will to Win

JOHN EGAN AND JAGUAR

The Will to Win

JOHN EGAN AND JAGUAR

John Underwood

W H ALLEN

First published in Great Britain in 1989 by
W.H. Allen & Co. Plc
Sekforde House, 175–9 St John Street
London EC1V 4LL

British Library Cataloguing in Publication Data

Underwood, John
  John Egan and Jaguar: the will to win.
  1. Great Britain. Motor vehicle industries: Jaguar Cars Ltd
  I. Title
  338.7'6292'0941

  ISBN 1–85227–185–X

Set in Meridien by Phoenix Photosetting
Printed and bound in Great Britain by
Mackays of Chatham PLC, Chatham, Kent

For Jack and Ella

Contents

Illustrations

───────────────────────────────

(*Unless otherwise indicated, photographs are reproduced courtesy of Jaguar Cars.*)

Hectic trading on the Stock Exchange floor (*Press Association Photos*)

The scramble for shares at Barclays Bank (*Press Association Photos*)

Guy Edwards dragging Niki Lauda from his blazing car, Nurburgring, 1976 (*Guy Edwards*)

The winning Jaguar XJR-8 racing car in the 1987 World Championships at Fuji, Japan

Tom Walkinshaw, the brains behind the Jaguar racing team

The XJ40 undergoing rigorous testing, complete with camouflage panels

Over 100 support staff were needed at Le Mans, 1988 (*Alain Lockyer*)

Victorious Jan Lammers leads the Jaguar convoy at Le Mans

Lammers and members of the Jaguar team celebrate victory (*Alain Lockyer*)

The 1989 Jaguar racing team (*Guy Edwards*)

Jaguar cars rely on traditional craftsmanship and new high technology

Sir John Egan

The board members of Jaguar Cars

Jaguar's US headquarters

Jaguar's Japanese headquarters

Acknowledgements

THIS BOOK would not have been possible without the help of many past and present employees of Jaguar Cars. Some asked not to be named: others I can thank openly. I am particularly grateful to David Boole, Jaguar's director of Communications and Public Affairs, and also to his assistant, Bridget Tedds. Seven other directors of Jaguar Cars granted me interviews, sometimes several times. They were Jim Randle (Engineering), Roger Putnam (Marketing), Kenneth Edwards (Personnel and company secretary), Patrick Audrain (Purchasing), Michael Beasley (assistant managing director) and John Edwards (Finance). The seventh was the chairman and chief executive, Sir John Egan, without whose assistance this book would have been infinitely more difficult to write.

A number of other senior Jaguar executives gave freely of their time, including Gerry Lawlor, who introduced me to the robots at the Castle Bromwich plant; John Morgan, who explained much about the company's overseas sales; and Thomas E. McDonnell of Jaguar Cars Inc., the New Jersey-based subsidiary that sells Jaguar cars into the North American market. Many former Jaguar personnel also helped me, including Bob Berry, Bob Knight, Hamish Orr-Ewing and Andrew White. Mr White, a former Jaguar manager, wrote several books about Jaguar cars. Sadly he died as this book was being prepared.

I am also grateful to: Liz Austin of the Institution of Mechanical

Engineers; Fenella Rogers of the London Chamber of Commerce for obtaining copies of Sir John Egan's public speeches; staff at the *Blackpool Evening Gazette* and Kenneth Shenton at Blackpool's Arnold School for information on Sir William Lyons's early life; John Costin of General Motors and John Neil of Unipart for their insight into Sir John Egan's management philosophy; and Guy Edwards and Tom Walkinshaw for help with my research into Jaguar's racing programme. I am also indebted to a number of people in the City of London, particularly Christopher Will of Shearson Lehman Hutton and Gavin Launders of Kleinwort Benson. I would also like to thank Christopher Hird for access to his papers on the privatisation of Jaguar. In the West Midlands both the Engineering Employers Association and the Transport and General Workers' Union provided invaluable assistance. At the former I particularly wish to thank Dr Cedric Thomas, and at the latter, Ron Newcombe.

I also received help from Geoffrey Robinson, a former chief executive of Jaguar and Labour MP for the company's home constituency, and from the Rt. Hon. John Moore MP, Conservative minister responsible for the privatisation of Jaguar, who granted me a lengthy interview.

I am grateful to Collins Publishers for permission to quote from Sir Michael Edwardes's *Back from the Brink*; to the *Sun* and *The Sunday Times* for permission to quote from articles by Sir John Egan published in 1987 and 1984; and to the *Daily Mail*, London, for the extract quoted on p. 145.

Several academics gave me helpful advice, including Rick Brown (University of Bradford Management Centre), Padma Nathan (Henley Management College) and Professor Garel Rhyss (University of Wales). Press officers at Mercedes-Benz and BMW also gave me their co-operation.

I would like to thank Alain Lockyer for help in obtaining a number of the photographs used in this book. (Where an appropriate acknowledgement for photographs has proved impossible, the publishers will gladly rectify any omission in future printings.) Many thanks also to David Weiland for his assistance during the research phase, and Gill Gibbins of W.H. Allen for her support and encouragement over many months.

Introduction

WHEN THE popular ITV series *The Sweeney* was launched in 1974, the title sequence included a car chase. In the first series the police were driving a Jaguar. By the time the second series was made they were driving a Ford Granada. *The Sweeney* summed up all that was wrong with Jaguar in the 1970s. It was a car for bank robbers and barrow boys; respectable people like policemen drove something more reliable.

In Dallas, Texas, there is a Jaguar dealer who likes to play a small practical joke on his new customers. When they arrive at his immaculate premises he leads them down a long corridor towards a room where the car is waiting. As they walk he apologises for the fact that the car is not as clean as it should be, but promises to give it a full valet when it comes in for a service. Then he apologises for the fact that the windscreen wiper does not work but assures the customer that it will be fixed. By the time the hapless buyer arrives at the end of the corridor and the end of a catalogue of faults, he or she is beginning to wonder whether it would not have been wiser to purchase a BMW. The door opens into a completely dark room – then several spotlights illuminate a perfect, glistening, matchless new Jaguar. Few buyers fail to appreciate this amusing touch or the expensive personal gift on the front seat.

Under the stewardship of Sir John Egan, Jaguar was transformed from an organisation losing a million pounds a week to a company that was hailed as the jewel in the crown of Mrs Thatcher's economic 'miracle'. As the bull market of the 1980s raged Jaguar was privatised, immediately becoming a popular wonder share. In less than three years the value of the company's stock rose almost fourfold. Production jumped, turnover leapt and profits raced ahead. But in the boardroom at Coventry a time bomb was ticking away. When Jaguar was privatised a special golden share was retained by the government to ensure that the company was not immediately taken over by a large competitor. That vital holding remains in existence until the early 1990s when it will be redeemed, leaving Jaguar to the tender mercies of the market. Little did anybody think at the time of privatisation that when the golden share expired corporate raiders would be travelling the world looking for tempting takeover targets and that a company like Jaguar could easily fall victim.

Jaguar now seems a perfect product of 1980s Thatcherite Britain. It appears to be governed by traditional values, but behind the leather and polished wood trim is the hard cutting edge of new technology. On the front cover of the annual report an elderly craftsman works on a hand-cut walnut veneer, while in Coventry the cars are built by robots. The ethos of Jaguar may seem to be that of its paternalistic founding father, Sir William Lyons, but today's management style borrows rather more heavily from Japan.

In the 1980s the Jaguar car company has been recast. It is no longer a manufacturing-led company, it is a marketing-led company in which 'satisfying customers' is the key to success. But all the marketing in the world will not sell cars if demand is weak and despite the best efforts of dealers like the one in Dallas, Jaguar's sales in the paramount North American market have fallen. Profits are down too – in the six months to June 1989, Jaguar ran at a loss for the first time since the early 1980s. On the afternoon of 19 September 1989, Lindsey Halstead, of the American Ford Motor Company, telephoned Sir John Egan and told him that Ford proposed to buy 15 per cent of Jaguar's shares – the maximum permissible while the golden share remained in place. His call was the prelude to an increasingly familiar corporate contest. This book tells the story of an independent British company, and shows how it became the target of foreign predators.

1

Money in the bank

THE VILLAGE of Mulsanne in the Department of Sarthe in northern France is known for poultry and fine wine: capons in sparkling cider are a local speciality. According to a local stone memorial it is also the spot from which Wilbur Wright made his first-ever flight in Europe. In every other sense the village appears entirely unremarkable. Mulsanne is approached along the *route nationale* RN 138 that runs from Alençon to Tours. Like many roads in this part of France it is a perfectly straight, tree-lined avenue. This road, however, has been recently resurfaced.

For 51 weeks of every year Mulsanne is just another sleepy French village, but for a few days in the middle of June it is awoken from slumber. The village is five miles from Le Mans, the town that gives its name to the 24-hour endurance race, and for these few days the RN 138 here is closed to the public, echoing instead to the roar of the fastest, most powerful motor racing cars in the world. The 3½-mile stretch of road leading into the village becomes the longest 'straight' in motor racing. Seven-litre engines that produce 700 horsepower at 7000 revolutions per minute shatter the peace of the Sarthe countryside. The French call it 'la ligne droite des Hunaudières' after the hotel-restaurant halfway between the village and Le Mans. Racing enthusiasts know it simply as the Mulsanne straight.

The Le Mans circuit is a collection of kinks, bends and chicanes. The final bend before the Mulsanne straight is called 'Tertre Rouge'. As a prototype sports car accelerates into the straight you can near the driver changing up through the gears. The whining pitch of the engine climbs higher and higher. The sound carries across the flat countryside and only dies when it is swamped by the sound of the next car passing through.

As the driver leaves 'Tertre Rouge' he faces the moment of greatest danger. He will pump the accelerator hard to the ground and suddenly the car will be travelling at almost 250 mph – faster than Formula One Grand Prix cars ever travel. The speed itself is not especially dangerous. Danger comes because it takes over 60 seconds to travel the 3½ miles of the straight. There are no bends, no gear changes, no deceleration. In fact there is nothing to concentrate the mind. A driver must fight constantly to ensure his attention does not wander to the trees, to the sun's rays, to the scattered buildings along the road. Sometimes a driver will try to save fuel by tucking in behind a rival and allowing the lead car's slipstream to pull the slower car along. The lead driver may start to weave and twist to break the other's advantage. Occasionally two drivers will enter the Mulsanne straight together. One may choose the left-hand carriageway, the other the right. They will spend what seems like an eternity travelling side by side at 250 mph.

Le Mans is a race of compromises. Team managers need to maximise speed while minimising fuel consumption. They must build in enough downforce to stop the car from leaving the ground at 250 mph while at the same time ensuring it is not too difficult to handle through the slow corners. Speed and safety vie for attention. As the Jaguar works team prepared for the 1988 Le Mans race, the Mulsanne straight held, for them, particularly chilling memories. In 1987 Win Percy had been driving a Jaguar XJR-8LM along that straight when he suffered a 'blow-out'. As his left rear tyre disintegrated, any hope of controlling the car was lost with it. The XJR-8LM hit the crash barrier, turned over and screeched along the road upside down at more than 200 mph before coming to a halt. Fortunately for Percy, the main structure of the car remained intact and his helmet, which had been dragging along the road, saved his life. No other racing driver has ever survived a crash at that speed. After the 1987 race it was decided to resurface the Mulsanne straight and to install new triple-layer crash barriers.

Behind the pits area is a concrete car park. For the weekend of the Le

Mans race it takes on the appearance of a tented city: the rich and powerful nomads of the international racing circuit descend on Sarthe for a contest which, to them, has taken on the mantle of a sacred event. Each of the race teams has its own compound, a bizarre mixture of marquees, luxury caravans and repair trucks. For 24 hours this compound will be home for drivers, mechanics, team managers and assorted hangers-on. Above the main tent flutters the team's national flag or perhaps its corporate pennant. Some teams have even gone to the trouble of laying Astroturf between the tents. The Porsche compound is decorated with beautiful, fragile flowers that seem inappropriate against the backdrop of powerful engines and fast racing cars. Beyond the edges of the main encampment are the smaller, scattered tents of the camp followers, the racing fanatics who follow the circus from track to track.

For the 1988 attempt on Le Mans the Jaguar racing team developed their most powerful car ever. A tuned version of the V12 engine was engineered into a body shell designed and developed to give maximum downforce and low drag. The connecting rods were made of steel and titanium, the fuel injection was controlled by a sophisticated electronic management system, and at full speed the car spat out fumes from twelve individual exhaust pipes. It owed its superb road-holding to an aerodynamic design that helped 'suck' the car down on to the road, ensuring that it would grip the road surface more effectively, especially when cornering. This was particularly useful, given that most racing circuits consist of a large number of corners separated by a few short straights. The Le Mans circuit, however, consists of a series of bends separated by the long Mulsanne straight. Too much downforce on the straight would place excessive strain on the car and slow it down, so the bodywork was redesigned to lower the drag when the car was travelling at top speed but without losing too much downforce on the bends.

When the Jaguar racing team managers were satisfied they had the right design they decided to improve their chances of victory by entering no fewer than five XJR-9LMs at Le Mans. Leaving nothing to chance, they hired the best drivers in the world. Even by motor racing standards, Jaguar's line-up read like an international *Who's Who* of the rich and glamorous, the fast and the faster.

The best-known driver was John Watson, who had won several Grand Prix in the late 1970s and early 1980s. Born in Belfast, he had first driven, in his father's car, at the age of nine. Before joining Jaguar he had driven for the company's arch rivals, the Porsche racing team. Watson was partnered in No. 3 car by Raul Boesel and Henri Pescarolo. Boesel was a 31-year-old Brazilian who now lives in Miami. In his youth he had been more interested in showjumping than in motor racing. At college he had won the Brazilian National Showjumping Championship and for a while it seemed he would follow his father into the family's highly successful property development business. His interest in racing sprang from a visit to a local kart race. In just five years he climbed to the very top of the motor racing tree with a place in the March Formula One Grand Prix team. In 1987 he switched to racing prototype sports cars, becoming the World Champion driver in his first year. Frenchman Henri Pescarolo is now just about the most experienced Le Mans driver in the world. He has driven the 24-hour race on no fewer than 22 occasions and has won the race four times.

Apart from Watson, Boesel and Pescarolo, Jaguar had brought in the top American drivers Danny Sullivan, Davy Jones, Price Cobb and Kevin Cogan as well as the talented Danish driver John Nielsen. There was room for just two Englishmen, one of them Martin Brundle. Brundle was the young favourite of the Jaguar fans. When he was in his early twenties he had partnered the veteran racing driver, Stirling Moss, in a series of saloon car races and it was not long before he was offered a contract by the Tyrrell Formula One team.

But the most formidable array of driving talent was reserved for the No. 2 car. Dutchman Jan Lammers was brought up in the seaside town of Zandvoort, home of the famous Dutch racing circuit, where he worked as a teenager. He won national and international championships at every level of motor racing before moving up to Formula One in 1979. By Le Mans 1988, he was one of Jaguar's most valued drivers.

Lammers's Scottish partner was John Colum Crichton-Stuart, Earl of Dumfries, better known as Johnny Dumfries, another who had graduated from karting to Formula One and built a reputation for himself as a test driver, working variously for Williams, Lotus, Brabham, McLaren and Ferrari. In 1986 he joined Ayrton Senna in the prestigious John

Player Special Lotus Grand Prix team before turning to sports car racing. He had driven for all three of the top manufacturers – Jaguar, Porsche and Mercedes – and at the 1987 Le Mans had set a new lap record. The third driver in the No. 2 car was Englishman Andy Wallace, who at just 27 years of age was widely recognised as one of Britain's most promising young drivers. He had never driven the Le Mans circuit until the week before the big race. He had certainly never before driven such ferociously fast cars as the Jaguar XJR-9LMs. His youth and inexperience were matched only by his determination. The line-up of Jaguar drivers was completed by Irishman Derek Daly and Australian Larry Perkins.

The drivers are supported by a team of over 100 people. Engineers, mechanics and designers are supplemented with crew chiefs, refuelling technicians, time-keepers, signallers and radio experts. There is even a company fire-fighting team. Behind the scenes are medical staff, physiotherapists and caterers.

The drivers' preparation for the race – a strict diet and a course of exercise – is overseen by a team of doctors, but in the days leading up to the big event a healthy diet gives way to an orgy of junk food, pizza and pasta. Endurance racing is a sedentary sport, but drivers nevertheless use a great deal of energy. The need for stamina prompts them to store carbohydrates in the body as long-term energy, to be released over the 24-hour period. On the morning of the race itself the drivers may feel a little sluggish, but adrenalin will pep them up and as the race wears on the stored energy will be released. At 250 mph a driver's pulse rate can rise to over 200 beats per minute compared with the standard rate of 60 or 70, and the body will use a great deal of energy.

Throughout the race the drivers will need to drink plenty of liquid. The temperature in the cockpit of a Jaguar racing car can rise to 150°F, so drivers sweat profusely and lose a great deal of body fluid. Some make use of a drinking bottle fixed to the interior of the car and fitted with a flexible tube that connects with a mouthpiece inside their racing helmet. A driver can take a few sips as he hurtles along the Mulsanne straight without taking his hands off the steering wheel.

When the driver hands over to a team mate he has a long high-energy drink before retiring to his caravan in the team compound. He will do some exercises to avoid stiffening up and may then have a massage, courtesy of a team physiotherapist. He will eat and rest but he will not sleep. Adrenalin will keep him going for well over the 24 hours of the race. Like Olympic athletes, some of the drivers have their own training coaches and for many it is not simply a matter of preparing for Le Mans: there are other motor sporting commitments for them in the period leading up to the race. Some of the drivers must fly in from America and overcome the effects of jet lag before they can perform at their peak.

Three p.m., Saturday, 11 June. A year of corporate preparation and a week of practice and scrutineering have ended. The 'warm-up lap' of the 8½-mile circuit has been completed and the pace car has turned from the home straight into the pit lane. A blur of bright colours rushes across the starting grid. The noise of the howling engines drowns every other sound as it reverberates around the roof of the main stand. Le Mans 1988 is under way.

The Porsche of Hans Stuck goes into an immediate lead followed by another Porsche and the Jaguar of Jan Lammers. It is not long before Lammers has overtaken both cars. It soon becomes clear the race is to be a duel between the purple and white of Coventry and the red and yellow of Stuttgart: with the race just minutes old, Jaguar and Porsche cars hold the first fifteen places between them.

The frontrunners soon suffered their first setbacks. The most favoured Jaguar, driven by Brundle and Nielsen, ran into a gravel pit shortly after turning out of the Mulsanne straight. In a calculated gamble, the drivers had decided to run their car without a rear roll bar in an attempt to lessen the structural strain, a decision which made them slower on the straight, which in turn forced them to use more fuel; so in order to keep to their fuel limit they had to drive much harder round the bends. As the pressure on the drivers built up, an accident became almost inevitable. Fortunately nobody was hurt. The leading Porsche of Stuck, Ludwig and Bell was also in trouble, losing several minutes when a reserve fuel tank failed to operate, leaving the stricken car to limp round the circuit almost out of fuel.

Competition was intense. In the first three hours the lead changed fifteen times as Jaguar struggled to deal with an unforeseen problem. The resurfacing work on the Mulsanne straight had made that section

of road unexpectedly flat and true, upsetting Jaguar's precise calcula-
tions about fuel mixture and aerodynamics. Each car had to be brought
into the pits for minor adjustments without which they would have
been travelling too slowly or consuming too much fuel. As evening
approached, the fastest Jaguars and Porsches would sometimes swap
the lead twice in a single lap. The insistent, professional roar of the
Jaguars seemed to signal some special will to win. Yet the Porsches
sounded altogether lighter, as if stripped bare, ready for action.

As darkness falls even the most fervent fan finds it difficult to follow the
intricacies of endurance racing. There is an exodus from the circuit to
the 24-hour funfair. It is this carnival atmosphere that gives Le Mans its
unique attraction, with stalls and sideshows, bars and restaurants,
games and competitions spread round the perimeter of the track. In a
special reception area the Department of Sarthe makes the most of its
annual marketing opportunity. 'Have a taste of Sarthe,' exhorts the
welcoming banner. Journalists and VIPs are plied with local sparkling
wine, chicken and mushroom casserole and hard-boiled eggs stamped
with the slogan 'Love: 24 *heures du Mans*'.

A shop run by Jaguar's sponsors, the Gallaher cigarette brand 'Silk
Cut', sells Jaguar books, Jaguar radios and other Jaguar merchandise.
Another stand offers Jaguar designer clothes for sale. There is a mobile
Jaguar exhibition centre featuring a company racing car that revolves
on a turntable before an admiring public. Both the suited corporate
salesmen and the bare-chested French stall holders do a roaring trade
with the 50,000 British fans who have travelled to Sarthe for the race.
One wears a sheet round his shoulders in the fashion of a cape bearing
the slogan 'Brundle – No. 1 Top Cat'. Another devotee carries a rough
stave with a company flag above a Union Jack. Jaguar is nothing if not
British.

Every other spectator is wearing a sun cap with built-in radio aerial
and ear phones. This cheap headgear enables the fan to receive constant reaction, speculation, gossip and lap timings through the local
radio commentary. Each cap has a team logo on it – Porsche, Mercedes,
Jaguar. The Jaguar caps are the first to sell out. The main commentary is
provided in French but there is also a low-powered FM radio station,
Radio Le Mans, that gives an English language commentary in the area

round the racing circuit. It is expensive to organise and operate; it therefore needs a sponsor. Jaguar Cars have offered their support.

In the all-consuming drive to squeeze every ounce of publicity out of their racing programme, Jaguar took every square inch of advertising space on the giant spectator stand immediately opposite the team's pit position. If a Jaguar driver wins at Le Mans he will bring his victorious car to a halt directly opposite this stand. Wherever they point their cameras the press photographers will get a lensful of Jaguar's corporate logo. The leaping cat will spring into every celluloid frame, it will adorn the front pages of newspapers round the world and Sir John Egan, Jaguar's chairman and chief executive, will marvel once again at how valuable the company's racing programme really is.

Those who are involved with the financing of Jaguar's bid for glory are sworn to secrecy over the figures, but they will confirm that it costs less than mounting a Formula One challenge. The best estimate is that Jaguar's racing programme costs around £30 million a year, much of which comes from sponsorship – a lot of money, but cheaper than advertising. Jaguar is certainly not at Le Mans for the prize money: the race entry fee is just over £1000 and the winner receives little more than £3000. When Sir John launched Jaguar's 1988 racing programme with a lavish reception at the Royal Automobile Club in London's West End, he said racing was '. . . a cost-effective way of advertising our products'. The publicity cost-to-benefit equation is only the tip of the iceberg. 'Our engineers learn from the entrepreneurial spirit of the race engineers,' he explained, and Jaguar expects that spirit to be reflected within the company. Racing success helps build the morale of Jaguar's workforce. Hundreds, sometimes thousands, of Jaguar workers travel to race meetings to watch the team in action and when the star drivers visited the main factory they were besieged for their autographs.

A racing presence helps attract young, talented engineers to the company and racing is also a valuable sales aid. Wherever Jaguar races there is a dealer within 20 miles and that dealer will use the race meeting as an opportunity to flatter and pamper prospective customers. Just as importantly, the racing programme also acts as a useful test bed for production components: Jaguar's production departments genuinely value the feedback they receive from the racing team.

But the most important perspective on the company's racing programme is the part it plays in supporting and building the Jaguar image. Market research carried out amongst Jaguar owners has revealed that they 'expect' Jaguar to be involved in international motor racing. Yet racing may still seem an odd way to promote luxury cars, especially those with the understated cachet of quality and excellence that belongs to Jaguar. The corporate image is based on a degree of restraint. Many Jaguar owners have, or like to think they have, an aura of 'older money' about them, unlike the younger Porsche owner who is more likely to have made a small fortune in the City of London during the 'Big Bang'. Jaguar proudly boasts that as many as four hides are used to cover the seats of just one car; that the burr walnut veneers are hand-cut by craftsmen, which means that no two cars will ever have an identical set of fascia and door cappings; that every Jaguar engine is assembled by hand; and that the limousine's carefully designed front seats are adjustable in eight different ways and covered in hand-stitched leather that is matched both for grain and colour.

Combined with this image of old-style values is another of modern, hi-tech design and performance. The average Jaguar buyer now expects his or her car to exhibit the quality and reliability that come only with computer-aided design and manufacture. That is where the company's racing programme comes in. Performance and reliability on the racing circuit help reinforce the image of those qualities on the road. And for Sir John Egan, image is inextricably linked with demand. 'You try to make your image as strong as possible,' he says, 'and the result is that demand for your goods will grow. If you successfully build your company image it is like putting money in the bank.'

2

The pride of Lyons

IT IS A commonly held view, in the motor industry and elsewhere, that there is 'something' about Jaguar cars that marks them out from every other car. Implicit within this observation is the notion that this special attribute is of real, positive value. It is often defined as the car's classic lines or its elegant curves or its feline shape. Sometimes the quality engineering will be mentioned or the very English mood of the car, with its fine leather upholstery and its hand-cut walnut veneers. More often Jaguars are simply said to have some special mystique, image, mythology or even personality. Most commonly critics and enthusiasts ascribe to them a combination of all these qualities and may perhaps throw in a very practical comment as well: that Jaguars are, for example, outstanding value for money or that the basic shape of the car does not date very quickly.

It is difficult to define this peculiar 'Jaguar' trademark but one thing is apparent. While other companies make cars that are designed by designers, Jaguar makes cars that are styled by stylists – at Jaguar the word 'designer' is reserved for technical engineering staff. It is also possible to make a clear observation about the basic shape of Jaguar cars. They tend to be very low, very wide vehicles in which the relationship between wheels and bodywork is such that a car appears to have 'haunches' at the back: a Jaguar looks uncannily like the leaping cat after which it is named. The one factor, however, that really makes a

Jaguar car a Jaguar is often ignored or overlooked. Ever since the company was formed in 1922 every new Jaguar car has stemmed from the inspiration of one man – Sir William Lyons.

William Lyons was born in Blackpool in 1901, the son of an Irish musician who had met and married a local woman, Minnie Barcroft, during a tour of the Lancashire seaside resort. William Lyons senior decided to settle in Blackpool and set up what became a thriving small business: Lyons's Music and Pianoforte Warehouse.

The young William Lyons was educated as a day pupil at Arnold House, a school founded in 1896 by its first head, Frank Truswell Pennington. The wealthy ruling class of Blackpool thought he was the perfect teacher who could offer an education they felt was fitting for their sons. The pupils in his care, however, saw Pennington as a hard taskmaster with an intimidating appearance, but if he might seem somewhat terrifying by present-day standards he was also a man who recognised that education involved more than success in examinations alone. He believed in education in its widest sense, holding that his school should encourage and kindle in its pupils a wide range of interests and a thirst for knowledge.

In the young William Lyons, Frank Pennington found a source of great irritation. Lyons was not one of the school's academic achievers. He was keen on running and he is mentioned in the school magazine as a member of his House soccer team but his major interest in life was motorcycles and therein lay the cause of F. T. Pennington's exasperation. Had Lyons been interested in his school work as well, the head might have looked more kindly upon him but Lyons's interest in motorcycles was to the exclusion of his studies.

According to an old schoolfriend he was a 'dunce' who was 'always in trouble'. Homework was not handed in on time, Lyons was kept behind after school hours in detention and Pennington often suggested that he would never get anywhere in life and that his place would be better filled by a more enthusiastic scholar. Neither Lyons nor Pennington was sorry to part company in 1918. William's father wanted him to join the family firm but instead he went to work for a Manchester vehicle manufacturer. His stay there did not last long. An entrepreneurial spirit was stirring in him and he came back home determined to start his own business.

For a while after his return to Blackpool Lyons worked in the retail motor trade. He bought and sold various motorcycles and took part in numerous competitions, including sprints on Southport Sands. He also spent some time languishing in his father's firm but the business opportunity for which he was searching did not appear until the early 1920s.

The Lyons family were then living on the corner of King Edward Avenue and Holmfield Road, a few hundred yards from the Blackpool seafront. In 1921 another house, on the other side of the road, was purchased by a family called Walmsley, from Stockport. Tom Walmsley was a wealthy coal merchant who had decided to retire to Blackpool. His son, another William, made motorcycle sidecars.

From his corner house William Lyons could look across the road junction to a narrow alleyway that ran past the back of the Walmsley home. It was up this alleyway that William Walmsley carried the materials needed to construct his sidecars. But Walmsley's were no ordinary sidecars. While standard models were dull and drab, his motorcycle 'chairs', called Swallows, were stylish, attractive and aerodynamically designed. William Lyons decided to buy one and as a result of his purchase he struck up a friendship with William Walmsley.

Lyons could see great potential in Walmsley's new product. It had all the fundamental qualities that were later to characterise the cars Lyons created. The Swallow sidecar was not in fact revolutionary in either concept or engineering: it was simply a racy, attractive version of a very standard design. Today it might be said that Walmsley's product was perfect for 'niche merchandising'. In 1921 William Lyons simply spotted a gap in the market.

Lyons tried to persuade Walmsley that the two of them should set up in business and increase production but at first Walmsley was not convinced. Eventually, early in 1922, he was persuaded and the two partners began trading as the Swallow Sidecar Company. They had four employees and an overdraft facility of £1000 guaranteed at the local branch of Williams Deacon's Bank, half by Walmsley's father and half by Lyons's father. The sum proved woefully inadequate but through repeated appeals to their bank manager the company was allowed to exceed its overdraft facility and keep its head above water. In the early days of the business William Lyons senior had to sign the cheques since his son was not yet 21 years old. On 4 September 1922 all that changed when Lyons came of age. Although Walmsley was eight years older than Lyons and therefore the senior partner, it was Lyons who was in charge of the cash. Every Saturday morning he went to the bank to collect the wages but usually arrived after it had closed. It meant that he often kept Swallow's employees waiting for their money.

The company was established on two storeys of an old building in Bloomfield Road, near the Blackpool football ground. The business plan, if it could be called that, was to build ten sidecars a week on chassis supplied by Montgomery's of Coventry. Swallow even offered optional extras: you could have electric instead of acetylene lighting! Within a year Swallow had its own stand at the national Motor Cycle Show and the company's sporting sidecars were displayed as accessories by no fewer than four motorcycle manufacturers.

The business went from strength to strength, flourishing on the wave of the post-war boom, but Lyons nevertheless felt that the market for motorcycle sidecars was limited. He wanted to broaden the company's horizons, to move into the world of motorcars, so he began to investigate the possibility of building a high-quality coachwork body on to a standard Austin Seven chassis. It was 1926, the year of the General Strike, and economic depression was about to engulf Britain. Some might have thought it the worst possible time to develop an expensive 'up-market' product. Lyons thought otherwise and his belief that the luxury car market would be little affected by economic slump has subsequently become an accepted axiom of the motor industry. By the middle of 1926 Swallow's production of sidecars was rising steadily, the number of employees had grown to 30 and the company needed to move into larger premises. The move was accomplished with minimum fuss and Lyons was able to advance his plans for a new car.

William Lyons was a great admirer of the Austin Seven, a car he felt to be 'wonderful value for money', but he thought the upright, square-rigged body was 'a very stark affair'. His plan was to give the car an attractive, luxurious look with a degree of refinement. In 1927 he bought two Austin Sevens and rebuilt them with new bodywork to produce an open-top two-seater and a saloon model. The cars' origins were barely recognisable. Lyons took the saloon to London where he showed it to Bertie Henly, a partner in the rapidly expanding Henly's retail motor business. Henly placed an immediate order for 500 of the new so-called Austin Swallows, but stipulated that his firm must have exclusive distribution rights in the south of England. Lyons, astonished at this speedy success, promptly agreed. He had no idea how he was going to make 500 of the new cars but he returned to Blackpool full of enthusiasm. The next few months would be a period of make or break.

The inability to cope with rapid expansion is one of the most common factors in the collapse of small businesses. The capacity of the Swallow works was just 12 cars and 100 sidecars a week, and when Austin Seven chassis began to arrive at the Blackpool railway station in quantity, Lyons could not cope. As the station yard filled to capacity, the station master became increasingly irate. Lyons and Walmsley made two important decisions: manufacture of cars would take precedence over motorcycle sidecars and the company must once again move into larger premises.

The first decision was underlined by a change of company name to the Swallow Sidecar and Coachbuilding Company. The second involved a major reorientation of the business and could not be achieved immediately. Swallow's supplies were coming largely from the Midlands and the type of labour the company now needed was also based there. So instead of moving into new premises in Blackpool the two partners decided that the company should relocate further south. After searching for several days Lyons found a disused munitions factory for sale in Coventry, one of four separate buildings on the same site and five times the size of the Blackpool plant. The company did not have the capital to purchase the factory outright so Lyons negotiated with the owners to lease it at a fair rent. The building required almost total renovation but when a contractor gave Lyons a price for repairing and repainting it the quote was found to be in excess of Swallow's total assets. Lyons and Walmsley hired a number of labourers and did the job themselves. In September 1928 the company moved to Coventry.

The first cars produced by Swallow were, by present-day standards, terribly botched jobs. The detachable roof was liable to spring open as the car was driven along and when Lyons found that his coachbuilt bodies would not precisely fit the Austin Seven chassis he generally employed brute force rather than engineering excellence to solve the problem. He discovered, for example, that he could not fit his own radiator cowling over the Austin radiator filler neck because the neck was half an inch too high. His solution was to place a piece of wood on top of the neck and to strike it a hefty blow, creating a depression in the brass header tank and reducing the height by the required amount.

The business was run in much the same way. Lyons had complete faith in his own judgement. He knew exactly what he was doing and why he was doing it but he always opted for improvisation and 'make do' and he was proud of that fact. He would tell the story of how he once received a requisition for a wheelbarrow. He sent it back, asking, 'What is wrong with the two buckets you have got?' He earned the reputation among his employees of being tight-fisted. As late as 1959 the Jaguar production lines consisted of trestles that were pulled along by chains. When they were eventually replaced, it was not with state-of-the-art technology but a second-hand track purchased from another motor manufacturer. Lyons believed that if you attempted to maintain the minimum cost base in business there was no factor that could seriously impede growth. In the late 1920s that simple creed was a recipe for business success on a grand scale. There is still much truth in it today. But as the years passed, Lyons failed to grasp that the increasing sophistication of automobile manufacture required investment on an almost unimaginable scale. His decision in the years after the Second World War to 'make do' with inefficient, poor equipment nearly brought about the extinction of Jaguar Cars in the late 1970s.

Lyons had another failing too: he rarely delegated important decisions to his managers or co-directors. His failure in this respect meant that few of his senior colleagues developed business skills or management expertise and when Lyons approached retirement his company faced a crisis of continuity. It is a tribute to Lyons's personality and a reflection of the times in which he lived that despite this failing his colleagues had little but praise for him.

Lyons can be criticised for his lack of long-term vision but it is a criticism that can only be made with hindsight. He was undeniably a shrewd businessman and his business principles were pure simplicity: a highly competitive pricing policy and value for money. To achieve these he identified six key factors crucial to the success of a luxury car manufacturer. First, he recognised the supreme need for a product that was capable of generating substantial consumer demand. Second, he acknowledged the need to manufacture that product with mass production techniques. Third, he believed the manufacturer should provide a good follow-up service. Fourth, he believed in running the production operation as economically as possible. Fifth, he tried to purchase components at the best possible price, consistent with certain standards of quality. And sixth, he recognised the need to concentrate exclusively on the luxury sector of the car market and to cover that sector with a range of models. The test of his perception is that 60 years on luxury car makers, from Germany to Japan and from Coventry to Detroit, and still trying to put his principles into practice.

The move to Coventry was not universally welcomed by the Swallow workforce: most adjusted to their new surroundings but families were split up and many people commuted at the weekend between Blackpool and Coventry. But it spurred William Lyons to even greater efforts. He worked a sixteen-hour day aiming to raise production from 12 cars a week to 50 a week within 3 months, realising that this would require the introduction of mass production techniques, as hitherto the framework of each Swallow car had been machined and assembled by an individual body-maker. The technique that was rapidly being introduced into the volume car business involved breaking down the manufacturing process into separate functions and assigning one worker to each. Lyons tried to institute the same system in his factory but at first it seemed the scheme would fail. The body-makers approached him *en masse* and told him it was too complicated. They urged him to return to the old production methods, but Lyons would hear none of it. He pressed on and eventually made the system work. Soon the company was reaching his production target of 50 cars a week.

Lyons was later to claim that the introduction of volume production techniques to the luxury car market represented a 'whole new approach' to the manufacture of specialist cars. It is doubtful whether Austin Swallows could at that time genuinely be classed as luxury cars, even less as true competitors of the likes of Bugatti; but Lyons's company certainly became a luxury car maker and it prospered, which is more than can be said for those specialist car makers that failed to introduce mass production techniques. In the years leading up to the

Second World War, Britain could boast numerous luxury car makers. Few of them remain in existence today.

As well as introducing mass production Lyons also brought in the payment system known as 'piecework', which involved payment by results. He conducted a crude 'time and motion' study to discover roughly how long certain production jobs took, then assigned a value to each process that corresponded with a weekly wage of around £5. Thus, if a particular task took one fifth of the working week it would be assigned a value of £1. He then printed a quantity of voucher books, one for each car produced, each voucher corresponding with a particular task. When a worker had completed that task he simply signed the voucher and presented it to the foreman for counter-signature. At the end of the day the vouchers were handed in to the wages clerk and at the end of the week the worker was paid a wage that corresponded with the number of vouchers he had signed.

For Lyons piecework represented a perfect guarantee that labour overheads would never be exceeded: the production of a car would cost a precise sum of money whether it took three days or three weeks to complete. From the workers' point of view the important thing about piecework was that timings and job rates should be fair. If they were not the employees would need to work unpaid overtime in order to earn their basic wage. Accounts now differ as to whether Lyons did pay fairly or not, but by his own account the Swallow workers often toiled deep into the night. The Swallow workforce was not always compliant, however. Lyons introduced piecework shortly before the move to Coventry and the new workers who were taken on during the first week in the Midlands signalled their objection to this method of payment by marching into the stores area where the completed vouchers were kept in bins and emptying the contents of the bins all over the floor. Lyons reacted in a typically unyielding fashion. He told the workers that piecework was there to stay and if they did not like it they could go and work somewhere else. Despite the fact that Britain was in the grip of mass unemployment, some chose to leave.

William Lyons held very strong views about trades unions. He believed that businesses existed to make profits and that trades unions stood in the way of that aim. For their part the trades unions felt that he was an old-fashioned manager with an appalling attitude towards his employees. When piecework payments were introduced, for example, it was not enough for him successfully to implement the new system – he insisted on having large notices displayed on the factory walls saying 'No Daywork Paid'. All the same, his methods were so successful that within a year of moving to Coventry the Swallow Company had expanded into the neighbouring factory and increased production to 100 cars a week. Profits were racing ahead and the company's range of cars had been extended as planned. At the 1929 Motor Show the Swallow stand included not just the Austin Swallow but also the Standard Swallow, the Swift Swallow and the Fiat Swallow, all cars with Swallow bodies built on to production chassis.

In appearance the new models were longer, sleeker and more stylish than the original Austin Swallow. By common consent Lyons had a flair for shaping cars that was quite exceptional. He was not an innovator but he had a crystal-clear perception of what his cars should look like. He often made preliminary sketches but because he had no great gift as a draughtsman he tended to work rather like a sculptor or model-maker, creating every experimental shape in three dimensions. Lyons would reject dozens of prototypes before having the 'body' brought to his home at Wappenbury Hall in Warwickshire. Only when he could see the embryonic car standing outside his front door could he be sure of whether the design was right or wrong. The key to his thinking was deceptively simple and correspondingly hard to define. In the words of Bob Berry, a former press and public relations director for Jaguar, 'If it looked right, it had to be right.'

The Swallow business was really beginning to prosper but Lyons was concerned that his bodywork styling was largely dictated by the design of the underlying chassis, often preventing him from achieving the truly sleek lines he sought. So, in 1930, Lyons had a chassis of his own designed, conceived to accommodate either the Standard-built 16-horsepower engine or the larger 20-horsepower version. The chassis was specially built by Rubery Owen and was delivered direct to the Standard Motor Company. Standard's chairman and managing director, R. W. Maudslay, agreed to build his company's engine, suspension and transmission on to it for delivery to the Swallow works. Maudslay, not altogether unreasonably, wanted the new car to be called a Standard. Lyons resisted his demand and after a long argument between the two men it was agreed to call this hybrid skeleton the 'SS1'.

There has been much speculation over the years as to what the initials 'SS' stood for. A press release issued by Jaguar's North American subsidiary shortly after privatisation in 1984 declared that 'SS' stood for Standard Swallow, though an earlier company document, currently held in the British Library, said 'SS' stood for Swallow Sport. Before his death Lyons intimated that the name might have been Standard Swallow or it might have been Swallow Special: the matter was never properly resolved. Whatever the truth of it, the argument over the name had undoubtedly originated in and reinforced Lyons's absolute determination to establish a marque of his own.

The SS1 was introduced on 9 October 1931 at the Olympia Motor Show in London where it caused a sensation. The elegant lines, the long bonnet and the 'low-slung' effect offered a degree of style virtually unknown to the average British motorist. It was certainly extraordinary value for money – it looked like a thousand-pound car but cost less than a third that price. The *Daily Express* carried a large front-page photograph and described the SS1 as a 'dream' car. Lyons signed up dealers and distributors throughout the country.

Sales grew encouragingly but, as with the earlier Austin Swallow, the new car was better on style than on performance, failing to achieve much success in road rallies but scoring in the so-called 'comfort' or 'coachwork' competitions. Despite Lyons's business skills, the company still had no after-sales service organisation, which led to major problems when defects began to show up: windscreens leaked, roofs leaked, the engine did not perform well and the rear seating was meagre to say the least. Quality had been lost in the drive for production and if Swallow was not to lose its reputation something had to be done. Even Lyons admitted that the SS1, 'did not quite live up to the promise of its appearance'. That was something of an understatement.

What was needed was a new body and a new engine designed to complement each other in order to achieve a car that had both good looks and good performance. But that would require major investment, the development of an engineering department and the opening of a machine shop. Typically, Lyons adopted a more thrifty approach. He began work on the design of a new body shell and hired an engineer called Harry Weslake to help design a modified version of the Standard Motor Company's 6-cylinder engine. Weslake was promised a bonus for every brake horsepower above 90 that he was able to coax from the engine. The Standard 6-cylinder was a fine engine but with modification it proved possible to increase its output from 70 horsepower to over 100 horsepower. When the alterations were complete Lyons was pleased with the engine's performance but predictably enough his obsession with image meant that the engine's appearance pleased him almost as much. He was later to observe, 'It made a good-looking unit.'

Over the next few years the production of Swallow's other products tailed off as the quantity and variety of SS cars increased. There was a 9-horsepower version (the SS2); an SS coupé design; open-top and saloon models; an SS1 drophead; and, in 1934, the final SS derivative, the SS1 Airline saloon. The SS marque was firmly established.

Eventually the word 'Sidecar' was dropped from the company name and in October 1933 Lyons registered a subsidiary company called SS Cars Ltd, later to become his main operating company. Although four-wheeled automobiles had taken over from sidecars as the company's most important product, manufacture of sidecars continued for some years, the supply of chassis being subcontracted to a number of different companies until 1935 when Grindlay's of Coventry took over the job. Grindlay continued to supply chassis until the outbreak of the Second World War and in 1945 the sidecar business was sold to the Helliwell Group, which in turn sold it to Tube Investments.

Throughout the years of their partnership William Lyons and William Walmsley had grown apart. If Walmsley had had the original idea from which their business had sprung it was certainly Lyons's business acumen that had developed it from a tiny affair operating out of Walmsley's garage into a major concern. William Walmsley, in Lyons's view, was frivolous, childish and lacking in business vision. To Walmsley, William Lyons was a business adventurer. The two men argued incessantly and eventually decided to split. When, in 1935, their company was floated, Walmsley sold his shares and retired. Lyons retained his 50 per cent of the business and later acquired additional shares in order to establish a majority shareholding. Walmsley dabbled for a while with the design and manufacture of caravans but in later years he withdrew altogether from business and devoted himself to his model railway on which he lavished much love and attention.

According to the late Andrew Whyte, a former press and public relations officer at Jaguar and author of an authoritative history of the company, William Walmsley was a 'rough and ready' man while William Lyons was a 'terrible snob'. In his later years, when Lyons was asked about his former partner, he would simply say, 'Terrible man! Terrible man!' In the official company history of Jaguar and its subsidiaries the name William Walmsley does not appear once. When William Walmsley died in 1961 two Jaguar directors went to his funeral. William Lyons did not attend.

3

Swallows and Jaguars

WILLIAM LYONS was now chairman and managing director of a public company but his majority shareholding allowed him to continue ruling over it like some personal fiefdom. His attitude to the workforce, to his managers and even to his co-directors remained cool and aloof. The business was run as if it was still Lyons's private company. The quality of the SS range of cars was gradually improving but Lyons's priority was to launch his new car with the engine that had been modified by Harry Weslake and which Standard had agreed to manufacture. A new chassis was being designed by Bill Heyness, later to become vice chairman (engineering) and Lyons himself worked on the body shell.

One overriding problem remained. What should the new car be called? The Swallow Coachbuilding Company had been acquired by Lyons's new holding company, SS Cars Ltd, but confusion over what exactly the initials 'SS' stood for meant the marque was not establishing itself in the public consciousness. Lyons decided that the new car needed a model name rather than just a set of ambiguous initials followed by a number. One day in 1936, Lyons asked his publicity people to provide him with a list of animals, fish and birds. In his own words he 'immediately pounced on "Jaguar" for it had an exciting sound to me'. It also reminded him of stories told by an old friend who had joined the Royal Flying Corps towards the end of the First World War. Based at Farnborough, he had worked as a mechanic on the

Armstrong Siddeley 'Jaguar' engine and he used to regale Lyons with stories about his work and about the famous engine. Consciously or not the name 'Jaguar' had become indelibly fixed in the young Lyons's mind. The company remained SS Cars Ltd but the new product was called the SS Jaguar. Shortly after the Second World War, when Lyons decided to change his company's name from SS Cars to Jaguar Cars, he wrote formally to Sir Frank Spriggs, the managing director of Armstrong Siddeley, to ask his permission, which was willingly given. Lyons then jealously guarded the name and although he later gave the British Aircraft Corporation permission to call their new jet fighter the Jaguar, he refused permission for the name to be used by a joint BAC/French development company.

With the name settled William Lyons was ready to launch his new car. It was introduced to the dealers and distributors with an extravagant reception held at the Mayfair Hotel in London. The car, with its Jaguar lines already clearly defined, was displayed on a circular dais. With characteristic style, Lyons invited his guests to guess the price of the SS Jaguar and to write it on a card provided for the purpose. When all the cards were gathered in they were added together and an 'average' guess was calculated. As a body, the dealers and distributors thought the car would sell for £765. When Lyons announced that the actual price was just £395 there was stunned amazement.

Among the Jaguar range was the SS Jaguar 100, a designation intended to underline the fact that the engine developed 100 brake horsepower and that the car could reach 100 mph. It was William Lyons's first genuine 100 mph car.

Demand for the SS Jaguars was strong and sales rose throughout the 1930s. In 1937 SS Cars introduced a major new industrial process. Wood-framed bodywork was replaced by all-steel panels; these were pressed by outside contractors and then assembled at the SS factory. The new process helped reduce weight, increase body strength and speed up the process of manufacturing, but before those savings were achieved the plant was in chaos. With a wood frame there was plenty of scope for physical adjustment: with metal pressings that was not possible. Not only would the panels not fit together, but there were also supply problems and in 1938 SS Cars came perilously close to making its first annual loss. The situation was retrieved during the summer months and from then until the outbreak of the Second World War William Lyons's factory produced some 250 SS Jaguars a week.

The 1930s saw Lyons become increasingly involved in motor sport and at the same time he began to sell a significant number of cars abroad. Unlike the earlier SS vehicles, the Jaguars achieved sweeping success on the rally circuits of Europe. In the late 1930s Jaguars won the Paris-to-Nice Rally, the RAC Rally, the Welsh Rally and the gruelling Alpine Rally.

The outbreak of war saw the run-down of the car business as the SS Company was turned over to the production of military hardware. Lyons's near legendary adaptability stood him in good stead. During the war his company made fuselages for Stirling bombers and Meteor jets; components for a host of other aircraft including Spitfires, Lancasters, Mosquitos and Oxfords; and no fewer than 100,000 military trailers and a multitude of other sundry war items. The SS Company even carried out some experimental work, developing four-wheeled alternatives to the motorcycle combination that was the favoured transport of airborne assault forces. It is likely that these new vehicles would have gone into production but for the fact that by 1944 aircraft design had advanced to the point where much heavier payloads could be lifted into the front line, thereby reducing the need for light transport. The company also had repair contracts for the Whitley and Wellington bombers. When the first Whitley bombers arrived at the Coventry factory, Lyons estimated that they would take a month to repair. Some of them were still there a year later: he had not allowed for the strict test rules laid down by the Aeronautical Inspection Directorate. For once his 'short cut' methods were not acceptable.

The SS Company's contribution to the war effort was substantial but the years 1939 to 1945 were also years in which William Lyons achieved much that would prove to be of value when hostilities ended. War work enabled him to build up a large machine shop, for example, an investment he had not previously made and which was achieved in part because of a contract to build the new Manchester bomber. Lyons constructed and partly equipped a new factory before the government decided to cancel the Manchester and re-establish the Whitley bomber, which had been assigned to the reserve list. The Coventry factory was also greatly improved thanks to a rebuilding programme put in hand to repair war damage.

By March 1945 the initials 'SS' had taken on a new and sinister meaning throughout Europe and it was then that Lyons decided to adopt the name 'Jaguar' not just as the model name for his cars but as the name for his company too. As the war drew to a close the Jaguar Car Company prepared to return to its main purpose, the production of luxury automobiles.

Post-war austerity measures made it difficult to obtain the materials needed to build cars. Steel was in particularly short supply: it was rationed and allocations depended on export performance. Before the war Jaguar had been able to sell just about all the cars it made on the domestic market, so exports had been a low priority. Now Lyons set out to convince the government that he could sell cars abroad. He prepared a document explaining how much steel he wanted, how many cars he could make, how many could be sold abroad and which countries he would be exporting to. He then presented the document, in person, to Sir George Turner, Permanent Secretary to the Ministry of Supply. Within two weeks Jaguar had been granted all the steel it asked for and the scene was set for a massive export drive.

In the late 1940s the world was desperate for motorcars of any type: production capacity in many countries had been destroyed during the war. William Lyons established links with dealers and distributors throughout the world and at one time exports rose to almost 80 per cent of Jaguar's output. The first official shipment to America crossed the Atlantic in January 1947. It was the first of many.

Lyons wanted the best dealers and distributors to represent Jaguar and he was prepared to take risks if he felt a new, small company would put in more effort than a larger, long-established firm. In Australia, for example, Lyons was unhappy with his pre-war distributor. When it became known that he was contemplating a change a small dealer, Bryson Motors, cabled Jaguar in Coventry and offered to sell 2000 cars over the next 12 months. A relatively unknown newcomer was proposing an astonishing twenty-fold increase in Jaguar's Australian sales — but Lyons took the chance and appointed the dealer. The gamble paid off. Jack Bryson just missed his self-imposed sales target but only because Jaguar failed to supply all the cars he wanted. Within two years the new distributor had taken over the Sydney showrooms of his predecessor. In the United States Jaguar's east-coast distributor also distributed Volkswagen cars. According to William Lyons, the post-war Jaguars were so popular the distributor was able to insist that when a dealer took delivery of a Jaguar he had to take two Volkswagens!

Even before the war had ended, Lyons had turned his mind to the company's development and one matter had troubled him in particular. The engines for his cars had been largely redesigned by Jaguar's Harry Weslake but they were based on a Standard engine and were still manufactured by Standard. It was a matter of dispute between the two companies as to which one had ultimate rights in the hybrid power unit. Several firms had approached Standard asking to be supplied with the 'Jaguar' engine and it had taken all Lyons's substantial powers of persuasion to convince Standard not to sell the product to any other company.

Lyons felt that he could not honourably break with Standard because in order to produce the modified engine they had agreed to make a major investment in production plant at a time when Lyons himself could ill afford such an investment. As it happened, at about the same time that Lyons was considering this problem, executives at the Standard Company had been debating precisely how their company should develop after the war. They decided to concentrate production on just one model and to discontinue the 'Jaguar' engine. Lyons was informed of their decision and after some discussion they agreed to sell him the special 'Jaguar' plant at a generously discounted price.

Lyons could barely believe his good fortune. Not only did this deal represent security for his company, it was also the final step towards his ultimate corporate goal of a self-contained motor manufacturing company. He swiftly arranged for transport to collect the plant and he paid for it immediately. Standard had made a big mistake. They had lost a potentially profitable product and had helped a major competitor to establish a secure presence in the market place. It was not long before they proposed to Lyons that he should sell the plant back to them and that once again they should manufacture the engine for him. Lyons politely declined their offer. Standard's John Black made several approaches and pressed Lyons to reconsider. Lyons's response was characteristically blunt. 'No thank you, John,' he replied, 'I have now got the ball, and I would rather kick it myself.'

William Lyons had now built sidecars and coachwork, he had made a major impression upon body design and established his own marque, and he had improved a production engine and installed it in a new model, but one major challenge remained. He had not yet developed a new engine from scratch and combined it with his own chassis and bodywork to create a wholly original automobile. This was to be his next project.

He began with the engine. His development team included Harry Weslake, Bill Heynes and Wally Hassan, a highly regarded experimental engineer who had joined Jaguar shortly before the war. The brief was to develop a 6-cylinder unit. The letter 'X' was used as the engine designation prefix and, as the specification changed, each new development was given a letter of the alphabet. By the time the team reached 'XK' they had designed one of the greatest automobile engines ever produced.

The original intention was to test the new engine in an experimental car that would not be produced in any great numbers. Lyons developed yet another sleek body shape and the new prototype was called the 'XK120' because it was supposed to have a top speed of 120 mph. Lyons chartered a plane and flew the press to Belgium where the car with its new engine was demonstrated on a closed-off section of the Brussels-to-Ostend autoroute. It covered a 'flying mile' and reached a speed of no less than 132.596 mph. No production model had ever been driven that fast before. Demand for the 'prototype' was so great that Lyons changed his mind and decided to market the vehicle: instead of building a limited number of aluminium-on-wood bodies he went ahead with a major programme of steel pressings and produced the car in volume. The first XK120s were open two-seaters. Fixed-head and drophead coupé models were soon to follow.

The success of this remarkable car was based on a simple premise: that customers would appreciate the combination of luxury styling and sports car performance. With the XK120, William Lyons proved the accuracy of that belief and never looked back. The XK120 and its immediate successors, the XK140 and the XK150, were so successful that they stayed in production until the Jaguar E-type was introduced in the 1960s.

Having established the effectiveness of the XK engine, Lyons introduced it into Jaguar saloons and incorporated it into the Jaguar sports cars that were so successful throughout the 1950s. As production climbed from 1000 cars a year immediately after the war to 10,000 cars a year in the early 1950s, so Jaguar once again outgrew its production facility. Lyons was unable to obtain permission to extend his factory but he was offered the opportunity instead to buy a million square feet of space at Browns Lane, Allesley, in northwest Coventry, on condition that Jaguar undertook production of the Meteor tank engine which was needed for the post-war rearmament programme. Lyons agreed and so Jaguar moved to its present site.

The history of Jaguar in the 1950s was dominated by the company's success on the race circuits of Europe and with steel allocations based on export performance there was no better way of increasing the company's continental profile – and its sales – than by winning at Le Mans. Throughout the 1950s Jaguar practically made the famous 24-hour race its own but there were other victories too. XK-powered cars won a host of classic competitions including the Tourist Trophy Race, the Alpine Rally, the Liège Rally, the Tulip Rally, the Acropolis Rally, the RAC Rally and a number of races at such famous 1950s circuits as Dundrod, Sebring, Spa and Reims. A new range of highly successful Jaguar saloons went on sale and in that decade, for the first time, Jaguar produced 20,000 cars in a year. In recognition of William Lyons's achievements and the Jaguar contribution to British industry, the Queen visited the Coventry factory in 1956 and knighted the chairman later the same year.

By the end of the decade the publicity that came from motor sport, combined with the opening up of a worldwide distribution network, ensured that the Jaguar name was known and revered from Coventry to California. But one event, in 1955, had a greater impact on the future development of the company than all the victories at Le Mans put together. Ironically it went barely reported at the time.

William Lyons and his wife Greta had three children, two daughters and a son. Neither of the daughters was interested in motoring but the son, John Lyons, was a keen motor racing enthusiast. In the summer of 1955 John Lyons travelled to Le Mans to watch the company cars take part in the 24-hour race. He was driving his own Jaguar on a road south of Cherbourg when he was involved in a horrific road accident. He was killed. The tragedy had little immediate impact upon the way in which William Lyons ran his business but it meant that he had no obvious successor.

The death of an only son was a tragedy that befell two other great motor magnates. Bugatti's son died in an accident and Enzo Ferrari's son, Alfredo, died of cancer. All three companies made cars that were the dream visions of one man. In each case the son's death tempted the patriarch of the business to continue at the helm for longer than he should have done. In due course each of the companies faltered and stumbled when in the natural cycle of commerce they were required to inject new blood but failed to do so. By the time Sir William Lyons retired in 1972 Jaguar had been run by its founder for almost 50 years. He had given a great deal but he had failed to introduce basic modernisation, management systems or new technology. The man who succeeded him, Jaguar's former racing manager, 'Lofty' England, had gained little experience of running a large company in a modern economy and when he took over as chairman and chief executive he was himself approaching retirement.

Yet even when faced with disaster Lyons seemed able to turn adversity to advantage. In 1957 fire destroyed almost half his factory. Sir William galvanised workers, suppliers and building contractors into helping him rebuild his empire. At first it seemed as if production would be halted for many months but in fact rebuilding work started within 48 hours. Limited production was resumed within nine days and the factory was back to normal output levels within six weeks. One irony behind this achievement was that, having been coaxed on to a piecework system of wage payment, the workforce had to revert to a day-rate system in order to clear up the mess that resulted from the fire.

By 1960 Jaguar had yet again outgrown its factory site. The need to expand further came at the very time the Conservative Government was pressing companies to move into areas of high unemployment. Factory extensions in Coventry would not be permitted, therefore the only way in which Jaguar could expand in the Midlands was by acquiring Midlands companies. Just two miles from the Jaguar plant, Daimler occupied a factory site at Radford. When Sir William Lyons learned that Daimler's owners, the Birmingham Small Arms Company (BSA), were keen to sell he went to see the chairman, Jack Sangster, and made an offer. The two men struck a deal very quickly and Jaguar acquired another factory similar in size to its own plant but one which was at that time under-utilised. The deal also doubled the size of the Jaguar workforce to more than 8000. Along with the Daimler premises Jaguar acquired a 56-acre site, a successful bus and armoured car business, a government contract for the manufacture and supply of Daimler's Ferret armoured vehicles and a company with a prodigious history: Daimler was one of the oldest car manufacturing concerns in the world.

Daimler cost Jaguar £3.4 million but when the deal was practically agreed a dispute arose between Lyons and Sangster over some pension provisions involving the relatively small sum of £10,000. After much discussion it became clear that each man genuinely felt the other should foot that particular bill and neither was going to give way. In the end they agreed to toss a coin. Sir William Lyons won.

Jaguar moved its machining and engine production to the Radford factory and Lyons began the process of effectively integrating the Jaguar and Daimler marques, for example introducing the Daimler V8 engine into a Jaguar body shell. Today Jaguar uses the Daimler marque in some markets but not in others. In Germany, for instance, the name would lead to confusion with Jaguar's arch rival, the wholly separate Daimler-Benz company that manufactures Mercedes automobiles.

Daimler was the first of several acquisitions and although it was bought principally to allow Jaguar to expand it also offered the company the opportunity to diversify. Daimler was already an active participant in the bus market and provided a perfect base from which Jaguar could launch itself into the heavy commercial vehicle market. Plans were well afoot for just such a move when news broke that Guy Motors of Wolverhampton, a truck manufacturer, had been placed in the hands of the receiver. Enquiries revealed that Guy's had been making an average loss of £300,000 a year for the previous four years and though Sir William was far from convinced that it was possible to salvage anytl ng from the remains of the company, he made a very low offer for the business and it was accepted. It was not long before Lyons had turned Guy Motors around, transforming a £300,000 a year loss into a £300,000 a year profit. Just three years after its acquisition by Jaguar the firm launched a new range of heavy-duty trucks called the Guy Big 'J' range.

In 1963 Jaguar acquired the Coventry Climax business by an exchange of shares. A Jaguar press release at the time said, 'This acquisition has been made to extend still further the range of products manufactured by the Jaguar organisation.' Certainly the company's fork-lift truck and fire pump businesses were highly profitable, but part of the attraction of Coventry Climax was undoubtedly its formidable racing reputation: the company's engines had won many top races, including five consecutive Monaco Grand Prix. The company also had one further attraction. Lyons was aware that even though Jaguar had now developed its own engine and tackled the early problems of poor performance, his engineering team still needed to be strengthened. One of the automobile engineers he most admired was Wally Hassan, the man who had helped Lyons develop the Jaguar XK engine. Hassan had left Jaguar shortly after the XK was launched to join Coventry Climax. By purchasing the company Sir William Lyons once more gained access to Wally Hassan's skills. A year later Lyons made his final purchase when he bought the Wolverhampton company, Henry Meadows Ltd. Again the acquisition of this company and its workforce helped to widen Jaguar's product base, this time into light engineering, but the main reason for the purchase seems to have been Jaguar's need to augment its manufacturing facilities. The Henry Meadows plant was adjacent to the Guy Motors factory.

The Jaguar Group was now making buses, trucks, coaches, military vehicles, engines, fire pumps and marine gearboxes, but the core business was still luxury cars. In the late 1950s and early 1960s a bewildering succession of new Jaguars appeared on the market. The last derivative of the XK sports car was launched as the XK150, the Jaguar Mark II medium-sized saloon was launched with a choice of 2.4-, 3.4- or 3.8-litre engines and the larger Mark X saloon was introduced with a 4.2-litre engine but probably the company's best-known car ever was the E-type Jaguar sports car which appeared in 1961.

The E-type caught the imagination of a generation. The Morris Mini-Minor, designed by Sir Alec Issigonis, was the popular car of the Swinging Sixties, achieving sales of a million in just five years, but at the quality end of the market the E-type sports car captured the spirit of the decade more successfully than any other car, perhaps more successfully than any other product. It had an image for its time and it is a tribute to Sir William Lyons that he recognised the fact. Yet even as the E-type was being launched the British car industry was facing problems that would come close to destroying it. Post-war austerity had given way to a boom which in turn was being threatened by competition from overseas manufacturers, in particular those from the Far East. In Britain it seemed that the only way to combat these problems was to bring the country's main motor companies together through a merger. This was the period when the phrase 'big is beautiful' achieved common currency.

In more recent years large conglomerates, especially large state-run conglomerates, have become rather less fashionable than they were in the 1960s. Now, it seems, 'small is beautiful'. It has been suggested that Sir William Lyons had the foresight to oppose the merging of several motor companies, at first under the banner of British Motor Holdings, later under the title British Leyland Motor Corporation, but in fact he was a staunch advocate of merger. 'I was an enthusiastic protagonist,' he once said, 'as I believed this was both necessary and desirable.' Sir William was involved in wide-ranging discussions with a number of car makers but at first little progress was made. Then, in 1966, he succeeded in negotiating a limited merger with the British Motor Corporation (BMC). As a result he lost his majority shareholding in Jaguar but retained nominal control over the Jaguar cars operation within the newly formed British Motor Holdings. Apart from the perceived need to grow larger in order better to compete on an international scale, Lyons had several other reasons for wanting to merge with another company.

He had no natural successor and in his judgement his fellow directors were ill-equipped to assume the mantle of leadership. Some were approaching retirement but all of them suffered from the fact that they were company directors in name only. It is said that until the merger with BMC Sir William Lyons did not hold formal board meetings and rarely delegated major decisions, and his co-directors therefore had little real experience of running the business. Lyons had become the victim of his own autocratic management methods. To compound this problem he also had a potential supply difficulty. BMC had recently acquired Pressed Steel, the company that made Jaguar's body pressings and Lyons was concerned that they might decide to cut off his supplies. Fortunately for him, Sir William had a good relationship with both Joe Edwards, the managing director of Pressed Steel, and with Sir George Harriman, the chairman of BMC, and thus was able more easily perhaps to negotiate a merger with a company that presented a potential threat to Jaguar's existence.

Aside from these reasons Lyons was also concerned about being taken over: this was a period of major restructuring within British industry. Moreover it is widely believed within the car industry that by 1966 Jaguar was unable to finance the massive investment that would be necessary to develop a new range of models. Though Sir William later denied that this played any part in his thinking, it is conceivable that Jaguar needed an injection of cash but that Lyons did not recognise the fact. One thing he did perceive, though, was that in the 1970s and beyond it would become easier to provide luxury and refinement in cars and that the main pressures on specialist car manufacturers would come from the volume car makers. He was proved right.

Sir William Lyons was a hard taskmaster, a paternalist and an autocrat; it is a measure of his coolness that he only ever addressed people by their surnames. But he was also a perfectionist with a unique gift for styling cars and a sure knowledge of what the public would buy. His knowledge of the motor industry was unrivalled and his vision of how it would develop was almost prophetic. The motor industry recognised his supremacy and heaped honour after honour upon him until his death in 1985, aged 83.

Almost 20 years before his death Sir William had listed four steps that a specialist car maker should take in order to prepare for what he then saw as the inevitable increased competition in the late 1960s and early 1970s. He said that a luxury car maker should keep up with the rapid advance of new technology, should be prepared to change the model range more frequently, should offer standards of refinement, handling and comfort that volume manufacturers could not match, and should promote the product in such a way as to endow it with an aura of exclusivity. His four steps to success could have been written specifically for John Egan.

4

Decline and fall

IT IS COMMONLY believed that the automobile was an American invention. In fact it was first developed in Europe, but between the First and Second World Wars exploitation of their vast domestic market encouraged North American car makers to introduce techniques of mass production. The attendant reduction in costs triggered a boom in the US car industry and by the end of the Second World War almost 90 per cent of the world's car manufacturing took place in the USA – most of it intended for home consumption.

Mass production systems were introduced by European car makers during the 1950s, even for relatively small-scale production runs, and specialisation became something of a European strength. Small cars were developed in Italy, large cars in Germany, luxury cars in Britain and rugged cars in Sweden, all exploiting their own markets and those in the rest of the world. The European domestic market was growing swiftly: after a period of austerity the post-war years saw the development of a long and sustained boom. In 1950, 7 out of every 8 cars were made in America; by 1960 the figure had dropped to 7 out of 13; by 1970 it was just 7 out of 21. More cars were being made in Europe than in the USA.

In the early 1950s the Japanese were building just 3000 cars a year; by the early 1960s that figure had risen to 300,000; by the early 1970s it had erupted to over 3 million a year. The Japanese Government had encouraged the indigenous car industry with a careful combination of financial incentive and domestic market protection. Foreign investors were kept out and a wholly new industrial culture was developed, involving company unions, jobs for life, total employee commitment and novel management techniques. Low wages and the latest in new technology allowed the Japanese to build cars that were cheap but very reliable. This new industrial order helped to create the Japanese economic miracle and throughout the 1970s that miracle mesmerised the world. Production of Japanese cars rose from 3 million to 7 million in just 10 years and the only place for the cars to go was abroad; the Japanese domestic market was far too small to soak up anything like these numbers.

At first Japanese import penetration in Europe and America was not thought to be a problem. The Japanese made small cars and the rest of the world believed that the biggest profits were to be made through sales of large cars. In 1973 the energy crisis that followed in the wake of the Arab-Israeli war sent a warning shot across the bows of the complacent European and North American car makers. When oil prices quadrupled they found themselves badly exposed to a slow-down in the world car market and a switch towards smaller models, but as the market picked up again they chose to ignore the warning signs. In 1979 the second and much more serious oil crisis struck. This time the world was plunged into recession and most car makers were ill prepared to meet the challenge.

In Europe the problem was an excess of production capacity, caused by the belief that big was beautiful: in the 1960s and 1970s many European car companies had merged, convinced that a greater market share would make them more profitable. In America the problem was not over-capacity but over-sized cars: the American manufacturers were still building 'gas guzzlers' and in the turmoil that followed the second oil crisis Chrysler almost went bankrupt and General Motors saw its production practically halved. Of the big three, Ford was best placed to deal with the crisis but even Ford found it difficult.

Industrial disaster was averted in the US thanks to a voluntary trade agreement between America and Japan which effectively restricted Japanese exports into the USA. On the face of it the agreement was a timely solution to the crisis, but in reality it failed to solve the underlying problems and only served to put off difficult decisions, since efficient Japanese production practices were not implemented by US car makers. Moreover, in an attempt to circumvent the voluntary trade agreement on imports, the Japanese began to establish their own car factories, called 'transplants', right across America. Perhaps the most sensible response to the persistent Japanese threat came from General Motors. Recognising that automobiles were increasingly being produced in relatively unsophisticated, low-wage economies, they used the brief respite offered by the voluntary trade agreement to diversify rapidly into hi-tech business operations outside the car industry.

To be fair, the world car industry had been hampered by a succession of calamities that were difficult to predict. The Korean War caused a period of cutback, the Suez crisis had the same effect and it was certainly a singular misfortune that at the very moment when Jaguar's Radford plant stopped making fuel-efficient buses and started to make the thirsty Jaguar V12 engine, the Arabs went to war with the Israelis, triggering a massive rise in the price of petrol. But even allowing for these 'environmental' factors, the performance of British managers was dismal.

British companies in the vehicle sector suffered from all the same problems as other European and the American manufacturers, plus many more. In the years after the Second World War Britain had rapidly lost its status as a super-power. It had lost an empire and its position as a major manufacturing nation. What Britain did not lose was the outdated attitudes and prejudices that had informed industrial management in the years leading up to the Second World War. British industry, and in particular the British car industry, was resting on its laurels. Instead of the sophisticated marketing techniques pioneered by the Americans, British manufacturers relied on intuition. Instead of the new technology installed by the pacesetting Japanese, Britain relied on antiquated plant and machinery. Instead of running their businesses professionally and efficiently British managers adopted an amateur, 'botch job' approach.

Successive governments hardly made the job any easier for them. Incomes policies led to labour problems, the post-war export drive diverted resources away from modernisation and Britain's failure to join the Common Market served only to underline management

xenophobia. Perennial crises over the balance of payments were traditionally tackled by managing consumer demand. Hire-purchase restrictions were a favourite ploy, either to stoke up the economy or, more
usually, to stop it from overheating. The car industry was particularly
badly affected since cars were still luxury items and many were bought
on hire-purchase. Between 1950 and 1970 hire-purchase restrictions
were altered, on average, almost once a year, creating economic up-
swings and downturns that made sensible commercial planning very
difficult. The net result was to discourage investment or innovation, to
reduce profits, to increase labour tensions and generally to make the
industry less competitive.

In pursuit of the economic goal of full employment, successive
governments also attempted to persuade firms to set up in, or move to,
areas of high unemployment. Grants and loans were made available to
those companies that co-operated, and Industrial Development Certifi-
cates required for the building of new factories were withheld from
companies that would not move. Thus the apparently laudable aim of
ensuring full employment resulted in the dispersal of motor manufacturing to regions far from the main markets and to a restriction on
expansion for those companies that would not move. Once again
industrial competitiveness suffered.

The boom that followed the Second World War had disguised the
underlying problems of industry, and British industrialists had failed to
capitalise on the good times by restructuring their companies and
modernising their management systems. The pre-war belief that everyone had to 'work their way up from tea boy' still held sway. Training
was not a priority and graduates were not encouraged into the car
industry. The intellectual calibre of British managers was very low,
their ability to lead and motivate was severely restricted and knowledge
of modern management techniques was almost wholly absent. Worse
still, managers often shrank from their responsibility to manage. At one
stage in the 1970s Jaguar managers were described as 'cowardly' by the
chairman of an industrial tribunal for failing to support a worker who
had allegedly been victimised by his own union. Management attitudes
towards the workforce typically veered from belligerent hostility to
weak subservience. During the 1960s the concept of a Britain peopled
by self-seeking, workshy employees gained currency. It was typified by

the Peter Sellers film *I'm Alright, Jack*, about a trade unionist who stood in the way of progress, and an impression of the Coventry car worker as a greedy, overpaid, politically motivated lout was reinforced by the popular press, eager to find a scapegoat for Britain's increasingly obvious economic ills. The strike-prone worker became an integral part of what was dubbed the 'British disease'.

Britain certainly suffered a surfeit of strikes during the 1960s and 1970s but the extent to which that was a significant factor in the decline of the car industry is at least debatable. The expectation of high and rising wages had, in any case, been fuelled by managers in the immediate post-war years when they were keen to stop skilled labour moving to their competitors and were prepared to pay handsomely in return for loyalty. Whatever the reason, by the 1970s it was said, quite accurately, that Britain's car factories were practically under workers' control: union shop stewards assumed the role of supervisors, determined the throughput of work and even controlled the hire of labour. Management had all but withdrawn from the shop floor. Disruptive labour disputes were often deliberately provoked by managements keen to avoid stockpiling during periods of reduced demand, yet this was rarely reported in the popular press. 'Strikes' and 'lay-offs' became central themes of public debate but the real, underlying labour problems involved lack of investment, outdated work practices and poor training.

In 1966 Jaguar and the British Motor Corporation had merged to form British Motor Holdings. Two years later, with the encouragement of the Wilson government, BMH merged with Leyland to form the British Leyland Motor Corporation, its aim to achieve commercial strength through economies of scale. When BLMC was formed, too many dealers were trying to sell too many cars made by too many workers in too many factories; BLMC was simply a collection of car companies lacking any real cohesion. Each company wanted to retain a degree of independence – none more so than Jaguar – but economies of scale demanded the subordination of company pride to the need for corporate rationalisation. At the time of this second merger BLMC was the largest UK motor manufacturer, commanding 40 per cent of the home market. In little more than 10 years, as the company's problems piled up, its market share crumbled to just 20 per cent.

For Jaguar, this crucial period of change in the industry coincided with the period when Sir William Lyons and so many of the people who had joined his company in the 1920s and 1930s retired. In 1968 Arthur Whittaker went, Sir William's deputy chairman since the days of the Swallow Company. In 1969 Bill Heynes retired, the man who had been in charge of Jaguar engineering for over 30 years. In 1972 Wally Hassan, largely responsible for the design of the Le Mans-winning XK engine, also retired as did Sir William Lyons himself. The BL press release said simply, 'After half a century as chairman and chief executive of the organisation he founded, Sir William Lyons, chairman of Jaguar Cars Limited and a deputy chairman of the British Leyland Motor Corporation, will retire from both boards on 3 March, having reached the age of 70.'

Lyons was replaced at Jaguar by his then deputy chairman and long-time friend F. R. W. 'Lofty' England. He had joined Jaguar in 1946 as service manager, later becoming service director. In the 1950s he had managed the highly successful Jaguar racing programme before becoming in succession assistant managing director, deputy managing director, joint managing director and, finally, deputy chairman. With the possible exception of Lyons himself nobody knew more about the Jaguar Car Company. What Lofty England lacked was not a deep-seated knowledge and appreciation of the company and its cars but modern management skills. He took over Jaguar at a time when the company and its parent, BLMC, were facing serious problems of long-term decline and he was ill-equipped to meet the challenge. A former Jaguar director who worked closely with England explained: 'The need to change direction in many different areas, almost simultaneously, was not a situation with which he had any experience.' It would have been difficult enough for a fully trained manager, but for England it proved impossible.

One of the first problems England had to deal with in 1972 was a major strike by 2000 Jaguar workers which led to several thousand lay-offs and a complete production stoppage. The strike lasted eleven weeks, the longest in Jaguar's history, and it was an important milestone in the decline of the British Leyland Motor Corporation.

Ironically the dispute was the result of BLMC's attempt to replace piecework – the payment system Sir William Lyons had favoured –

with measured day work, a form of payment which made financial planning more predictable. With piecework there was a financial incentive to work, whereas with measured day work supervisors were supposed to provide the incentive. Ron Newcombe was a shop steward at Jaguar in 1972; today he is an official of the Transport and General Workers' Union. He explained that 'In reality it did not work. We ended up with three times as many supervisors and no more work done.' Measured day work was a classic example of 'too little, too late'. It was a necessary commercial reform but by the time Leyland managers tried to implement it, they had lost their authority. New supervisors were installed without adequate training and they failed to win the respect of shop floor workers.

During the piecework strike Jaguar made one of its worst corporate decisions ever. With its image and reputation, to say nothing of its production potential, severely dented by industrial strife, the company decided to launch a new car, the 140-mph Jaguar XJ12 powered by a 5.3-litre, 12-cylinder engine. The XJ12 was supposed to be a major initiative aimed at winning a greater market share from the German Mercedes company, but with production at a standstill and tight picketing around the factory it was impossible to supply dealers with XJ12s to sell. At the very moment when media interest in the new model was at its height just three of the new cars were available for public inspection: one at the Jaguar showroom in London's Piccadilly, another at the BLMC showroom in Piccadilly and the third at the Coventry Municipal Art Gallery, where an exhibition about the history of Jaguar cars was being staged. None of these new cars was for sale.

It was not long before BLMC management decided to replace Lofty England with a younger, more dynamic boss at Jaguar. In 1973 England was asked to become chairman of Jaguar Cars and a Leyland man, Geoffrey Robinson, was appointed managing director. It soon became clear that England's role was non-executive and that Robinson had the real authority.

5

Into the abyss

GEOFFREY ROBINSON was born in Sheffield, the son of a furniture manu-facturer and an Italian opera singer. He went to school in London before studying modern languages at Clare College, Cambridge, and Economics at Yale University in the United States. Robinson was a Labour Party member and during the period of Harold Wilson's premiership he worked for the party as a research assistant. Later he joined the Industrial Reorganisation Corporation, the government body charged with assisting small companies to merge into larger corporations; consequently Robinson was able to watch the develop-ment of BLMC at close quarters. After Harold Wilson's defeat by the Conservatives in 1970 Robinson was offered a job as Leyland's financial controller. In 1972 he was appointed managing director of Leyland Innocenti, the company's Milan-based subsidiary, which he turned into one of Leyland's few overseas profit centres. In 1973, when he arrived at Jaguar, he was just 34 years of age. Several years later, following his period as managing director at Jaguar, Robinson went on to become the Labour MP for Coventry North West, the constituency that includes the main Jaguar factories.

By all accounts Robinson was seen to be a talented man of substantial intellect who worked hard and played hard. He threw himself into his new job with complete conviction. He took a room at the Post House Hotel just a few hundred yards from the company's factory in Coventry

and from this base attempted to turn Jaguar into a modern and successful car maker. To begin with he was still involved with the management
of Innocenti and frequently flew back to Milan for the weekend before
returning to Coventry ready for another full week's work.

Robinson decided that Jaguar's success depended on a major
planned investment programme, the lack of which had helped to stifle
Jaguar's potential over the previous 50 years. He reckoned he would
need £60 million, a sum far in excess of anything Jaguar could afford
from its own resources. But, Robinson argued, if the creation of the
British Leyland Motor Corporation was not about providing investment for the small car companies that could not otherwise afford it,
what was it about?

Despite his socialist beliefs and his close working relationship with
the trades unions, Robinson was not going to give the workers a free
ride. His plan was to double production capacity within two years. He
would increase production and secure jobs but in return he wanted
increased flexibility and changes in working practices. His relationship
with the trades unions was the exact opposite of Sir William Lyons's. He
drew them into the decision-making process and fostered a spirit of
co-operation. He respected trades union representatives and they
respected him. Ron Newcombe says Robinson had 'a tremendous, infectious personality. His impact on the shop floor was really tremendous.
He convinced a lot of people that Jaguar was a good company and that
he'd got a sense of direction for it.' Robinson's management colleagues,
people reared in the more cynical industrial attitudes of the 1960s, were
not always so enthusiastic about his style, but if they thought he would
be soft on the unions they were in for a shock. In many ways Robinson's plans for Jaguar were very similar to John Egan's a decade later.
Both men wanted to increase production to the elusive figure of 60,000
cars a year, both recognised the need for major investment and greater
flexibility and both began with a management shake-up that saw the
introduction of young, new blood. But two crucial factors separated the
Robinson era from the Egan years. Robinson's strategy was production-
led rather than marketing-led; and while Egan had just about every
'environmental' factor running his way, from the exchange rate to the
industrial climate, Robinson was dogged by oil crises, inflation and
corporate interference.

Bob Berry, a senior Jaguar executive who worked under both Robinson and Egan, says that Robinson did succeed in freeing production bottlenecks, something which had defeated even Sir William Lyons. Robinson, he says, 'broke the bottleneck of Jaguar in the context of supply. He was a recovery expert through the manufacturing supply route. Robinson was the first man really to get Jaguar manufacturing by the throat because he saw that if we could get the manufacturing rate up we could then start creating a lot of noise in the market place . . . It was certainly one of the hardest-working times I can recall simply because we were not only fighting an internal battle but we were fighting the battle of the market place as well.'

When Robinson felt he was not getting the support he required either from the unions or from his managers he would not mince his words. There were many heated arguments during the Robinson era – but people were allowed to speak their minds without feeling their jobs were on the line. Bob Berry recalls that after one fierce row which resulted in Robinson changing his mind about a particular issue, Robinson sent a bottle of champagne round to Berry's house with a note which read, 'I appreciate you more than you will ever know.'

The Robinson formula began to work. A renewed commitment by workers and management meant that in 1974 Jaguar sold over 32,000 cars, a figure that was not equalled until the company was privatised a decade later. But Jaguar faced mounting difficulties: the Arab-Israeli conflict led to the first international oil crisis which knocked the bottom out of the car market; American dealers could not handle the volume of cars Robinson wanted to ship them and only by switching deliveries at the last minute to the European and domestic markets was disaster averted. In the words of Bob Berry, Robinson 'came in at the worst possible moment . . . nobody tried harder than he did . . . he just got overtaken by events'.

The main 'event' which knocked Geoffrey Robinson's plans off-course was the energy crisis; it proved to be the final straw for Edward Heath as well as for BLMC. The crisis struck as Britain entered Phase Three of the Conservative government's pay policy. A national 50 mph speed limit was swiftly announced, then petrol rationing coupons were distributed and 'the three-day week' was introduced to save energy.

Early in 1974, with the miners on strike and the country in chaos, Prime Minister Edward Heath called a general election. Fundamental questions were raised about the way in which Britain was governed and who was really in charge of the country. The electorate clearly thought Edward Heath was not in control and duly returned Harold Wilson to office.

In 1973 BLMC had declared a pre-tax profit of £50 million but by the early months of 1974 the company was running at a loss. In addition to economic problems associated with the oil crisis, inflation was also taking a heavy toll and it soon became clear that planned investment programmes would have to be scaled down. In July BLMC tried to persuade its bankers – Barclays, Lloyds, Midland and National Westminster – to support a reduced investment programme but the company's financial position was deteriorating rapidly and while the banks were still considering the proposition BLMC's annual results became available. Net liquid assets of £50 million had been turned into net liabilities of £35 million. The company was heading rapidly towards the limit of its overdraft.

On 27 November the British Leyland Motor Corporation and its bankers met the Department of Industry to discuss the deteriorating situation. It became clear that the banks were not going to bail the company out. There were two alternatives. The first was radically to contract the size of BLMC with all that that meant for exports, employment and the long-term prosperity of the company. The second, as Lord Stokes, Leyland's chairman, succinctly explained in evidence to the House of Commons Expenditure Committee, 'was to get some money from somewhere'.

Events moved rapidly. After a flurry of meetings in early December the Secretary of State for Industry, Tony Benn, announced that the government would underwrite a £50 million extension of the British Leyland Motor Corporation's overdraft while an inquiry was carried out into the company's prospects. It was to be chaired by Sir Don Ryder, Industrial Adviser to the Prime Minister, Harold Wilson, and chairman designate of the new National Enterprise Board – the government vehicle for regenerating British industry. Mr Benn also made it clear that the government intended to introduce a measure of public owner-ship into BLMC; in due course the government's shareholding was to be administered by the NEB. Mr Benn told the House of Commons that the Ryder team's remit was 'to conduct, in consultation – I stress that – with the corporation and the trades unions, an overall assessment of BLMC's present situation and future prospects'. Sir Don was also given some confidential guidelines on matters which the government felt would need to be covered. He was told to look at BLMC's current financial position and to assess its future financial needs, to examine its recent performance and to look at the role of employees in the company's decision-making process.

In March 1975 Ryder presented his report to Tony Benn; at the end of April an abridged version was made public. It said that because of massive under-investment in the past a large proportion of BLMC's plant and machinery was old and inefficient and would need to be replaced immediately. It also said that the amount of money needed was far beyond that which the corporation could provide from its own profits. The implication was as clear as it had been when stated by Lord Stokes: 'Very large sums would be needed from external sources to finance the action required to make BLMC a viable business.' The money was to come from the government and the report estimated that when inflation was taken into account more than £2 billion of capital expenditure would be required over the years 1975 to 1982 and that £750 million of working capital would be needed as well. The Ryder Report also proposed a new structure of councils, committees and conferences to bring workers into the company's decision-making process. BLMC was intended to become a model of industrial democracy with new consultation machinery that allowed the workforce a say in company strategy.

The report's most controversial proposal, however, concerned the broad structure of the company. Ryder proposed that all British Leyland Motor Corporation car manufacturing activities should be brought under the wing of 'a single integrated car business'. The report recognised the arguments in favour of separate identity for companies like Jaguar but effectively rejected them in favour of centralised allocation of resources such as design and marketing. The report said BLMC could not afford to develop and sell competing models, that it had to minimise the number of body shells, engines and components it used and concluded that this would not be possible if companies like Jaguar remained separate entities. Ryder envisaged rationalisation but no major redundancies. The alternative to bailing out BLMC was far too horrific to contemplate: in 1975 the concept of consigning half a million people to the unemployment queues was barely considered. The Wilson government accepted the recommendations of the Ryder Report and took a major shareholding in the company: British Leyland Motor Corporation became British Leyland Limited, with Alex Park as chief executive, Derek Whittaker as head of the car division and Tony Thompson as chairman of the Jaguar 'operating committee'.

Over the next few months criticisms of the Ryder Report began to surface. In the autumn the House of Commons Expenditure Committee reproached Sir Don for relying on a BLMC management study of its own future: the study assumed a 'fairly free availability of cash'. Such an assumption, the committee observed wryly, 'is unlikely to have rigid economy as its central theme'. A group of executives working in BL's export department compiled a paper suggesting that the volume sales forecasts contained within the report were so optimistic as to cause real concern. But it was the new structure of British Leyland that drew greatest criticism; within the motor industry it was widely believed that merging different marques under the BL umbrella would lead to a loss of identity, independence and pride.

Just two weeks after the Ryder Report was published Geoffrey Robinson resigned as managing director of Jaguar Cars. He felt the Ryder proposals would never work: 'The whole thing was madness,' he said. Robinson believed that Jaguar should remain autonomous and wanted nothing to do with a report that recommended the exact opposite. The company shop stewards threw an impromptu party for him in the works canteen and as he arrived he was given a standing ovation. When Derek Whittaker visited the main Jaguar factory the concern of both workers and managers was made very clear to him. It was the strength of their expressed feelings that persuaded Whittaker to introduce changes within a few days of Robinson's departure. Jaguar was given a small degree of independence in the form of its own 'operating committee' and a promise that Bob Knight, Jaguar's engineering chief, could head his own department which would be wholly separate from the much larger and centralised Leyland engineering department. Nonetheless, many people at Jaguar felt such concessions did not represent autonomy but were merely token gestures. Jaguar, they believed, was about to go through its darkest hour.

The problems caused by years of under-investment at Jaguar were compounded by the new organisation and management structures of British Leyland; symptomatic of these problems was the case of the Jaguar paint shop. For many years Jaguar body shells had been built at Castle Bromwich near Birmingham and then transported to Coventry for painting and assembly. By the time Geoffrey Robinson arrived in 1973 the need for a new paint shop had become pressing. Along with just about everyone who worked at Jaguar, Robinson believed that the new plant should be constructed at the main Jaguar factory in Coventry and he duly proceeded to include a new paint facility in his expansion plans. An Italian company, Interlack, was commissioned to build the plant, and the steel needed for the new factory was ordered and arrived on site. But with the appointment of the Ryder team in December 1974 to investigate BLMC and its subsidiaries the investment programme was frozen. By the time Leyland next came to consider the Jaguar paint facility the Ryder Report had been published and Geoffrey Robinson had resigned. The parent company decided that the new paint shop should serve more than one plant and would therefore not be built at Coventry but at Castle Bromwich. The steel that had been delivered to the Browns Lane factory became a rusting memorial to the Ryder Report. It remained in a heap on the main Jaguar site in Coventry until it was resold at a handsome profit. The siting of the new paint plant was an early test of British Leyland's new consultation machinery. So far as workers at Jaguar could see, it clearly did not work. Despite their protests, Leyland management went ahead with its plans for Castle Bromwich.

The new paint technology that Leyland decided to introduce was called Thermo Plastic Acrylic. As well as voicing doubts about the paint shop site, the unions at Jaguar tried to dissuade Leyland from introducing this particular system. As former shop steward Ron Newcombe recalls, the unions argued 'quite vehemently and campaigned quite strongly against its use because we knew they had tried it in other areas – they certainly tried it in the States – and it was an abject failure'. The problem with TPA was one of sophistication. It was a high-technology paint process that tended to show up minor imperfections: consequently it should only be used on car bodywork that was flawlessly and accurately constructed. In the mid-1970s Jaguars were neither flawless nor accurate. According to Geoffrey Robinson there was a problem with the quality of Jaguar body panels caused by poor tooling: 'Bill Lyons wanted a first-class body shell off third-class tooling.' On top of that craftsmen occasionally had to use hand-moulded lead to achieve the required lines. Unfortunately the lead tended to melt at around the same temperature at which the paint was applied in the TPA process, making the work a technical nightmare. Jaguar people claimed that the TPA process was so bad that nine out of ten cars had to be repainted, creating bottlenecks and production shortfalls. As if that was not enough, the process proved so difficult to get right that Jaguar owners were restricted to a choice of just five colours.

The row over the paint shop was indicative of a wider malaise. Jaguar workers and managers were frustrated over their loss of identity and what they perceived to be their product's declining status. Because the Jaguar was a specialist car, the building of which required certain specialist skills, they had felt themselves to be an elite, the aristocracy of the Midlands car industry. They made a special product and wanted special treatment. With the increasing use of technology throughout the international car industry, Jaguar workers felt that they were defending the last bastion of skilled craftsmanship in an industry domi-nated by volume car makers. Ron Newcombe says, 'We resented the involvement of British Leyland . . . because I think there was a certain degree of pride working for a company that built what was considered to be the best motorcar in the world.' Geoffrey Robinson had recog-nised that spirit very quickly and deliberately built on those feelings of pride. When he left Jaguar the British Leyland management tried to reverse his philosophy and to break the elitism at Browns Lane once and for all. Newcombe recalls that 'We were treated a bit like lepers by Leyland because of our general attitude and our anti-Leyland position.'

Over the next few years British Leyland took a succession of deci-sions that in turn saddened, disappointed or appalled the people at Jaguar. When the Jaguar XJS grand tourer was launched in 1976 the celebrations were held not in Coventry, Jaguar's home territory, but at Longbridge, a factory which was constantly in the news, not least for its poor industrial relations record. In the view of many it was not just an inappropriate place to launch a new luxury Jaguar, but actually the worst possible place. Leyland understandably saw it as a perfect opportunity to underline the company's new unified structure, but Jaguar wanted nothing to do with it.

The parent company also radically altered Jaguar's pricing policy. Under Sir William Lyons the Jaguar philosophy was to build the cars as economically as possible and to sell them at prices which represented genuine value for money. British Leyland felt that Jaguars were underpriced and anyway Rover was supposed to be Leyland's 'cheap' quality car — so Jaguar had to become an 'expensive' quality car. This, of course, did nothing to help Jaguar sales and only served to underline the problems that arose for Leyland if its ownership of both Jaguar and Rover meant that the two companies could not compete in the same sector of the market.

At one time British Leyland tried to get some good publicity by putting Jaguar cars into European touring car races. It is widely believed that Jaguar engineers did their best to hinder and thwart Leyland because they did not want 'their' Jaguars racing under the Leyland flag. Ron Newcombe recalls that British Leyland even tried to stamp its corporate image on the Jaguar factory colour scheme: 'Everything that was painted . . . was painted blue and white. They might sound silly things but they are not. They were significant in terms of real identity.'

As Leyland's various car marques were progressively integrated into one giant division, cost control began to break down. Buyers working for other British Leyland marques found that they could not purchase component parts as economically as buyers working for Jaguar because the Jaguar people had relationships with suppliers that sometimes went back to the days of Sir William Lyons's SS company. The new, higher cost of components was rapidly established as the norm for all parts of British Leyland, including Jaguar. Eventually the structure and organisation of British Leyland became so complex that it was impossible to tell whether any particular model was being produced profitably, let alone being sold profitably.

The number of changes to the Leyland hierarchy and structure was positively bewildering. In the late 1960s Jaguar was part of British Leyland's Specialist Car Division, along with Rover and Triumph. In August 1970 the company escaped the first major reorganisation at

Leyland but in October 1972 it was split from Rover/Triumph. In June 1973 it was merged once again into a Specialist Cars Division. In February 1974 Specialist Cars was split into Jaguar, Rover/Triumph and Parts Divisions. In November 1974 Leyland's Volume Car Division was split in two, with the Body and Assembly Division separated from the Power and Transmission Division. In 1975 Jaguar effectively ceased to exist with some people reporting to Body and Assembly and others reporting to Power and Transmission. Later the company was to go through further metamorphoses but in the mid-1970s the reaction of workers and managers alike was one of shell-shocked disbelief as the company staggered from crisis to crisis. In the words of Patrick Audrain, later to become Jaguar's purchasing director, 'The whole thing had doom written all over it.'

In August 1977, Don Ryder (by this time elevated to the House of Lords) resigned as chairman of the National Enterprise Board, the body which oversaw the government stake in British Leyland. Ryder's position as both chairman of the NEB and author of the plan to save Leyland placed him and his NEB colleagues in some difficulty: a criticism of British Leyland's performance was, in effect, a criticism of Lord Ryder's plans for the company. His departure opened the way for less inhibited discussion and almost immediately there was a groundswell of opinion for 'changes at the top' of British Leyland.

Over the two and a half years in which Leyland had supposedly been run according to the Ryder plan the company had effectively atrophied. It did not make much of a profit, but then it did not make much of a loss, and it had not been a major drain on the national exchequer because it had drawn just a small proportion of the funds it had been allocated. The reasons for that were that it had tackled hardly any of its structural problems, there had been practically no rationalisation of plant and little new technology had been introduced. Perhaps the most disappointing thing of all was that British Leyland had failed to introduce common management systems throughout its operation and had failed to instil a sense of common culture among its workers and managers. Other large car corporations, like General Motors, had managed to bring disparate car companies under a single corporate banner: British Leyland had not. On top of all this, the company's market share was still falling and productivity was getting worse all the time.

It was judged to be time for a senior management shake-up and in 1977 Michael Edwardes was invited to take over at British Leyland. Edwardes was born in 1930 in South Africa where he studied law at Rhodes University. His father was the half-owner of a company that held the Exide battery distribution franchise for South Africa's Eastern Province. In 1951, H. V. Schofield, a director of Chloride, the company that owned Exide, happened to be visiting South Africa and young Edwardes found himself at dinner with the visitor. He obviously impressed Schofield because he was invited to join Chloride as a management trainee and spent two years in Britain before returning to Africa as a Chloride manager. In the years that followed he helped to develop Chloride's Africa operation, then returned to England where he became chief executive and finally chairman of the company. Between 1971 and 1977 he engineered a massive increase in earnings for the Chloride group: profits rose from £3½ million a year to £26 million a year.

Edwardes says he is not a capitalist in the strict sense of the word: he says he is more a professional manager. Be that as it may, his performance was impressive enough for him to be invited on to the National Enterprise Board by Harold Wilson. In many ways his relationship with the Labour government of the late 1970s was significantly more cordial than his relationship with the Conservative government that followed it.

When he took over at Leyland, Edwardes noted all the problems that others before him had noted, and more besides. Apart from the declining market share, poor profitability, low productivity and the tarnished image, he pinpointed the problem of an ageing model range and the difficulty of bargaining with 17 trades unions in over 50 factories. He too believed that the Ryder Report was seriously flawed and though others had identified poor management as a serious problem at British Leyland, Michael Edwardes was the first to do something about it. In his book on the five years he spent at the company Edwardes says its managers '. . . lost their will to manage. Britain and the world blamed the unions, and turned their backs on British Leyland products. But the real blame lay with management, for they failed in their duty to manage.' Consequently Edwardes's most predictable action was to reverse the ethos of the Ryder Report. Instead of lumping all the car marques into one division he began the process of reasserting marque identity. Austin-Morris was split from Jaguar-Rover-Triumph, and Land Rover was established as a separate entity. The name Leyland was reserved for commercial vehicles and the name of the holding company was formally changed from British Leyland to BL in an attempt to play down the role of the central bureaucracy. Edwardes pressed ahead with a string of new models including the Metro, the Maestro and the Montego. He tackled manning levels and productivity by rationalising the BL operation and closing loss-making factories. But his most important contribution to the health of BL was the removal of literally scores of bad managers, many of them senior executives. An American psychologist was brought in to evaluate the effectiveness of BL management and executives were put through gruelling tests to prove their strengths and expose their weaknesses. Some left, many more were forced out; technically they may have 'resigned' but in reality they were sacked and paid off. Edwardes discovered that of those who were good enough to stay the vast majority were in jobs to which they were unsuited: people with a special capacity in a particular area had simply been deployed in the wrong place.

In 1979 the Conservative Party was elected to office and the pound began temporarily to grow stronger in anticipation of Mrs Thatcher's monetarist policies. That was fine for the City of London; it was not so good for manufacturing companies like BL. With a strong pound British cars sold abroad earned less sterling, while foreign imported cars were suddenly a lot cheaper. BL found itself less competitive at home than ever and less competitive abroad as well. Once again events had conspired to strike at the very moment when the results of better planning and operation should have been felt. Simultaneously with this domestic economic problem occurred the second and rather more serious oil crisis which was about to send the world economy into slump. The results were inevitable. Having instituted one round of closures and sackings Edwardes was now faced with the prospect of embarking upon a second.

As well as staff reductions Sir Michael Edwardes (he was knighted in 1979) also attempted to reform work practices. In 1980 he forced through a 92-page document that wiped out 30 years of custom and practice in the British motor industry. It marked the end of what was called 'mutuality', the agreement whereby even the smallest alteration in work practice could only be introduced after exhaustive and lengthy negotiations and usually after some sort of extra payment that effectively reduced productivity. But despite his efforts to improve productivity and work practices, Edwardes could do little about the strengthening pound. If BL was to survive it would need a further injection of government cash. A Labour government had been persuaded to finance the Ryder Report in the mid-1970s. Edwardes now had to persuade a Conservative government – a government sworn to the principle of not supporting lame ducks – to provide further cash support of around a billion pounds to keep BL afloat. He did it by persuading Mrs Thatcher that the cost of keeping BL going during her first year in office would actually be quite low. The political decision to support BL was then presented as the company's 'last chance'. Only later did it become obvious that BL would need even more cash, in fact hundreds of millions of pounds, but by then the government was ensnared. Mrs Thatcher never forgave Sir Michael for deftly forcing her hand. He had squeezed more money out of the Conservatives than had ever been available from Labour.

While Edwardes did battle with the bureaucrats from Whitehall and the politicians from Westminster the various BL car marques began their planned reassertion. Throughout the three years from 1975 to Michael Edwardes's arrival at the end of 1977, one man, Bob Knight, had kept the flame of Jaguar company loyalty alight. Knight was the head of Jaguar's engineering department and the man around whom all opposition to BL focused. Knight's successor, Jim Randle, recalls: 'Bob was an extraordinary chap. One of the best analytical engineers I've ever come across. He was a fairly lonely man too. He never married. He had a tremendous devotion to his mother and father. I don't think anyone was ever very close to Bob. But a quite remarkable chap to whom Jaguar owes a very great debt . . . We spent countless nights worrying about how we would stave off the various attacks that were made by British Leyland on Jaguar engineering.'

Superficially Knight appeared to relish the political infighting and admits 'I became good at it,' but deep down he was an engineer and, he says, only a 'reluctant participant in corporate politics'. Despite his reluctance he became a subtle, sophisticated operator with a burning desire to do what he felt was right for Jaguar Cars. He spent hours plotting his strategy and when all else failed he simply filibustered. Often his approach involved 'sheer determination to fight the battle and to continue to fight the battle'. As Jim Randle says, 'Bob used to bore people to tears. He used to go on and on and on to such a point that they just gave up and let him get on with it.'

Under Edwardes, Bob Knight was appointed Jaguar's managing director. According to another former colleague it was 'a role for which he . . . was totally unsuited and he took it for no other reason than that he saw that if he was the managing director then it strengthened his ability to maintain a Jaguar engineering function'.

Bob Knight was a manufacturing engineer through and through; he had many strengths, but marketing was not one of them, as Michael Edwardes recognised. Given that Jaguar now had to stand or fall on its capacity to sell luxury cars Edwardes set about the task of finding a manager who could lead Jaguar into a new era. 1979 saw Percy Plant as nominal interim chairman and in 1980 John Egan was appointed chief executive of Jaguar Cars.

The succession of bosses who walked in and then out of Jaguar's Coventry factory in the 1970s had left the workforce thoroughly bewildered and demoralised. After 50 years with Sir William Lyons at the helm Jaguar had gone through eight chairmen and chief executives in eight years. With the arrival of Egan, Michael Edwardes hoped he would be able to inject a degree of management stability at Jaguar in an appointment that would underline the perceived importance of marketing. Edwardes felt some people at Jaguar were enthusiastic about the cars but not quite so enthusiastic about running a successful business. In a sense Jaguar summed up all BL's problems: it was manufacturing-led rather than marketing-led. In the words of Bob Berry, 'It was the inevitable result of the way the business was set up . . . There were periods when they tried to change it to a marketing-led company but frankly it never happened.' It was about to happen now, though, and even Michael Edwardes would be surprised at just how successfully Jaguar would be transformed.

6

A knight to the rescue

WHEN JOHN EGAN arrived at Jaguar the reputation of the company's cars was at an all-time low. They were seen, especially by the people who owned them, as poorly produced, poorly serviced and liable to break down with frightening regularity. Anecdotes illustrating the decline of the Jaguar name were legion. Some were doubtless apocryphal. The sad reality was that many were all too accurate.

It was said that Jaguar cars were the best thermometers in the world: the engine would start at 33°F but never at 32°. It was said that they were the perfect status symbol for the very rich, because owning a Jaguar implied you could afford heavy repair bills. It was said that the only way to keep a Jaguar on the road was to own two – since one would always be in the garage. It was said that at parties Jaguar executives lied about who they worked for in order to avoid more jokes or abuse, or worse. The Jaguar was called the 'Friday night/Monday morning' car because dealers tried to close their sales on a Friday and sell the customer's trade-in vehicle over the weekend – that way it was easier to cope with irate customers: when they returned on Monday morning appalled at the Jaguar's poor quality they could be told they could not have their own car and their money back because the old car had been sold. Worse than this, it was said that junior managers at BL were being offered luxury Jaguars instead of mid-range company cars because the Jaguars simply could not be sold. And cruellest cut of all: it was said that these BL managers preferred the Austins because the Jaguars were so unreliable.

Egan had been approached by Sir Michael Edwardes in 1979 and invited to become managing director of BL's specialist car division which at that time comprised three separate marques – Jaguar, Rover and Triumph. Egan declined the invitation. He says, 'I believed at the time that I did not have a general theory which was able to be used on all three. I saw them as three companies. So therefore I wasn't confident I'd be able to do what had to be done . . . Secondly, I think he [Sir Michael Edwardes], at the time, was being very unrealistic about how much of British Leyland could actually be saved. A lot of it clearly couldn't survive.' But Edwardes was not to be deterred and later suggested to Ray Horrocks, chief executive of BL Cars, and Berry Wilson, BL's personnel and organisation director, that it might be worth approaching John Egan again and asking him to join BL to take control of Jaguar alone.

One might wonder why Egan was tempted to leave his relatively secure and senior job at Massey Ferguson for this highly dubious privilege. He certainly thought about the decision very carefully. Writing in the *Sunday Times* in May 1984 he said that when he took the job he estimated Jaguar's chances of survival to be 50-50 at best: 'What probably tipped the scales for me', Egan wrote, 'was memories of being a schoolboy in Coventry during the 1950s. Jaguar then had an almost magical appeal to me – a great brand image is hard to destroy, although many had tried.'

Egan thought Jaguar had come under constant attack from British Leyland executives during the mid-1970s. 'At one stage,' he said, 'Jaguar signs at the entrance to the factory were torn down, only Leyland flags were allowed to be flown on the premises and telephonists were threatened with disciplinary action if they answered callers with "Good morning, Jaguar Cars". Instead they were supposed to say "Good morning, Leyland Cars" and if any further address was needed "large car assembly plant number one".'

The Jaguar image was battered and bruised but Egan thought there was a fighting chance that it could be nursed back to health. He believed the company name was really worth something and that was undoubtedly a major factor in his decision to take the job he was being offered. There was, however, another factor. Egan was firmly of the view that the Ryder plan for the future of British Leyland had been ill-conceived and was wholly wrong. Instead of being submerged under the BL banner Egan believed that Jaguar should be allowed, quite literally, to float off on its own. Although privatisation was not formally on the agenda for Jaguar Cars, Mrs Thatcher's Conservative Government had just been elected for the first time with a mandate for a wide-ranging privatisation programme. So when he was offered the top job at Jaguar, Egan sought, and was given, a firm assurance that Jaguar would be allowed to go its own way and that he would have power and control over the company's affairs: 'I doubt whether I would have taken the job . . . unless I had a clear understanding that that company [Jaguar] was going to be independent.'

Given that assurance, Egan then had to assess what was possible and what was impossible. He tried to answer one simple question. It was not 'Can Jaguar be turned around?' but 'Can Jaguar be turned around on the basis of its present product range?' Egan knew there was neither the time nor the money to introduce new models.

On paper the Jaguar range was beginning to look dated. The company's main product, the XJ6 saloon, had been in production for twelve years, the XJS grand tourer for five. The industry's wisdom was that if they were not yet outmoded they soon would be. Egan rejected that view: he felt both cars were stylish and appealing. What was indisputable, however, was the cars' widely held reputation among owners for poor reliability. Egan could hardly reject that and he did not. What he questioned was the reason for the reputation. According to Bob Berry, Egan was at first 'entirely unconvinced' that reliability was a major problem: he thought the sales department was using it, building it up, as an excuse for failing to sell more cars.

In his judgement of the models and their reliability Egan arguably made serious miscalculations. But sometimes people make the right decision for the wrong reasons and Egan told Sir Michael Edwardes he would take the Jaguar job.

John Leopold Egan was born on 7 November 1939 at Rawtenstall in Lancashire. His family was already steeped in the motor business: the family firm of James E. Egan was a Rootes dealership. John Egan lived in Burnley Road, Rawtenstall, and went to the local Bacup and Rawtenstall Grammar School, joining as a fourth-former and leaving with seven O-levels when the family moved south to Coventry. In the Midlands he went to Coventry's Bablake School before taking a degree in petroleum engineering at Imperial College, London. He graduated in 1961 and in 1962 joined Shell International for whom he spent several years prospecting for oil in the Middle East.

While working for Shell he came to the conclusion that his job was more about business than about engineering and that he therefore needed to broaden his understanding and knowledge of the world of commerce. In 1966 he enrolled in the first business studies course at the London Business School. At that time the school, which had been set up a year earlier, was still part of the University of London and Egan was awarded the University's MSc, the equivalent of today's MBA, or Master of Business Administration. His classmates in 1966 included Seymour Fortesque, later to become the general manager of Barclays Bank; Derek Lewis, the managing director of Granada Television; and James Arnold Baker, the chief executive of BBC Enterprises. Twenty years after graduating the class of '66 gathered to toast their success with a reunion at London's Savoy Hotel. Egan retains his links with the LBS as a member of the Business Liaison Committee; its Centre for Management Development now trains senior Jaguar managers.

On graduating Egan was offered a number of jobs and decided not to rejoin Shell but to work for General Motors. In 1968 he became general manager of the AC Delco replacement parts operation. At that time General Motors had two companies in the UK – General Motors Ltd and Vauxhall Cars. AC Delco was a division of General Motors Ltd but it manufactured parts for all General Motors products including Vauxhalls. Colleagues from that time remember Egan as a creative manager who in the words of John Costin, the sales manager of AC Delco, 'was always particularly interested in trying new things. "Change" was something he always liked . . . I think we all learned a lot from him.'

In 1971 John Egan moved on and upwards, joining British Leyland where he eventually became director of BL Parts and Service, in which capacity he was responsible for the rapid development of the company's highly successful spares and accessories operation, Unipart. Until Egan arrived the spares business had been the poor relation of the motor trade. He began its transformation into a high-profile, slickly packaged retail sales operation. Egan left British Leyland in 1976, shortly after the company began implementing the Ryder plan, a plan he felt was doomed to failure. He joined Massey-Ferguson as marketing director of the company's construction and machinery division, based in Rome, later becoming Corporate Parts director.

When Egan arrived at Jaguar in the middle of April 1980 he must have thought back to his days at the London Business School and wondered what the academics would have made of his chances of saving the company. Since his period of business study in the mid-1960s, corporate turnaround strategies had become an increasingly important topic of academic research. Books like *Corporate Collapse – the Causes and the Symptoms* by J. Argenti had almost become required reading in Britain's business schools. Research carried out at the University of Bradford's Management and Administration School shows that there is remarkable unanimity among academics on the basic causes of business failure: bad management, poor financial controls and adverse environmental factors such as exchange rate fluctuations, government-imposed credit controls or international oil crises were mentioned by most authors. Interestingly, only one study indicated that strikes were a significant factor in company failure.

Having considered the problem, Egan must also have considered the academic solution. Again there is extraordinary agreement among most researchers on the basic steps that need to be taken in order to turn round a company facing collapse. The first is almost always a change of top management; it is often the inability of the old management to recognise the need for change that leads to the final crisis in a business failure. In the case of Jaguar the problem was, in part at least, that the management was constrained by the orders of its superiors at BL, and many of the managers at BL were more concerned with saving the volume car business than with saving Jaguar. Nonetheless Sir Michael Edwardes certainly thought there was a need for new blood at the company. He later wrote that, 'John Egan believed what other Jaguar executives would not: that mounting losses made Jaguar's demise a certainty, unless the turnaround could be accomplished quickly . . .'

According to the business school gurus the second step in a business turnaround consists of a rapid evaluation of the problem. Step three is usually the most painful, in that it involves emergency action, like redundancies, to stem short-term losses and reduce the cost base. If that works, the fourth step sees the company stabilise its operation and the fifth stage of recovery entails a return to satisfactory rates of growth.

In the rarefied atmosphere of some university campus it could not look simpler. For the man who had to put the theory into practice it must have looked dauntingly difficult. As John Egan sat down and worked through the list of problems he would need to tackle he must have been tempted to pack up and go home. Apart from the blindingly obvious things like the cars' reputation for poor reliability and the fact that they were not selling, he also faced low morale among the workforce, poor rates of productivity, intolerable supply problems, high warranty costs, wretched customer service, shoddy workmanship and obsolete machinery. As if that were not enough, BL had put up the price of Jaguar cars, on top of which half the workforce was on strike and the factory was virtually at a standstill. The company was in such a parlous state that there was a real risk of it closing down before the strike was over. Egan was in serious danger of becoming the first chairman of a motor manufacturer never to produce a car.

The dispute was not a simple argument over 'pay and conditions'. It was, once again, a more complex conflict involving issues of motivation, pride in the product and even elitism. Sir Michael Edwardes was trying to impose a series of new work practices and a common, five-tier pay structure upon hourly paid employees through-out BL. He said that any worker who arrived for work on a given date would be assumed to have accepted the new terms and conditions. For many Jaguar workers, once the highly paid craftsmen of the motor industry, this meant a big drop in the pay league and even those who were not adversely affected by the new pay structure felt that it was yet another attack on Jaguar's image and integrity as a luxury car manufac-tured by skilled craftsmen.

They found support from an unexpected quarter. John Egan, arch opponent of industrial action, understood their pride in the product they were making. He too felt the Jaguar was potentially a top-quality car and he was soon made aware of the fact that the trades unions had spent a great deal of time complaining to his predecessors that they were being asked to build substandard automobiles.

Throughout the long weekend of 26–7 April, John Egan, the senior Jaguar shop stewards and officials from the Transport and General Workers' Union sat down and discussed their mutual problems. There was one other person at that first meeting, a representative of BL's personnel department. It seems there was concern at headquarters that Egan might not stick to the corporate line on the implementation of the new pay structure. According to Ron Newcombe the personnel man attended the meeting 'to ensure that the BL policy was applied and that Egan toed the line. It was there, clear to see.' Egan indeed had to tread a careful path. He could not upset Sir Michael Edwardes's plans – after all, Jaguar was still part of BL – but he clearly wanted to send a signal of sympathy and understanding to the workforce. Again in the words of Ron Newcombe, an experienced trades union official not easily fooled, especially by a new boss desperate to end a strike, 'he [Egan] gave the impression that he wanted to help resolve the grading problems and . . . more than gave the impression that he supported a lot of the views that we expressed to him.'

Another shop steward at the same meeting described Egan as being on a 'high', excited, keen to get to grips with the job in hand, raring to go. For the first time Jaguar workers were seeing the almost evangelical motivating technique Egan was to use often in the future. He raised the emotional temperature of the meeting by confronting the company's problems, asserting that they were soluble but declaring that they could only be solved if everyone worked together. Then, as he banged the table with his fist, he asked, 'Are you with me?' The response was not as positive as he might have hoped but then he was dealing with people who had suffered an almost constant reorganisation of their working lives for well over a decade. What Egan was promising, in the short term at least, was more of the same and they wanted to see some results before they were prepared to trust him. However, that first meeting with the representatives of the workforce generated enough goodwill to ensure a speedy end to the dispute. Leyland agreed to look at ways of boosting Jaguar workers' earnings with productivity schemes, a grading appeal mechanism was set up and the new pay structure was introduced.

Contrary to public belief, John Egan is not a workaholic. He certainly works hard – during the crucial months of 1980 and 1981 he worked very hard – but he also makes time for his family. He is married and has two daughters, one in her early twenties, the other a teenager. The family lives in a comfortable home next to Warwick Castle and there's a country house at Sidmouth in Devon. If Egan is fanatical about anything it is probably exercise. He used to play rugby for Imperial College. Today he swims, runs and plays squash, boosting his natural vigour and stamina. He also has an abiding interest in music.

The man who became boss of Jaguar Cars in 1980 is a late product of Mrs Thatcher's Britain. The basis of his political views is to be found, not surprisingly, in his background and his experience. He was working his way through the ranks of British industry during the most acute period of national economic decline. The 1960s saw the end of the post-war boom and in the 1970s the rejuvenating effect of North Sea oil had barely begun to be felt. On more than one occasion Egan has pointed out that between 1960 and 1980 the output of British manufacturing industry slumped dramatically. As he saw it, 'Great Britain, once "the workshop of the world", had become an industrial also-ran.' He blamed this spectacular decline on a wide range of factors. He believed that managers were to blame because they did not invest enough money in things like training and research. He believed the trades unions were to blame because they were not interested in the well-being of the companies that employed their members. He believed the City was to blame for adopting short-term perspectives when manufacturing industry needed a long-term overview. He blamed government for offering little incentive (if Conservative) or being downright meddlesome (if Labour). In short, he believed that nobody treated industry with the seriousness it deserved and that the most talented people in the country therefore chose other careers when they completed their university education.

He felt the motor industry was a perfect example of his thesis. When he took over at Jaguar the company was, he said, 'the sickest part of a sick industry'. Never lost for a colourful metaphor, he once said that when he arrived at Jaguar the company was 'about to become another tombstone in our national industrial graveyard'. Just ten years earlier, in 1970, the British car industry had been employing half a million people and making two million cars a year. Half that production was exported and barely one in ten cars sold in Britain was imported. Within the decade exports and employment had been cut in half and imports had risen sixfold. Speaking at the Cambridge Manufacturing Forum in 1984 he summed up his view of Britain's industrial decline with these words: 'In the late 'seventies I believed that Britain was probably no longer capable of manufacturing goods to world standards of quality and productivity and that therefore Britain's industrial decay was inexorable.'

The one factor that reversed Sir John Egan's perspective was the election of Margaret Thatcher in 1979. He believed she alone could create the enterprise culture that would encourage business to thrive and prosper. Speaking to the London Chamber of Commerce in 1986, he touched upon the four aspects of Thatcherism which he felt had helped to create a 'climate of endeavour'. He said Mrs Thatcher had reduced top rates of income tax, thereby encouraging wealth creation; she had brought competition to the City of London; she had embarked on a long-term programme of privatisation in the belief that private enterprise was more responsive to the needs of customers; and she had introduced curbs on trades union power.

Egan had, indeed still has, strong views on trades unions. At the time of the 1987 general election he wrote in a major political article for the *Sun* newspaper, 'Labour's promise to repeal all Tory Trade Union legislation would spell a return to the industrial relations jungle of the 'seventies. None of us should forget the chaos that existed then, the intimidating mass meetings and the violent secondary picketing.' The *Sun* may seem a surprising vehicle for his political views since it is hardly the preferred reading of most Jaguar owners, but Egan is a potent symbol of Thatcherism to many *Sun* readers, the successful face of capitalism, the man who saved a great British company that had fallen on hard times and made it great once again. The headline across the feature read 'Six Reasons Why You Must Not Vote Labour.' Anyone with any doubts about Egan's personal political views soon had those doubts dispelled. 'Were Labour to be elected today their muddled policies would set the clock back 20 years,' he wrote. 'Only Margaret Thatcher can provide the inspiration Britain needs to maintain its recovery.' And he did not confine himself to the economy or to British industry. On defence he wrote, 'We must not forget that nuclear weapons have kept the peace in Europe for over 40 years. Labour's defence policy is muddle-headed.'

Egan had been prompted to write the article because 'a very jittery Conservative Party PR man actually frightened me to death'. Egan was frightened by the prospect of Mrs Thatcher losing the 1987 election and a few days before polling day a number of public opinion surveys had suggested that was precisely what might happen. The day after his conversation with the Conservative Party official Egan called Jaguar's PR director into his office and suggested a concerted attack on the Labour Party. According to one senior executive at Jaguar, some of Egan's colleagues voiced concern at the prospect of the Jaguar chairman writing such a blatantly biased party political tract and tried to dissuade him from it, but Egan felt so strongly that he decided to go ahead. '99.99 per cent of company chairmen are politically neutral,' he says, 'and I think that's a great mistake. I think our success as a company required a robust economy and there was no way a Labour government was going to create a robust economy. I think our long-term existence and survival as a company demanded a competent government and the only competent government around was Mrs Thatcher's. I think every thinking businessman should have got stuck in . . . to make sure she was elected.'

The *Sun* article revealed the thrust of Egan's thinking about trades unions. He believes them to be outmoded institutions that neither understand nor sympathise with his theory of wealth creation through industrial co-operation. He says they have a simple philosophy based on more money for less work and opposition to all change. He believes they deliberately stand in the way of his company's drive for profitability. In this area at least his thinking is strangely out of tune with much modern management theory and practice. His contention that the unions are irresponsible is itself out of date and hard to sustain. In the year he joined Jaguar Cars the company lost almost a million employee hours through strikes and stoppages. By 1983 that figure had dropped to a total of less than 5000 hours for the entire workforce. In the whole of 1983 Jaguar lost just 45 minutes per worker through industrial action.

Surprisingly, perhaps, Egan's hostility to the unions is not wholly reciprocated; their view of him is rather more balanced. Ron New-combe, the son of a Midlands miner, joined Jaguar in 1959 and worked for the company for 27 years, one of a group of young shop stewards who came to office in the 1960s. Eventually he rose to become chairman of the Jaguar Joint Shop Stewards Committee before leaving the company to take up a job as a full-time official of the Transport and General Workers' Union. His view of Egan is disarmingly straightforward: 'I might dislike a lot of things about him, certainly the way he treats the unions, but he is a brilliant salesman . . . He can sell sun to the Arabs!' Nonetheless, Newcombe finds it strange that Egan should demand complete loyalty. 'He expects everyone to have the same total commitment to Jaguar that he has got and he can't understand why they haven't.' For Newcombe the explanation why more people do not share Egan's enthusiasm is clear. Egan earns £4000 a week as Jaguar's chairman and chief executive; by contrast the average assembly line wage is just £200 a week.

It would be wrong, however, to see Egan's political views as slavishly Thatcherite. He does not, for example, subscribe to the view that 'the market' is always right or, at least, he does not believe that the City's analysis of the market is always right. On the battle between Mrs Thatcher and her Chancellor, Nigel Lawson, over the best way of dealing with exchange rates, Egan is uncharacteristically diplomatic. Along with Mrs Thatcher he believes that 'as our nation becomes more competent the pound will rise. It is absolutely inevitable.' He accepts that it is the job of industry to cope with a strong currency by becoming more efficient but in the short term he believes Mrs Thatcher is wrong to allow the pound to find its own level. He thinks the currency should be managed to iron out rapid movements and to help industry adjust gradually.

Egan also has some surprisingly non-Thatcherite views on education. He believes Britain's education system is elitist, needs a great deal more investment and should be encouraging more people to go to university. His views, once again, stem from his own experience and his needs as a manager in a major manufacturing company. In Britain he knows that the route to fame and fortune is often seen as an Oxbridge degree followed by a job in a merchant bank. He has discovered that in Germany more people go to university and the most talented aspire to a career in manufacturing industry with companies like his arch competitor, Mercedes-Benz. In public his criticisms of Mrs Thatcher and her administration are guarded. In private he can be scathing about government decisions that seem to him to be iniquitous. One Jaguar executive tells of Sir John's frustration and anger that while Jaguar regularly turns in profits, piles up exports and pays its taxes, it is a Japanese car maker that receives British government support for setting up a new factory in the Northeast.

Egan's political views are a strangely selective mix. He admires Mrs Thatcher for her policies of 'popular capitalism' and the encouragement she has given to the business ethic but as the advocate for manufacturing industry he seems to ignore, or at least to play down, the fact that under Mrs Thatcher's premiership Britain has slipped from running a trade surplus in manufactured goods to running a record trade deficit. Yet Mrs Thatcher remains a powerful role model for him. They share the attitudes, opinions and prejudices that come with a modest middle-class background. They have 'made it' and in their own way they are both the champions and the beneficiaries of the new meritocracy.

7

A question of culture

JOHN EGAN once said that if someone had suggested that the survival of a car company depended on that company reducing faults by 200 per cent, slashing its inventory of unsold cars to nothing and trebling productivity, 'You would have thought they were mad.' Yet that is precisely what Egan attempted at Jaguar and precisely what he achieved.

Egan was now master at Browns Lane. BL still controlled most of the company's management functions, including purchasing, personnel, sales and marketing, public relations and finance, but Sir Michael Edwardes had promised Egan an increasing degree of control as Jaguar became more successful. Egan recalls, 'The deal I had was that we could earn these departments as and when we had demonstrated that we could absorb them properly.'

The academic texts say that step one on the road to recovery is the appointment of new management. That was to be Egan's first task. Many of the executives who swiftly emerged as key members of the new management team were already working for Jaguar or BL. Egan's skill was in bringing together senior managers from outside the company and seasoned executives who had first-hand experience of how Jaguar worked. One of those who rose rapidly under Egan was Michael Beasley, a production engineer who joined Jaguar in the mid-1970s from Ford. After a short period with Leyland Cars he joined Jaguar first as a plant director, then as manufacturing director and today he is Egan's deputy. Another who was already working for Jaguar when Egan arrived was the softly spoken Jim Randle. Randle joined Rover as an apprentice in 1954, at the age of 16. By 1962 he had become a gifted and highly respected engineer and was given responsibility for the Rover 2000 project, but in the mid-1960s Randle decided to join Jaguar and when John Egan arrived, Randle took over as director of engineering. Ken Edwards, Jaguar's personnel director and company secretary, was already working at Jaguar when Egan arrived, as was Graham Whitehead, the head of the company's North American sales operation, but two key posts were to be filled by outsiders.

The transformation of Jaguar from a production-led company into a marketing-led organisation required the setting up of an entirely new sales and marketing department so Egan employed a firm of executive head hunters to find a person capable of leading the new marketing team. The head hunters came up with Roger Putnam, who had spent sixteen years in the motor industry, working his way up from salesman to sales director of the Lotus Car Company. He had never worked for any other car manufacturer. Putnam ran into serious trouble extricating himself from his Lotus contract and did not join Jaguar until the middle of 1982 but his eventual arrival marked the completion of the new Egan management team.

The other new face was perhaps the most important appointment of all. John Edwards was born in Chesterfield and went to a small grammar school just outside Sheffield. At university he studied production engineering but it was the financial side of the course that interested him most. On leaving university he joined Massey-Ferguson for a year before moving to Chrysler for four years. He then rejoined Massey-Ferguson and in 1979 began working for the company's European parts operation. Throughout his relatively short career he had been specialising more and more in finance. In 1979 his boss at Massey-Ferguson was John Egan. When Egan decided to accept the Jaguar offer he invited Edwards to join him as finance director. Edwards recalls, 'In 1980 a lot of people had written this place [Jaguar] off so there wasn't exactly a queue for the job.' Egan persuaded him he had little to lose and Edwards decided that at the age of just 31 he could afford to take a risk. In July 1980 he left Massey-Ferguson and joined Egan at Browns

Lane, thus beginning a formidable relationship – Egan the visionary, the ideas man, and Edwards the practical accountant who helped turn Egan's dreams into reality.

Now, with the backing of his own team, Egan could tackle step two of the turnaround: rapid appraisal of the full extent of Jaguar's predicament. Egan knew they did not have time for 'the luxury of a profound philosophical analysis'. Survival was the immediate priority and everything was subordinated to that one aim. Part of Egan's strategy was to engender a sense of 'crisis' in order to concentrate people's minds. He would call meetings at the end of the afternoon and keep people late to instil a sense of urgency: if the matter under discussion could not wait until the following day, it had to be important.

It did not take long to work out what was wrong with the company. Almost everything was wrong with it. Jaguar was a very sick company exhibiting a host of unhealthy symptoms and as Egan observed later, 'We had to improve our competitiveness by tackling each symptom in turn and more importantly in the right order of precedence. The company was so near to collapse that even mistaken priorities would have been fatal.'

So far John Egan had followed the classic industrial turnaround strategy. Step three should have been emergency action to cut costs and stem the outflow of cash. But instead of addressing costs as an immediate priority he chose to tackle another difficulty, a problem that arose from a conundrum he found very puzzling. He knew that whenever motoring journalists took a Jaguar car for a test drive they would end up writing highly complimentary reviews, but against that he also knew that sales had slumped and that the company was receiving an excessive number of complaints about reliability. Egan believed that hidden within this enigma was a clue to Jaguar's misfortune.

He was right. The contradiction between what the journalists wrote and what the owners felt did indeed hold the key to Jaguar's biggest problem but even Egan did not spot the precise explanation immediately. He reasoned that if the journalists were right the sales force could be exaggerating the significance of owners' complaints and using them as an excuse for failing to sell cars. He thought he had good reason to believe this hunch. After all, in the spring of 1980 Jaguar was still part of BL and at that stage Jaguar's overseas sales had been handled by a BL division called British Leyland European and Overseas Division. Egan was convinced that selling specialist cars was a specialist job and that the BL generalists could not possibly make a success of selling every type of car in every type of market.

The job of persuading Egan that fundamentally the journalists were wrong and the owners were right – that Jaguar cars really did have a major quality/reliability problem – fell to the man within British Leyland European and Overseas Division who carried the responsibility for looking after Jaguar sales.

Bob Berry was a long-standing Jaguar employee and enthusiast. After national service and studying for a modern languages degree at Cambridge he had joined Jaguar in the early 1950s. The company had been about to launch its famous assault on the Le Mans 24-hour endurance race when Berry wrote to the company offering his services as a translator. His offer was accepted. In the summer of 1951 he joined Jaguar's permanent staff and over the next 30 years he remained a loyal 'Jaguar man'. In the spring of 1980, however, Berry was not strictly a Jaguar employee. He reported instead to BL managers. The Jaguar sales and marketing functions were among the last that Egan was able to absorb and he found it 'immensely frustrating' that he did not control this vital area of the business – an area he believed was underperforming. During a series of high-level meetings, he tried to persuade Sir Michael Edwardes and Ray Horrocks to give him direct control of the selling operation but Edwardes refused to change the BL company structure. For Bob Berry the situation was even more frustrating, caught as he was in a power struggle between the paternalistic BL and the increasingly independent Jaguar.

Berry had, however, one advantage over Egan. After 30 years with Jaguar and BL in a range of different jobs he had built up a formidable league of dealers, distributors and enthusiasts who really understood Jaguar cars and the Jaguar company. In an attempt to persuade Egan that the basic problem rested with the quality of the cars themselves he decided to take a gamble. 'I organised a group of UK distributors . . . who I knew from years back were long-standing Jaguar devotees . . . to meet him and tell him at first hand what they thought of the car and the product and what we were doing.' Bob Berry wanted to persuade Egan it was the cars rather than the salesmen that were at fault.

The gathering took place two months after Egan had taken up his job. About 25 distributors arrived at the Browns Lane factory for the 'invitation only' meeting. They were ushered into the old boardroom at the Jaguar headquarters and there followed two hours of what Bob Berry euphemistically describes as 'very frank and open discussion'. What Egan discovered at that meeting was deeply shocking to him. The distributors explained, in effect, that the problem facing Jaguar was far worse than he had imagined. The cars may have been well designed but they were badly manufactured, badly assembled and badly serviced.

One of John Egan's great strengths is that when tackling a new problem he is not afraid to admit that others may know more about it than he does. He is prepared to accept fresh information from experts. He says, 'I felt there was a sales problem and bad as the quality was we could pump more in. I was pretty savagely relieved of that idea when we did try and sell them. They just couldn't be sold. You had to do a lot better job on the quality before they'd sell.' Following Bob Berry's meeting, Egan decided that his first priority at Jaguar had to be improving the quality of the cars. As Berry explained later: 'To Egan's eternal credit he did not fail to act on just about every one of the points that came out.'

The first step towards improved quality was an analysis of the scale of the problem. Even from this important meeting, Egan only had anecdotal evidence of its true size. He commissioned a study that involved interviewing hundreds of luxury car owners, not only Jaguar drivers but also people who had purchased Mercedes-Benz or BMW cars. The information gathered through the study was then combined with Jaguar's warranty statistics to help build up a picture of precisely how many faults needed to be tackled in order to make Jaguar's cars as reliable as their competitors'. The picture that emerged was even worse than had been feared. In Egan's words, 'The size of the task was daunting.' No fewer than 150 different faults were discovered. Egan felt that correcting them would require 'nothing less than [the] total re-orientation of the company and its resources towards quality and reliability'. It was now clear that the reason for the journalists' rave reviews was that they were not required to use the cars on a regular basis. They could appreciate the fine quality of the vehicle for a few hours or a few days but only if they happened to own a Jaguar would they learn about the breakdowns and the poor service. It was not the journalists but the owners and the dealers who had the true picture.

Egan knew that in the past many companies had tried and failed to improve the quality of their products. Jaguar would have only one chance to get it right. He decided that everyone, from managing director to assembly line worker, needed to be involved in the struggle, so he instituted a major programme of internal company communications to explain the overall company strategy, his broad quality objectives and specific local requirements. He set up a series of groups, at different levels within the company, to analyse and rapidly correct each fault and he adopted a slogan to symbolise the quality campaign. 'In Pursuit of Perfection' was his catch phrase. As he observed later, 'It looked as if it was going to be a long chase!' Multi-disciplinary Task Forces were set to work tackling the various faults. Less serious problems were dealt with by area managers in conjunction with plant directors. More significant defects were handled by an intermediate level Task Force chaired by Jaguar's quality director, David Fielden. The twelve most important problems were sent to a senior Task Force consisting of Jaguar's board of directors. Owners, dealers, engineers, workers and foremen were all drawn into the process. Anyone who could throw light on a problem was interviewed by the Task Forces. No stone was left unturned in pursuit of perfection.

One of the first facts to emerge was that Jaguar was 'importing' 60 per cent of all its quality problems. Six out of every ten faults emanated from sub-standard components supplied by outside firms. As this became clear the Task Forces were enlarged to include representatives from supplier companies; in one case a director of one of Jaguar's suppliers was brought in to lead a quality Task Force.

In order to persuade suppliers that when it came to quality Jaguar meant business, the company adopted a tough approach. They told suppliers the ground rules were being changed. Jaguar would analyse each component and set its own minimum acceptable failure rate. The company then insisted that suppliers achieve at least that level of quality and reliability. If they failed to do so they were forced to pay for it: not only were they charged the cost of replacement but also the cost of testing the faulty part and the cost of shipping it back to the supplier. On top of that they were charged the total field warranty costs, including parts and labour, that would otherwise be borne by Jaguar. Many suppliers were shocked at Jaguar's rigorous new attitude but in time the great majority were won over and improved their supplies. The few who failed to agree to the new terms of trade or who failed to achieve the new standards were immediately replaced. The quality of incoming components improved dramatically. Jaguar's purchasing director, Pat Audrain, recalls that, 'strangely enough money didn't come into it. There wasn't one supplier who said, "Well, I can fix it but it's going to cost you." Not one.'

Egan's approach was characteristically tough but it was not unfair: he gave the suppliers substantial help in their efforts to achieve his new standards of excellence. As Michael Beasley, Jaguar's assistant managing director, explained, the company adopted a 'carrot and stick' approach to its suppliers. 'We gave them some management support, we gave them some technical support . . . we made them realise that it costs us a lot of money but that, in fact, if they got quality right first time there was a saving not only to Jaguar but to themselves. And as a final penalty, if you like, we put the cost of the problem back where it belonged, with them. We only accept that a supplier can give us good quality. If he doesn't give us good quality we don't want to do business with that supplier.' Test rigs were built to simulate a host of different stress conditions. Identical test rigs were built for the suppliers and when Jaguar tested a component to breaking point the supplier was able to undertake exactly the same test in order to see if some improvement was feasible. Perhaps the most surprising aspect of John Egan's initial push for quality was that so few suppliers were replaced. Out of 1500 companies that supplied Jaguar only a handful failed to make the new, high-quality grade.

Egan's philosophy, when tackling technical business questions, is to address the fundamentals of the problem, to focus upon the essential core of an issue with great clarity. As his former colleague, John Neil of Unipart, explains, 'He is a very practical businessman and he combines an ability to communicate a vision in a compelling way with the willingness really to get in amongst the detail, if that is necessary to show people how it can be done . . . he eliminates a lot of complexity in the decision [-making] process so that people can see clearly what is expected of them.'

If the outward manifestation of Egan's management style was the re-establishment of quality and, by extension, of customer supremacy, the inward manifestation was nothing less than an attempt to promote an industrial cultural revolution. In 1980 Egan thought Jaguar was suffering from what he described as 'the British disease'.

His knowledge of this condition came largely from his period as a manager at British Leyland in the 1970s. By the end of that decade he was not prepared to believe that Britain was capable of industrial competition on the world stage. At the centre of the nation's misfortune, as he saw it, was unbridled trades union power, 'the British disease'. Certainly there were other contributory causes to this malady but at its core it was accurately characterised, in Egan's view, by the image of idle, strike-prone workers who were not prepared to do a fair day's work for a fair day's pay. Insofar as it is possible to define a pseudo-sociological industrial 'disease', the so-called British disease was rather more complex than Egan imagined, with a heavier emphasis on poor management and inconsistent government policies. Egan was convinced, however, that unless industrial attitudes could be radically altered – modernised, as he saw it – Britain stood little chance of becoming a world-class competitor once again.

Within Jaguar, Egan wanted to end what he felt was an 'us-and-them' attitude, an attitude he believed to be fostered by the unions. Egan regularly insisted that he had nothing against the workforce; it was its representatives, the trades unions, that stood in the way of progress. Of the workers he said, 'I have a profound belief in their abilities and the affection they have for the company.' The unions, however, he believes to be politically motivated, with aspirations basically at odds with those of employers and priorities fundamentally different from his own. He cannot understand how two groups of people, unions and employers, labour and capital, can have legitimate but differing aspirations. Success in the luxury motor industry depends on a cogent national industry strategy, relatively stable exchange rates and the ability of the government of the day to encourage free enterprise while at the same time operating subtle protectionism. It sometimes seems as if Egan has an almost naive belief that if only you could get British workers to work as hard as the Germans and the Japanese somehow success would be assured. If Britain has anything to learn from Germany and Japan it is that governments can and do encourage enterprise without allowing the free market to operate against the national interest.

Egan did not adopt a particularly belligerent or confrontational stance towards the unions. On the contrary, the changes he introduced were quite subtle, but his aim was clear. He wanted to encourage a degree of commitment to the company that was not simply restricted to the top tier of management.

His first job was to extend commitment into the ranks of middle management. In the days before Egan took control, managers at Jaguar had each developed personal goals which were often irrelevant to BL's corporate objectives and were sometimes in direct opposition to those objectives. In some cases these individual goals were company-related (the survival of the Jaguar engineering department, opposition to integration with Rover-Triumph) but sometimes they were personal and careerist (an attempt to get a job with another car company as quickly as possible). Egan created a degree of commitment in middle management that saw the subordination of these personal aims and aspirations to the one central, corporate objective of satisfying customers. Slowly at first, then more rapidly, managers began to see the future more clearly. Egan mapped out a common direction for them and exploited the political climate of the 1980s to encourage his troops along this predetermined route. The signposts were there for all to see: Thatcherism, market forces, consumerism, strict trades union laws. They all pointed in the same direction, John Egan's direction.

The job of winning over middle management was not particularly difficult; after all it was middle managers, along with top executives, who had most to gain from the rebuilding of the Jaguar legend. They simply needed to be convinced that salvation was possible and that if they backed him John Egan would work the required miracle.

Convincing the workforce was an entirely different proposition. Egan wanted to create a company in which everyone was working towards the same goal. Put simply, he wanted to create one happy family in which the familiar 'them-and-us' syndrome was consigned to the history books. He needed to win the hearts and minds of his employees and to do this he adopted a threefold approach. He established a sophisticated strategy of communications to ensure the workforce was informed about his aims and intentions. He introduced an advanced training programme to ensure that it was equipped to do whatever tasks proved necessary. And he started a series of 'family events' to win the hearts and minds not just of the workers but of their husbands, wives, children, parents and friends.

There were many strands to the communications programme. A company survey listed no fewer than nineteen different methods of communicating information about Jaguar, ranging from the external media to team briefings, management bulletins, quality circles, conferences, appraisals and audits, even down to the grapevine. (Quality circles involved small groups of workers and supervisors in deciding how to improve their productivity – in effect a form of self-management.) Apart from the usual panoply of posters, leaflets, staff magazines and suggestion schemes Jaguar also adopted several quite innovative ideas. For example, Egan introduced weekly briefings that were intended to involve every single employee. Egan himself wrote part of each management briefing paper which contained information on quality, productivity and sales performance. The plan was that information from briefings for plant directors and senior managers should 'cascade' down the company hierarchy, eventually, via superintendents and supervisors, making its way to the shop floor and assembly line through a ten-minute briefing which took place once a week during a scheduled tea break on a Monday morning. This shop-floor summary included information on any VIPs who might be visiting the factory, and information on Jaguar's racing results in Europe and America. The core of the briefing was common for the entire company but supervisors were encouraged to add their own 'local' material and to brief their sections in whatever manner seemed most appropriate. Some supervisors briefed their workers as a single group, others in smaller groups and some on a one-to-one basis.

Egan also introduced quarterly company videos to reinforce specific important messages. Quality was a regular theme in the earliest productions. Workers were taken off the production line in groups of up to 300, shown the video and then invited to debate the issues that were raised or to ask questions. A senior director was always present to reinforce the chosen message and to collect the brickbats. Egan said later, 'The interchange of views . . . ranged from the highly political to valuable identification of problem areas and suggestions for resolution of the problems.'

The production quality of these 'in-house' videos was extremely high. Egan believed that if video was to be a useful management tool it had to be produced to the highest professional standards. Consequently he expected the same quality from TV production companies as he expected from his component suppliers. Indeed, a company video was as important an element in the production of cars as a gearbox or an alternator, if it failed to galvanise the workforce it was as useless as a poor-quality part.

Money was no object in the battle to get the message over. One company video involved an interview with Egan conducted by the BBC *Newsnight* presenter Peter Snow. Another was produced in the slick style of a television news bulletin with an up-tempo theme tune and an animated title sequence. Introduced by the BBC's John Humphries, it began as a satirical news report set in the future. The top news stories involved references to Britain's 'King Charles' and to a summit conference between the American President, Clint Eastwood, and the British Prime Minister, Sir Bob Geldof, rapidly developing into a Jaguar company profile produced and presented in the same pacy style. The production did look remarkably like the television news bulletins that millions of people watch every night of the week. It had the same authority and appeal. It looked and sounded like objective truth.

Training was another important part of Egan's strategy for winning the hearts and minds of his workforce. After all, what was the point of spending hundreds of thousands of pounds on telling people why something should be done if you did not then teach them how to do it? Jaguar already had a significant reputation for training: in the 1950s a Jaguar apprenticeship had been highly regarded in the engineering business. The company operated no fewer than four different training schemes: one for technicians, one for craftsmen, another for commercial trainees and a fourth for engineering students. Jaguar apprentices were well trained and were expected to be able to turn their hand to any aspect of the business.

Jim Luckes, an apprentice in the early 1960s, remembers working in different parts of Jaguar's various factories and offices as well as running the London office for a while. He recalls that while most workers wore blue or brown overalls, 'apprentices wore green overalls to differentiate us from the rest of the chaps there . . . there was this most extraordinary assumption that if you wore green overalls you could do anything. I mean, you could walk on water.' Many of the apprentices were provided with company-approved accommodation in Coventry and a host of company social and sports clubs catered for their leisure needs. Within Jaguar the apprentices had a special position but their training, their status and their lifestyle was locked firmly in the Britain of the 1950s. By 1980 the company had a wider range of specific training requirements. It was necessary to develop a sharply focused training programme and to invest in it heavily. Egan decided that the key was to upgrade the importance of training and to extend it beyond the traditional areas of technical and craft instruction.

On the manufacturing side Egan was acutely aware that the trend within the automotive industry was towards cars that were less mechanically intricate but more electronically complex and that this would have a profound effect upon the number and type of technicians that Jaguar required. Egan responded by ensuring that training became an integral part of the forward product programme and by establishing a Computer-Aided Design Training Centre to upgrade the skills of hundreds of Jaguar's employees. For management Egan introduced a range of training opportunities. Company courses in traditional areas like financial control, negotiation and planning were focused towards a more communicative style of management and were complemented with increased training for line managers and external training at business schools. The company even developed a relationship with the Royal College of Art by sponsoring students, in return for which the company secured the services of first-rate graduate designers.

Another obvious area of importance was the dealership network. Dealer training had never been an important area for Jaguar but Egan introduced training in sales, product knowledge and management proficiency. He also commissioned a series of interactive videos, the latest form of educational audio-visual aid, that allows viewers to skip sections they are familiar with and test their knowledge in areas where they are uncertain. This meant dealers, salesmen and mechanics could learn about Jaguar cars at their own pace.

Over and above this wide range of training opportunities, Egan introduced what he called an Open Learning Programme intended to help individuals raise their general level of education. After a visit to a German car factory he was appalled to discover that the general educational qualifications of British workers were significantly lower than those of their German counterparts. Egan's Open Learning Centre now teaches everything from English for ethnic minorities to GCSEs to engineering degrees. There are over 100 different courses, requiring an average of about 30 hours' study a year. Thousands of Jaguar employees have signed up.

Whereas most British companies spend only a fraction of a percentage of their turnover on training Jaguar now spends 1.5 per cent of turnover on training – a total of £15 million a year. In 1987 the company was able to boast of employing 275 full-time apprentices and of having raised off-job training to more than 60,000 days a year, an average of five days' training per year per employee. By the end of the year Jaguar workers had accumulated almost a quarter of a million hours of private study on the Open Learning Programme.

The third strand of Egan's industrial relations plan was his attempt to win over the families of his employees. He introduced a number of events which were quite novel for the car industry. He held 'family nights' to which employees were invited to bring their friends and relatives in order to see how the company was progressing and to hear of its plans for the future. He organised bonfire-night parties, mini-marathons and trips to the pantomime for employees' children. He also started an annual 'Jaguar Open Day', a carnival with stalls, sideshows and competitions primarily designed to enable workers and their families to see round parts of the Jaguar factories they would never otherwise get to, or perhaps go for a ride in a Jaguar car. As an integral part of the launch of the new XJ40 Egan staged four 'J Days' at the National Exhibition Centre on the outskirts of Birmingham. 'J Days' were the company's opportunity to introduced the new Jaguar car to its own employees, an attempt to involve employees' families in the pride of achievement that attends a new car launch. Egan wanted to make sure that the workforce was treated to a car launch that was just as slick, just as glossy and just as professional as the one laid on for journalists and dealers. Egan also revitalised the company's sports and social club, building squash courts, swimming pools, tennis courts, a mini-gymnasium and an all-weather bowling green. He introduced inter-departmental sports contests and even the trades unions were surprised at just how successful they were.

It is difficult to escape the conclusion that Egan was trying to generate the kind of working atmosphere common in Japanese car factories, an atmosphere in which the workforce accepts wholeheartedly the corporate goals of the management. Indeed, Egan practically confirmed as much in a speech he gave in 1984. He said, 'Overall we have tried to create an environment at Jaguar which is the exact opposite of the purely instrumental approach which characterises the employee's attitude towards his company in so much of industry. We know the dividends this pays not only in terms of generating a much better atmosphere within our factories but also in our people's willingness to go far beyond the normal call of duty when problems arise. It is a simple philosophy. We believe that everyone working for Jaguar must be kept fully informed of its progress. This is the means we have adopted to encourage them to understand their place in a team working towards success and prosperity.'

For John Egan, communication was not simply a method of imparting information, it was a means of making contact and establishing a rapport with those around him. His management associates say he is good at communicating because for him it is a way of life; it comes very naturally. Bob Berry recalls that John Egan had 'this basic character of saying, "Well, okay, I don't know anything about that, tell me", rather than saying, "I don't like to display my lack of knowledge."' It came as no surprise, therefore, when Egan set up a company-wide communications programme called Speak-Up.

In 1986 the company had commissioned the London-based Charles Barker Communications agency to carry out an employee opinion survey, to discover what employees thought about internal company communications, about the company's management and about how Jaguar was performing. The results, in one area at least, were quite disturbing. According to the managers who now run the Speak-Up scheme, 'A significant number of employees had a worry about speaking up. Some felt that open discussion of conflicting interests was not encouraged as much as it might be, and that there were insufficient opportunities for formal upward communication.' For a company that prided itself on its internal communications that was very bad news indeed, and so Speak-Up was launched to rectify the problem by providing an opportunity for personnel to raise questions, voice comments or make complaints. It was intended to complement the company's Suggestion Scheme and Dollar Award Scheme, each of which provided cash incentives for ideas that improved the business. Speak-Up was the other side of the communication coin: it was not management communicating corporate strategy to the workforce, it was the workforce voicing fears and grouses to the management. Speak-Up was moreover a confidential scheme. Comments and complaints were coded and all identifying references were removed before they were passed on to a director for reply.

Not surprisingly, Egan's efforts to bring about a revolutionary shift in the industrial culture of the car industry met with distinct scepticism from many quarters. His efforts to break down the barriers between the two sides of industry were seen as little more than window dressing. TGWU official Ron Newcombe recalls one occasion on which the union challenged Egan really to make Jaguar 'one family' by scrapping the differences between hourly paid employees and salaried staff. Egan was told, 'It is alright you sitting up there and saying, ". . . we are together, we are all one family". We are not! It is "you" and it is "us" and it always bloody well will be "you and us" . . . You treat these people [salaried staff] differently from us and we are actually responsible for making the car, making the money, but we are at the bottom of the pile. They get all these perks, all these conditions that we don't!' According to Newcombe, Egan responded by suggesting that perhaps they should all sit down and talk about the possibility of creating one payment framework to cover manual workers and salaried staff. But Newcombe says nothing ever happened. 'He promised us a meeting . . . we then tried to pursue it at a later date and we got blocked every time.'

Ken Edwards agrees that 'the differences in employment conditions between hourly graded and staff employees is probably our last barrier to real teamwork and flexibility', but he insists that a programme to harmonise conditions of employment between the shop floor and the office has been initiated.

Top: the Lyons family home, a few hundred yards from Blackpool seafront. From here the young William Lyons used to look across to the alleyway at the back of William Walmsley's home *(below),* his imagination fired by what he saw as the possibilities of Walmsley's small sidecar business.

Top: Sir William Lyons (1901-85). He and Walmsley established the Swallow Sidecar and Coachbuilding Company, which in 1928 moved to a disused munitions factory at Foleshill, Coventry *(below)*.

Top: the Swallow sidecar, the sleek, stylish 'chair' upon which the success of the Jaguar Car Company was ultimately founded. Increasingly the new factory was devoted to the production of the Austin Swallow *(below)*, Lyons's and Walmsley's first car. Their initial order – from Henley's – was for 500.

Top: the SS1, Lyons's design powered by a Standard engine, which caused a sensation at the Olympia Motor Show in 1931; it looked like a £1000 car but cost just a third of that price. *Below:* the Jaguar XK range, launched in 1948, combined luxury styling with sportscar performance. When it was unveiled for the press it reached a speed of 133 mph; no production model had ever been driven that fast before.

Top: the Austin Swallow was the first car styled by Lyons and the new XJ6 (codenamed the XJ40) was the last car he helped design; he died shortly before it was launched. *Below:* the E-type, the car that caught the imagination of a generation. When it appeared in 1961 it represented a near-perfect combination of image, performance and price.

Lyons introduced mass production techniques to the manufacture of luxury cars. The manufacturing process was broken down into separate functions and each worker was assigned a particular job.

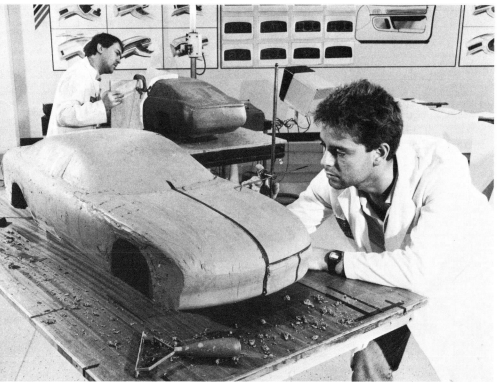

op: Jaguar's new Whitley Engineering Centre was built at a cost of £55 million and was largely modelled on the world-famous orsche Engineering Consultancy at Weissach. On the rig test facility *(above)* prototype cars can be proved under the most rigorous conditions. In the styling studio *(below)* Jaguar designers develop the cars of tomorrow in conditions of great secrecy.

When John Egan joined Jaguar in April 1980 the company was on strike. It seemed he might become the first chief executive of a car manufacturer never to produce a car.

Egan's big problem, when it came to winning the support of the workers, was that whenever an industrial dispute came to a head it was always the unions that had the last say. Egan may have explained the company's position in videos and briefings and company magazines but the effect of that was dissipated by the delay between the company's communication and the moment of decision on whether or not to pursue a dispute. That decision was always taken immediately after union officials had explained their feelings to the workforce. The nub of the problem, as Egan saw it, was that despite his best efforts the industrial culture of the 1960s and 1970s which suggested workers should turn to their trades union when they needed information or advice had not been broken down: shop stewards were still seen as the natural leaders of the men. Personnel director, Ken Edwards, says, 'We almost abdicated the leadership to whoever wanted to lead the workforce – and the shop stewards did that.'

This appalled Egan and prompted him to adopt a bold strategy aimed at seizing the leadership of the workers once and for all by offering an alternative leadership, a leadership trained and equipped by the company. The only group of people who could seize day-to-day control from the trades unions were the works supervisors, foremen who had traditionally been the filling in the sandwich that consisted of the workers on one side and management on the other. Their job had often been made impossible both by trades unionists who exploited their ambiguous position and managers who used them as scapegoats. Egan decided it was time to beef up the role of supervisor and to give each one of them the training they would need to assume the shop-floor leadership of the workforce.

This apparently radical and innovative idea had actually been pioneered by a Japanese car company. Nissan began the trend of giving more responsibility to supervisors, even using psychological assessment tests to choose those who were best suited for the role. The recession of the early 1980s gave further impetus to managers throughout British industry to assert management control and John Egan seized the opportunity with alacrity. Supervisors were selected more carefully, given specialist training, involved in new workplace practices and tested for management potential. Instead of promoting a shop-floor worker, almost as a reward for long service, the company started recruiting graduates into the supervisory role as well as using psychological assessment and aptitude testing to see which shop floor workers were best suited for the job. Skills tested included verbal and numerical competence, visual estimation and spatial recognition; candidates for supervisors' jobs were also given interviews at which their personal communications skills were brought under close scrutiny.

Egan's training managers came up with a host of courses aimed at equipping supervisors not just with the commercial and technical skills they would need but also with the social skills that would enable them to control team briefings and quality circles. The training developed as the role of the supervisor was itself gradually redefined. One course on 'Improving Supervisory Effectiveness' included components on industrial relations, meetings skills and making presentations to directors. It marked a significant change of emphasis away from the need for supervisors to be able to do their subordinates' jobs towards a more leadership-oriented role; they became in effect front-line 'managers'. Another course gave more experienced supervisors assertiveness training and taught them leadership techniques, self-analysis and how to manage time and change.

More recently the training of supervisors has taken a wholly new and self-assured turn. Longer courses have been introduced and methods which have hitherto been reserved for high-flying civil servants or officers in the armed forces are now being utilised. Jaguar supervisors are sent on character-building outward-bound courses. One such course took place at Poole in Dorset where, among other things, supervisors were sent on canoeing expeditions and given problem-solving exercises that required a subtle combination of brain and brawn. One task involved the crossing of a river using just two pieces of rope. Team spirit and lateral thinking were required if the trainees were to avoid a thorough soaking. Supervisors find they are able to build a certain comradeship as they live and work together in such new environments. Simply getting to know one another can be very valuable for solving production difficulties. When a supervisor discovers a problem that emanates from another part of the plant it is easier for him to approach the supervisor in that section and sort out the problem informally if they have at least met before. If they have met climbing a mountain together or fording a fast-flowing river, then solving a small production problem seems relatively easy by comparison.

Supervisors are also given management evaluation to seek out those who have the potential to go further in the company hierarchy. 'It's all about seeing who is going to turn out as a leader,' says Ken Edwards. The supervisors are assessed by a group of senior managers and a consultant psychologist, and required to complete a personality questionnaire and to take part in group exercises to test their management promise. They are also interviewed by an assessor and their aspirations and commitment examined closely. Supervisors' pay rates have been increased and in a further attempt to underline their new status their salary scale has been harmonised with low-level management grades. Those overseeing high-pressure production areas are given extra rewards and the number of supervisors is being increased. But leadership on the shop floor, like leadership anywhere else, is most effective when it is neither heavy-handed nor authoritarian. Whereas supervisors used to direct workers to behave in a certain way and to regulate the production process, they are now being trained to motivate employees and to lead by example. They are being educated in the art of taking the workers with them.

The results of this attempt to take over the leadership of the workforce have yet to be seen. If it succeeds John Egan believes he will be able to persuade the workforce to make common cause with management. If he fails he believes the job of turning Jaguar into a world-class car company will be infinitely more difficult. In the wider context of success and failure John Egan once said, 'I'm afraid of failure. I don't want the company to fail. I'll do anything to make sure it doesn't fail.'

One of Egan's earliest decisions had led to one of his most controversial plans. He arranged for a number of senior executives to visit the factories of Jaguar's competitors in Germany and Japan. Such visits may seem strange given the motor industry's reputation for secrecy about future model plans – they are, in fact, quite common and serve as a valuable means of communication about matters of common interest. Egan himself did not go to Japan. His image of the excellence of Japanese manufacturing and management techniques was so positive he simply did not want to be disappointed. Despite his later insistence that Jaguar's recovery had 'not been achieved by any mystical manage-ment techniques' the visits to Japan had certainly been followed by the introduction at Jaguar of what many people felt was the most mystical management technique of all time: the 'quality circle'.

Quality circles are commonly believed to be a product of the Japanese economic miracle. In fact they are based on quality control theories first developed in the United States. In the early 1960s, Pro-fessor Ishikawa of Tokyo, the so-called father of quality circles, was the first to put these theories into practice in Japan. Later, quality circles were taken up by American firms like General Motors.

A quality circle is a small group of workers along with perhaps one or two managers. They come from the same work area and they meet together voluntarily to analyse and (they hope) solve their own work problems. Although it hardly sounds like a revolutionary concept, it is actually one of the most contentious ideas currently being imple-mented in British industry. Quality circles introduce a continuous dynamic of change that is difficult for workers to argue with because they play a major part in initiating that change. Quality circles can undermine trades union structures and collective bargaining; they can result in job losses among quality control staff; and they can lead to productivity savings which may not be shared with the workforce.

For management all these 'disadvantages' are clear benefits, in addi-tion to which quality circles offer a range of other highly attractive possibilities. They can lead to better-quality products and a greater degree of quality consciousness among the workforce. They can be a useful tool in the development of an apparently more open manage-ment style. They can reduce costs, improve the use of resources and lead to a public perception of excellence and superiority that might not otherwise exist. But perhaps the most important thing about quality circles, from a management point of view, is that they break down the traditional structures of the industrial hierarchy. Workers become part of the company team, they seem to be more motivated and more involved in the company, they begin to feel a sense of common purpose with management. Instead of automatically looking to their trades union representatives for information and advice workers are encour-aged to look to themselves and to the company. A well-organised quality control programme can lead to an apparent breakdown of the 'them and us' attitude, transforming the workers' attitude not only towards quality but towards work itself.

It is not difficult to see why these ideas were regarded with deep suspicion by Jaguar's trades unions and as very valuable management tools by the company's executives. Of all the advantages it was the transformation of shop-floor attitudes that John Egan saw as the biggest benefit of all.

When quality circles were introduced Jaguar had to go through lengthy negotiations with the trades unions. A full-time co-ordinator was appointed and potential circle leaders, generally supervisors or more senior work superintendents, were enlisted. The leaders then approached colleagues they thought might be interested in joining the new circles. When a circle had been formed its members were taken to a briefing by the full-time co-ordinator who explained to them how quality circles worked and showed them a video of a circle in action.

Today the circles generally meet about once a fortnight in paid company time. Before they tackle real problems each circle has to choose a name and a logo for itself and adopt a code of conduct. The 'Seek 'n' Search' quality circle at Jaguar's Castle Bromwich plant operates by a typical set of rules sounding rather like the commandments of a mystical philosophy. One regulation urges members to 'participate according to the golden rule, keep an open mind and look for merit in the ideas of others'. Another rule reminds people that hierarchies are non-existent in quality circles: 'Everyone is equal during the meeting.' When a quality circle begins to examine real problems, members usually start with a relatively easy issue in order to build up group confidence and to avoid the morale-sapping effect of early failure. Information is gathered, the problem is explored and possible solutions are discussed. It is at this phase that one of the most intriguing aspects of quality circle work becomes apparent.

Circle members do not discuss problems in an unstructured manner. They use highly sophisticated management techniques which have to be learned and practised. Techniques like Pareto analysis, named after the nineteenth-century sociologist, attempt to separate the imporant aspects of a problem from the trivial aspects. Members also learn techniques like 'brainstorming', 'force field' analysis and 'cause and effect' analysis. They learn how to construct 'fishbone' diagrams and how to collect data accurately. They become more and more involved in taking low-level management decisions.

When a quality circle has a concrete suggestion to make it prepares a presentation for management, with the freedom to call upon audiovisual aids such as flipcharts, overheard projectors, photographs or slides to explain its presentation. Senior managers are called in to discuss the circle's findings and, if it seems appropriate, suppliers can also be summoned to the factory to see how their product could be improved. When the presentation is complete the management generally offers an immediate response before subjecting the proposal to more detailed examination.

There can be substantial rewards. Like many companies. Jaguar operates a company suggestion scheme through which any individual employee can make recommendations and which pays out a cash reward of up to ten per cent of demonstrable annual savings, with a fixed ceiling of £4000. Quality circle ideas also qualify for the suggestion scheme.

There is no doubt that quality circles at Jaguar have led to major improvements in the way cars are manufactured. At the Castle Bromwich body plant, for example, a quality circle researched a complex problem involving the way in which body panels were assembled. Certain panels did not fit together as well as they should have done. The circle investigated, recommended a series of changes and, in the words of assistant managing director Michael Beasley, 'The solution was a mile away from the initial perceptions of where the solution would be. There was valuable work done by a quality circle and that is done because the guys on the job said, "I've had enough of this and I want to fix it."'

There is no doubt, however, that some of the unions' worst fears about job losses resulting from quality circles have also been realised. Between 1980 and 1984, for example, the number of quality inspectors at Jaguar was halved from 700 to 350 as the responsibility for 'quality control' passed into the hands of production line workers. While Jaguar claims that quality circles are one of the most important innovations the company has introduced, others are not so sure. By 1989 approximately 2000 Jaguar employees were involved in about 200 quality circles. The figures look impressive but some workers suggest that they are deceptive. It is said that some quality circles fail to meet as often as is claimed: Egan is a strong manager who wants to believe quality circles are succeeding, so he is told they are meeting regularly when in reality they may not be. However quality circles are perceived within the company, there is no mistaking their impact outside it. As trades unionist Ron Newcombe explains, 'One of the things about quality circles is that if you tell the customer you've got quality circles in your factory, they think they're getting a better motor car – so let them believe it!'

8

Satisfying the customers

THE STORY OF Jaguar's transformation from lame duck to profitable super company ensured its position as the jewel in the crown of Mrs Thatcher's industrial policy. The popular image was of a company made great by an independent management that was allowed to thrive in a Britain made great by Mrs Thatcher. If Jaguar could do it why not every other company? Through the early 1980s the tributes of success were heaped upon John Egan's shoulders. The influential Institute of the Motor Industry awarded him its 1982 Gold Medal. In 1983 he was named Midlander of the Year. When the new XJ40 was launched the Institute of Marketing named him Man of the Year and in 1986, Industry Year, came Mrs Thatcher's grateful accolade. John Egan received a knighthood.

It had been apparent to Egan from very early on that Jaguar's success, even survival, would require more than improvements in quality and reliability, more than cutting costs and controlling cash flow. Selling luxury cars required specialist marketing skills, particularly in the world's largest luxury car market, the USA.

Egan recognised that the US market was fundamental to Jaguar's future and that Jaguar-Rover-Triumph Inc., BL's North American export operation, would play a key role in Jaguar's attempt to conquer that market. In 1980 nine out of every ten cars sold by JRT in the US were either MGs or Triumphs. With the pound strengthening against the dollar, every MG sold was losing JRT Inc. almost £1000 and BL announced the closure of both the MG and the Triumph factories. It was difficult to judge whether that was good news or bad. The more cars it sold the more money JRT Inc. lost, but with no cars to sell it would soon go out of business. The idea that a company, even the subsidiary export company of Britain's largest motor manufacturer, could survive solely on US sales of Jaguars, which had slumped from nearly 8000 a year in the early 1970s to fewer than 3000 a year in 1980, was regarded as optimistic at best and at worst downright laughable.

Faced with this apparently hopeless situation JRT Inc. tried every conceivable method of remaining in business. It did not matter how improbable an option might appear; if it was possible the executives at JRT Inc. examined it. They even looked at the possibility of selling Japanese cars.

Seven out of every ten people in the world who can afford a luxury car live in the United States. No world-class specialist car company can possibly flourish unless it has a significant presence in the USA and no other market is large enough to support a sustained company turn-around. Throughout the 1950s and 1960s Jaguar had sold around 5000 cars a year in North America. There were several reasons for the dramatic slump of the late 1970s. One was clearly the cars' appalling unreliability. Another was Jaguar's consistent inability to co-ordinate the timing of production and delivery and it was this problem to which John Egan next turned his attention.

In Britain the most important date in the retail motor business year is 1 August, the date on which the annual new registration letter is introduced. August consequently sees a boom in car sales and any manufacturer that is not ready to meet the increase in demand loses significant sales. In the United States, however, the most important month of the year is not August but September, when the next year's models are traditionally unveiled. Again, manufacturers who are not able to supply their dealers with enough new models for the beginning of the US selling year will certainly suffer.

In the late 1970s and through into 1980 Jaguar's performance in supplying the US market had been little short of lamentable. The company missed deadlines not by days or weeks but by months; sometimes new models would not arrive until the following April. On one occasion the US National Highway Traffic Safety Administration asked Jaguar why the cars for a particular year had not been included in a safety recall. The answer was that Jaguar had been so late in supplying the cars that year that the company had decided to skip it, and immediately begin production for the following year.

Egan's solution to this problem was to introduce a degree of simple old-fashioned management discipline: it was management that was failing and Egan made it clear that that was unacceptable. He wanted commitment to the customer and that required commitment to the dealer. The customer's needs were paramount and in order to satisfy those needs Jaguar had to supply the dealer not when Jaguar was ready but when the customer demand was at its greatest.

Timing problems were not confined to the supply of cars. Jaguar was also carrying an unnecessarily high parts inventory: too many parts were being stored on-site, which meant that space as well as money was being tied up. A component would arrive at the Jaguar factory, be stored for a while and eventually be used in the manufacture of a car. In due course the car would be sold and the cost of the component recouped – but the part had to be paid for within six weeks of delivery whereas the car might not be sold until weeks or even months after the supplier's invoice had been paid. Egan instituted a system of component ordering and supply known as 'Just In Time'. Instead of Jaguar holding substantial stores the suppliers were required to build up a store of components and to make smaller, more frequent deliveries from their own stocks. Components would then be integrated into cars very quickly and the cars would be sold and paid for before the suppliers' invoices fell due. The system was fine in theory but there were substantial teething problems: it became known as the 'Just Too Late' delivery system. Still, as with other innovations introduced by John Egan, 'Just In Time' eventually began to pay off and Jaguar's parts inventory was reduced to practically nothing.

At times Egan's approach to Jaguar's problems may have seemed oblique. It was only after he had set quality and timing improvements in train that he moved on to tackle the question of costs and poor productivity. Some businessmen would have given Jaguar's miserable productivity record a rather higher priority; but when he finally came to seize the nettle of inefficiency Egan attacked the problem with characteristic zeal, deciding that Jaguar's workforce had to be cut not just to a level the company could afford but to a level that would ensure productivity on something like the scale of Jaguar's competitors. Between 1980 and 1981 the number of employees was cut by 30 per cent. Managers, supervisors, assembly-line workers, craftsmen were all affected and those who remained were offered productivity bonuses to encourage greater efficiency.

Egan also improved productivity by introducing new plant and equipment, recognising that quality cars could only be built with quality tools. When he arrived at Jaguar in 1980 the company's machine tools were, on average, twenty years old. While Mercedes, BMW and Porsche regularly spend around ten per cent of net sales revenue on capital investment, spending at Jaguar in the late 1970s had been negligible. At every one of the company's factories the fabric of the building was badly in need of replacement: there was barely a roof that did not leak, barely a floor that was truly flat. By 1987 strategic investment in plant and technology had risen to over £130 million a year. In percentage terms it was even more than Jaguar's German competitors were spending, but then Jaguar had a lot of catching up to do.

Gradually the productivity savings began to come through. In 1980 Jaguar had employed 10,500 people and produced 14,000 cars, or 1.3 cars per person per year. By 1981, 7,200 people were producing the same number of cars, which meant that productivity had risen to 1.9 cars per person per year. Productivity continued to improve to 3 cars and then 4 cars per capita a year and by the middle of 1988 Sir John was able to tell a group of business journalists that productivity had risen to 4.6 cars per worker per year. Yet despite these steady improvements Jaguar still has a long way to go before it matches the opposition: the company's European rivals are making 6 cars a year for each of their employees. Nonetheless, Jaguar's productivity and other savings were at least enough to stem the flow of cash that in 1980 had been haemorrhaging out of the company at an alarming rate. Having cut costs, restored the potential for profitability and ensured Jaguar's immediate survival, Egan then set about developing a market-led strategy for the company's recovery plan.

It was significant in the turnaround of Jaguar that John Egan tackled the problems facing the company one at a time: 'You can't overburden a managerial system with too many things to do,' he said. Only when he had made significant progress in one area did he turn his attention to the next, and at each stage of the process he informed those around him what the next priority was. He believed that although it was necessary to deal with each of Jaguar's problems individually, they were in fact closely linked, which meant that the solutions to each problem were also linked.

The marketing departments of large automobile manufacturers spend a great deal of time and money trying to work out why customers buy one make of car rather than another. There are an infinite number of factors involved but when each consideration is weighed against the others, the account executives, the advertising men, the promotions people and the marketing consultants all come back to one phrase: 'customer satisfaction'. Of course, the satisfaction that derives from owning a Mini may be very different from that which comes from owning a Rolls Royce, but the owner of each car will have a set standard of anticipation against which he or she will measure performance. Each will expect a different top speed, a different rate of acceleration, a different fuel consumption, a different degree of comfort and style, but they will be as one in seeking, expecting, demanding 'customer satisfaction'. This was the bond that linked Jaguar's problems and its solutions.

Over several years the satisfaction that derived from owning a Jaguar car had been eroded. By 1980 there was no longer a pleasant sense of anticipation before a lengthy drive, rather the nagging fear of breakdown. A brilliant choice of colours was a thing of the long-forgotten past: if you wanted a Jaguar the choice was little more than white, yellow or red. Egan decided that the underlying mission that would inform all his actions at Jaguar was the restoration of customer satisfaction. It was the decision of a man who had set out on a crusade to convert his company, its workforce and its management to being led by marketing rather than by production: 'If I had to single out one operating principle which permeates all our business activities at Jaguar,' Egan said, 'it would be satisfying customers.'

The first step in Egan's customer-orientation programme was to refine and develop the customer-contact scheme Jaguar had undertaken in 1980 to pinpoint the quality problems. Each month Jaguar would telephone 150 new customers to ask them what they thought of their new car, how they thought it could be improved and what they felt was unsatisfactory about it. They were also asked about dealer service and their impression of Jaguar as a company. The initial call was made just over a month after purchase; follow-up calls were made after nine months and eighteen months to see how the customer was getting on with the vehicle. The customer-tracking programme was so success-ful that Jaguar decided to start ringing the owners of its rivals' cars: Mercedes-Benz and BMW drivers would receive telephone calls from Jaguar as the company tried to find out why they liked the wrong car. Egan said the research provided 'a wealth of priceless information'.

Jaguar also began carrying out regular public opinion surveys to determine whether people thought the company was well managed, profitable, old-fashioned, whether it marketed its cars professionally, had a sound future, cared about its customers, was conscious of quality and used modern manufacturing facilities. The importance of these surveys is that they help the company understand its own public image, and that in turn helps it to understand why people buy Jaguar cars or indeed why they buy Mercedes-Benz, BMW, Porsche, Audi and Volvo.

It is never easy for any company to improve its relationship with its customers; it takes time and effort. For a motor manufacturer it is particularly difficult because apart from such selective sample surveys the company has no direct contact with its customers. Jaguar cars are not sold to the public by the Jaguar Car Company, they are sold by dealers who have a franchise to sell the cars on Jaguar's behalf. Natur-ally enough, John Egan eventually turned his attention to the dealer network. As he saw it, the dealers were in the front line and they carried the responsibility for ensuring that Jaguar's good name was upheld: 'We certainly weren't going to let them treat that responsibility lightly.'

By 1980 the old Jaguar dealer network had almost ceased to exist. BL was selling 'up-market' cars alongside 'down-market' cars and the right to sell Jaguars was bartered like some trading chip in a bazaar. While Jaguar was under the control of BL, dealers who were tempted to leave the group were offered Jaguar franchises to persuade them to stay: there was little or no investigation into whether the dealer had the ability to handle the luxury marque or the market into which he could sell. In the words of Bob Berry, who now runs two Jaguar dealerships, 'There is absolutely no doubt the Jaguar franchise was used as a sweetener in popular franchising decisions of all sorts.'

Many dealers were not treating customers with the respect Egan felt they deserved but at first there was little he could do about it. He fought to take over the marketing and sales operation but to no avail; the sale of Jaguar cars remained under the control of BL for almost two years after he arrived. Predictably, when he did finally gain control of the dealer network he shook it up rigorously. He introduced strict minimum standards of service and customer attention that anyone holding a Jaguar dealership had to meet. He wanted exclusive Jaguar dealerships, he wanted smart, luxury showrooms; he insisted upon well-trained mechanics; he made sophisticated testing and diagnostic equipment a compulsory requirement; and if a dealer was not prepared to shape up and make the necessary investment he was fired. The number of UK dealers was slashed in half. One hundred and fifty dealerships simply vanished and the remarkable thing was that Jaguar sales went up and up. It seemed that the customer was less concerned about the proximity of the nearest dealer and more concerned about the after-sales service he or she received. As fewer remaining dealers sold more cars they were able to make greater investments in their own businesses and it seemed only natural that Egan should demand an ever-increasing standard of service from them. Certainly very few complained. Inevitably Egan made a few enemies; some of the dealers who had their franchises terminated found it difficult to understand where they had gone wrong – but they received compensation and, as Bob Berry explains, 'Tough decisions have been made and that's the nature of the business.'

The root of Egan's dealership policy was his belief that the sort of people who bought £25,000 cars were the sort of people who expected a high standard of service. Hardly a revolutionary 'discovery' – BMW and Mercedes-Benz had been following a policy of fewer dealers and higher-quality dealerships for some years but even so, when they saw the zeal with which Egan had attacked the Jaguar network, they were forced to re-examine their own operations.

If the pruning of the network was painful in Britain it brought squeals of indignation when Jaguar tried the same thing in America. The problem was exactly the same. In 1982 for every car a US Jaguar dealer sold, a US Mercedes dealer sold three. Jaguar dealers were not selling enough cars, which meant they were not making enough money, which meant they were not investing enough in the management, training and infrastructure that Egan felt to be essential. One of the subsidiary problems was that individual mechanics dealt with so few Jaguar cars their familiarity with the models left much to be desired. By the beginning of 1984 Jaguar decided they would have to purge one in five of their US dealers, a decision made all the more complicated by the fact that Jaguar had decided to act at the very moment when dealers felt the Jaguar franchise was beginning to look attractive once again.

American anti-trust legislation is notoriously strong and when Jaguar began to examine how it might terminate so many dealerships the company's American lawyers advised it was virtually impossible: the laws were drawn up in such a way as to ensure that Jaguar did not act arbitrarily and would have to compensate the dealers who were being sacked. The company was not to be put off, however, and invited the US National Dealer Advisory Council to draw up a satisfactory compensation package, eventually making what is called a 'blue sky', or goodwill, payment to every dealer who was sacked, amounting to $5000 for every car sold in the previous twelve months. The company also had to re-purchase the dealers' spare parts. The total buy-out package cost Jaguar millions of dollars.

Despite all the problems associated with the dealership pruning exercise, by 1986 Jaguar had reduced its US network to little more than 150 dealers. The measure of the operation's success in business terms was that between 1982 and 1986 the average dealer's sales rose threefold and annual US sales rose from just over 10,000 to almost 25,000.

A customer-contact programme was also introduced in the United States, carried out by the US automotive research company J. D. Power. Power's researchers actually recorded some of the conversations they had with Jaguar customers on audio cassettes and the catalogue of complaints made sobering listening. As they mused over the tapes senior executives working for Jaguar's North American subsidiary became angrier and angrier. The recordings were distributed and used as a psychological tool to galvanise middle management. Many of the complaints proved to be about dealer service. When a dealer was found to have fallen down on the job he was told to make amends, but all too often no action was taken. Jaguar ended up accompanying customers to the premises of errant dealers and insisting that problems were put right on the spot.

Slowly but surely the message began to get through. Jaguar was no longer prepared to accept second-best from its dealers, from its suppliers, from its management, from its workforce. The customer-tracking programme gave the company chapter and verse on where it was going wrong but more importantly it demonstrated to everyone involved with the company that henceforth Jaguar was going to take the customer seriously. The people who were most impressed with the programme were the customers themselves, especially those who received the market-research calls. They began to feel they were important to Jaguar, valued clients whose views mattered. It must have been a truly novel feeling.

So far as Egan was concerned the customer was king. One particular comment he made in his *Sunday Times* article of May 1984 has been taken up and used by business schools as the true definition of how a company can become customer-conscious. Egan wrote: 'Business is about making money out of satisfied customers – without satisfied customers there can be no future for any commercial organisation.' This uncompromising declaration became the cornerstone of Jaguar's marketing philosophy. The gospel was spread in a host of different ways, with videos, posters, quality indices, quality circles and simply by word of mouth. One of the most surprising things the company discovered was that improved quality did not necessarily lead to higher unit costs. Apart from the obvious warranty savings that resulted from fewer breakdowns, Jaguar executives also discovered that it was possible to build quality cars and components in a cost-effective way. It was largely a matter of planning and design. If a component was designed not just to fulfil a function but also for ease of manufacture, it often proved possible to offset the higher costs of quality with lower manufacturing costs.

This was just one of the many lessons that Jaguar managers were to learn over the next few years. Another was that sustained quality improvements had to be 'built' into a car: they could not be 'inspected' into it. When the manufacturing process for the Jaguar XJS was designed in the 1970s the car body was assembled and the engine was lowered into the car from above. This led to many quality problems not least of which was damage to the bodywork as the engine occasionally bumped against it. When it came to designing the assembly line for the new Jaguar XJ40 the process was reversed and the body was 'dropped' on to the engine block in order to avoid scratching the paintwork: quality was designed into the manufacturing process. It was this attention to detail that had led to a memorable demonstration of confidence in the company by the people whose support John Egan most needed.

As the Jaguar manufacturing operation in Britain began to pull itself up by its boot straps, the Jaguar sales operation in its most important market, the United States, was still in turmoil. In 1980, with the MG and Triumph factories about to be closed, many of BL's North American dealers had faced the imminent prospect of financial ruin. Some deserted the company, others were left struggling to sell a stock of vehicles that were suddenly unattractive because the range was about to be discontinued. BL did not have the cash to buy the cars back but it wanted them disposed of quickly. One man stood up for the dealers against the BL bosses in Britain. Graham Whitehead, at that time president of Jaguar-Rover-Triumph Inc. (he is now president of Jaguar Cars Inc.) told BL that the remaining dealers could not be left to sink without trace but would have to be helped and supported through the crisis, advice which saved the vestige of a dealer network that Jaguar was later able to seize and build upon. In the short term Graham Whitehead's commitment to the dealers earned him a great deal of goodwill.

Eighteen months later, when the earliest improvements had been made and when Jaguar was beginning to struggle out of the abyss, the company invited those US dealers over to Coventry. Despite the groundwork the company had done on quality problems the dealers were still sceptical about just how much could be accomplished by Jaguar Cars, but when they saw the transformation that had been achieved in attitudes and work practices, when they saw the pride and enthusiasm of the workforce they were genuinely astonished.

On their final night in Britain the US dealers were guests at a gala dinner. They were asked, during an after-dinner speech, if they could sell 9000 Jaguars the following year. (In 1981 the US dealers had taken just over 5000 cars.) They were so excited they bawled their agreement. Some were so enthusiastic they jumped up on to their chairs and screamed, 'Nine thousand! Nine thousand!' Anticipating exactly that spirited response, Egan had arranged for the band of the Royal Marines to be waiting in the wings. As the excitement reached its peak the band marched into the dining room playing 'America the Beautiful'. The dealers scarcely believed such style and flair possible from their British cousins. They returned to the USA fired with enthusiasm and began to sell and the following year saw them easily exceed the 9000 target. Michael Beasley believes that if the American dealers had not been won over, Jaguar 'probably would not have made it. So much relied on them taking those cars and having the confidence in us. In that respect it was a turning point.'

In the 24 months between the spring of 1980 and the spring of 1982 John Egan had got to grips with the main structural afflictions that had beset Jaguar Cars. Quality had been improved; supply timing had been given a degree of discipline; productivity had been pushed up through staff reductions and strategic investment in new plant and new technology; and the crucial 'sharp end' of the cars business – the dealership network – had been made more profitable and more responsive to customer needs. None of these problems had been completely solved, and indeed a definitive solution was neither possible nor, perhaps, even desirable. To believe that any of these problems had been permanently resolved would have been to believe that further improvements were not possible and over the succeeding years John Egan would strive for continual improvement, especially in the field of productivity. What had been achieved, however, was major progress in these four key areas, progress sufficient to see Jaguar transformed from a loss-maker into a company with a future. The turnaround of Jaguar Cars was achieved as a team effort but if any one group of people can be said to have dug Jaguar out, it was those American dealers. On that summer evening in the middle of 1981 they glimpsed the future, and their faith in the Jaguar legend was reborn.

9

Codename XJ40

WEST OF Montreal the Trans Canada Highway splits into three. The southern route runs to Toronto and on to the US border. The Lake Superior route follows the Ottawa river for 300 miles before dropping to the shores of the Great Lakes. The third route heads towards the tundra wastelands of northern Canada, a snow-covered desert fashioned by the expanding ice caps that covered Canada and northern Europe some two million years ago. The only relief in an otherwise barren wilderness is the myriad 'kettle' lakes left behind by the retreating ice. This is a subarctic wasteland where temperatures drop to minus 45°C.

March 1983. Just outside Timmins, Ontario, on a little-used road a few miles from the northern route of the Trans Canada Highway, two cars, headlights piercing the gloom, crunch across the ice. It is early morning. It is dark. It is snowing. The cars look strangely unreal, with light-coloured side-panels in stark contrast to the dark bonnet and boot. They do not look like any known production model but that is hardly surprising: they are disguised with specially made camouflage panels that hide the true shape of the bodywork. Each car is loaded with computerised monitoring equipment to analyse its performance. Expert test drivers have been hired to put the cars through their paces. The vehicles are prototype versions of the new Jaguar saloon, about to be tested in the same hostile enviroment that NATO uses to test its tanks. Secrecy surrounds the operation because Jaguar's competitors would dearly love to see what the new car looks like and to learn how it performs under test conditions. Industrial espionage is not unknown in the fast lane of the international motor business.

Those two cars, along with several others, would cover well over a million gruelling miles before testing in northern Canada was complete. In the rather warmer climate of Phoenix, Arizona other heavily disguised pre-production vehicles would be driven by non-expert drivers through the searing heat of the desert and up to the Colorado Plateau south of Grand Canyon. Over a million miles would be covered in Arizona too. In Australia, to the north of Sydney and around Cobar in New South Wales, prototype cars would accumulate almost two million miles of test driving on hot, dusty roads. Yet more cars would be put through proving trials in the desert sheikdom of Muscat and in the city side streets of Manhattan. They would be driven over the arduous test tracks at Gaydon in the English midlands and around the high-speed circuit at Nardo in southern Italy. Ninety pre-production prototypes would be used in these exhaustive trials. Some cars would be driven continuously for 25,000 miles. Some would be written off, some would last so long they would need to be put through the Ministry of Transport road test. Between them these 90 prototypes would cover over 5½ million miles. The new Jaguar saloon, code-named the XJ40, would be the most rigorously tested car ever to come off a British production line.

It was all a far cry from the test programme Jaguar undertook before it introduced the Mark X saloon in 1961. Then two men from the Experimental Department had driven down to Bayonne, just outside Biarritz in southwest France, and mapped out a route through the French countryside. In the words of the Jaguar *Apprentices' Magazine*, 'They had found a Jaguar dealer in the town, the Marmande garage, that would serve as a place to keep the cars and had the facilities to carry out any work that might prove necessary. A comfortable hotel had been found in the town not far away.' A few weeks later two pre-production Jaguar Mark Xs were taken to France and obligingly driven round the circuit. That was it. The result was a car that was still riddled with problems when it was launched.

When it came to testing the top-secret XJ40 John Egan's aim was 'to prove our cars in conditions ranging from the bitterly cold North Canadian winter to the blistering heat of Death Valley in the summer, *before* they get into our customers' hands'. The test programme was punctuated by regular meetings of Jaguar Service Managers from the Middle East, Canada, Germany and Australia, respectively the car company's hottest, coldest, fastest and roughest markets.

The XJ40 project was not simply the development programme for a new car: it was to be the consummation of John Egan's rescue plan for the Jaguar Car Company, the project that brought together all Egan's ideas. The XJ40 was to be manufactured with quality planned into it and reliability built into it. Computer-aided design would be used for the blueprint. Components would be reliable because they would be thoroughly tested. Productivity would improve because the car would be built with modern technology, including robots; ease of manufacture was a major priority. Shoddy workmanship would be a thing of the past because Egan's management techniques would galvanise the workforce and then the car's success would send morale soaring. These luxury dream machines would be delivered to the dealers on time, the dealers would service the customers properly, the customers would be deeply satisfied and the profits would come rolling in. That was the plan, the gamble.

The XJ40 project was born in the early 1970s. The main Jaguar saloon at that time was the XJ6, a car that was generally agreed to offer an elegant synthesis of saloon and sports car themes and which matched its good looks with sure handling. The XJ6 had been launched in 1968 and 'Lofty' England, who had taken over from Sir William Lyons as Jaguar's chairman and chief executive, thought it would remain in production for some time. Though he knew that it would take several years to develop a successor, he little realised that the project he launched in 1972 to develop a new Jaguar would take the best part of two decades to come to fruition, nor did he guess at the machinations that would ensue both to achieve and prevent it.

In the early 1970s Jaguar was becoming an ever more integral part of British Leyland and as crisis followed crisis in that troubled car company there were few resources that could be devoted to the development of the new car. There was, in addition, a bitter conflict of ideas about strategic priorities. Executives concentrating their efforts on saving the British volume car industry had little corporate commitment to the future of that industry's luxury car sector. Progress on the XJ40 was restricted to a few conceptual designs and even they were fundamentally flawed. There was no basic agreement between the Jaguar stylists and the British Leyland managers on what exactly the car should look like, or on what role or function it should fulfil within the corporate range. The Jaguar people wanted it to look like a development of the classic Jaguar theme while the British Leyland people wanted anything but that. As part of their attempt to impose a new design British Leyland called in Italian stylists. Their offerings were compared with the Jaguar in-house designs and did little to bridge the gap. The simple truth was that British Leyland was looking for a standard large car, rather like any other large car, while the Jaguar designers and engineers wanted to build a special large car – a Jaguar.

The Italians gave British Leyland what it wanted, a perfectly serviceable standard design that might just as easily have been a large Ford. In a sense that was inevitable. The specialist Italian design houses work for manufacturers all over the world, so their designs tend to be 'all-purpose' responses to design briefs. What they lack is a feeling for the database of information that comprises a company's design history. In this instance it meant that perfectly competent artists and designers were unable to come up with something that truly looked like a Jaguar. That did not bother British Leyland unduly but it meant that the Browns Lane Jaguar enthusiasts had to use all their guile and cunning to dissuade Leyland from proceeding with an unacceptable blueprint.

Throughout this period Bob Knight, the company's engineering chief, fought to keep British Leyland at bay. With the same tenacity he employed to keep Jaguar's engineering department in one piece he fought desperately to keep the XJ40 project on course. For him there was only one course, the Jaguar course. He would have no truck with design solutions or management solutions alien to the Jaguar heritage. Some campaigns he fought and lost: at one stage the project codename was even changed from XJ40 to LC40 (Leyland Car 40) to underline firmly who was in charge.

Jaguar's designers were particularly keen to anticipate future legislative changes, especially in America, where there was a trend towards tougher laws on safety, exhaust emissions and fuel economy. Second-guessing the politicians and the pressure groups was not easy and the slow, piecemeal development was not made any easier by two oil crises which effectively served to 'move the goalposts' for those engaged on the XJ40. Not only did they radically affect estimates on acceptable fuel consumption, but at one stage it was thought that they would reduce the size of the market for large performance cars, bringing into question the very existence of the XJ40. All these environmental business problems could have been sensibly tackled but the crisis that was engulfing British Leyland was beyond everyone at Jaguar. As losses mounted it became increasingly clear that adequate funds for the XJ40 project would not be forthcoming. The decision was taken to postpone the launch date of the XJ40 from 1978 to 1982 and to switch resources to a separate project that would revamp the Jaguar XJ6.

It is hardly surprising that much of the money that had already been spent on the new car was effectively wasted. One important fact did emerge, however. The world and the motor industry were changing so rapidly that when it did finally arrive the XJ40 would need to be an entirely new car. It could not be based on the XJ6. It would be designed from scratch and would have to incorporate state-of-the-art ideas and technology. By the time John Egan arrived at Jaguar, in 1980, the XJ6 facelift had been completed. Although his priority was to be the improvement of the 1980 range, he recognised the absolute need for a new model within the next few years. He immediately put 'Project XJ40' into a higher gear.

Egan knew that if the scheme was to have any chance of success, particularly in view of the uneasy relationship with BL, it would need forceful project management to drive it along. He set up a formal, high-powered team under engineering director Jim Randle, including two other board directors, Mike Beasley and John Edwards. Recognising that although a project's perceived status stemmed largely from the seniority of those executives committed to it, status alone was not enough, Egan also instituted management systems to cover communication, delegation and decision-making. Relatively minor decisions on timing and project control were delegated to departmental managers and three levels of review were set up: daily conferences to tackle detailed problems of manufacturing, purchasing and quality; weekly seminars to decide on priorities and tackle problem-solving; and monthly meetings to discuss the changing status of the project as well as future strategy.

By the middle of 1980 the new project team was prepared to make a presentation to the full BL board to obtain backing to take the car right through to production. The team proposed building a wholly new car with simpler manufacturing methods to improve productivity and quality. It also proposed to achieve better fuel economy through a reduction in weight and enhanced aerodynamics, with an improvement in performance as well.

The BL board had serious reservations, convinced that the oil crisis would lead towards smaller, lighter, more economical vehicles. Jaguar argued that the oil crisis would not significantly affect the luxury car market – except insofar as it would make Jaguar's three- and four-litre cars more attractive as the Americans 'downsized' from the six- and eight-litre gas guzzlers. In the end, board members were convinced and Jaguar won its backing for the XJ40. Given the initial reservations and the parlous state of both BL and Jaguar finances it may seem surprising that Sir Michael Edwardes's board agreed to allocate £75 million to the project. But having worked so hard to persuade Egan to join the company, Sir Michael could hardly give him less than total support at least for a brief honeymoon period. So the BL board agreed to support the XJ40 with a view to seeing the car on the road by the end of 1983. That stipulation ensured the continuation of undercover hostilities. Few people at Jaguar seriously believed that a top-quality luxury car that fulfilled all the company's requirements could be built from scratch in little over three years but as Jim Randle says, 'If we had put together a much more sensible time-frame it wouldn't have been saleable.' Jaguar had to allow BL to believe in an impossible deadline: a more realistic timescale could have prompted withdrawal of BL's financial support and Jaguar could have sunk without trace.

Luckily for Jaguar the quality of the XJ6 improved throughout the early 1980s, so too did sales, and with that improvement came an easing of the BL pressure to get the XJ40 on the road as quickly as possible. Egan was able to ask what the rush was all about, given the popularity of the car the XJ40 was supposed to be replacing. Over the next few years the launch date would be put back time and again until it came to the point where even Egan would joke about it. Jaguar's David Boole confirmed that the XJ40 was '. . . sort of ready in '84/'85 . . . it would have been possible to have launched it at that time. Had we done so, we'd have expected the customers to finish off the development process. I think that perhaps under a BL regime we would have been pushed to launch the car earlier, which would have been the wrong decision.'

The BL board backing was followed later by government backing and then the project team was finally able to concentrate its efforts on the new car. It soon learned, however, that its exacting list of required improvements would dictate several major compromises. The aero-dynamic improvements that would be needed to ensure greater fuel efficiency meant that the stylists could not do as they pleased with the bodywork. The need to incorporate state-of-the-art technology and a modern look had to be traded off against characteristic Jaguar features like walnut veneer and traditional instrumentation. It proved difficult to reduce noise without increasing the total weight of the car, but it proved just as difficult to improve fuel consumption without reducing the weight of the car. Jaguar was faced with the age-old problem of making its product more appealing to a larger, wider market without alienating its traditional, loyal customers.

Alongside these difficulties, further conflict of interest presented itself between parent and child. BL saw Jaguar simply as its luxury car producer. Jaguar saw itself not just in the luxury market but at the top end of the domestic executive car market as well. Egan knew Jaguar needed to improve its sales in Britain significantly if it was not to become over-reliant on the American market, and since Britain did not have a large luxury car market, that meant making the XJ40 appeal to both the luxury sector and the executive sector. BL's other large car company, Rover, was developing the Sterling, a car that would fight for a share of the market against the model at the bottom of the XJ40 range. If BL had guessed that Egan intended to compete with the Sterling it might have tried to veto the cheapest car in the XJ40 range, thereby forcing Jaguar into a vulnerable reliance on the US market. The only safe course for Jaguar was to delay the launch of the XJ40 yet again until such time as BL had no voice in Jaguar's corporate plan.

As Jaguar sales had plummeted in the late 1970s it had been assumed that at least part of the sales slump must have been due to the 'old-fashioned' interior design of the latest Series III version of the Jaguar XJ6. Its particularly British mood, created with a subtle blend of wood, leather and chrome, was presumed to be outdated. With this in mind the Jaguar stylists opted for a less conventional interior environment. Their problems began when the cars were first subjected to the public gaze in a series of car clinics.

The car clinic is an increasingly important management tool in the modern international motor industry. It involves the presentation and assessment of a prototype car alongside various competitors' cars and the vehicle that the new model is supposed to be replacing. The clinic, aimed at members of the public who have been carefully selected as potential target buyers of the new model, is held in an atmosphere of high security – the manufacturer does not want its competitors to know the presentation is taking place at all, still less to learn its venue, with the risk that industrial spies or prying journalists might try to steal an early look or even a photograph of the new car.

In the early 1980s Jaguar carried out XJ40 clinics in Britain, Europe and America. Hundreds of members of the public were asked to fill in questionnaires not just about the new car but about themselves. Trained researchers and consultant psychologists were on hand to explore their thoughts and attitudes and when the tests were over the information gathered at the car clinics was subjected to highly sophisticated analysis. What Jaguar learned about the interior style of its earliest prototype prompted a complete reversal of the XJ40 interior design philosophy. The public hated the hi-tech modern finish. They wanted the traditional wood, leather and chrome. People were not failing to buy the XJ6 because it was old-fashioned, they were failing to buy it because it was unreliable.

These clinic tests raised serious problems. Designing the 'traditional look' back into the car made it more expensive to build and more difficult to incorporate the new technologies that would ensure quality and reliability. There was another problem, too. While traditional owners wanted traditional interior trim, Jaguar was trying to expand the market into less conservative areas. Would those new Jaguar owners be just as keen on old-style British craftsmanship? Indeed, would anyone be prepared to sacrifice reliability for walnut veneer?

To solve these problems the XJ40 Project Team had to make several compromises. The traditional characteristics would be retained where they had an important visual impact but behind the fascia, out of sight, they would pack the new technology that would make the XJ40 a highly reliable car. According to Jim Randle, the development of the interior style 'was perhaps the most difficult process in the whole of the project's development'. Instrumentation for the new vehicle was a careful mixture of old and new. The traditional circular speedometer and tachometer were retained but the increasing number of hazard warning features on a modern car prompted the project team to develop a single electronic dot matrix screen incorporating all the warning functions in one display. A computer was added to help the driver assess fuel consumption, average speed and even estimated time of arrival. New seats were designed and an air-conditioning system was developed with a specification that it should work perfectly at any temperature between 52°C and minus 30°C. Egan explained that Jaguar's general design philosophy was to 'develop a specification on, say, air conditioning that will withstand the highest ambient temperature encountered in the Middle East and then standardise it on all our production. In that way we can be sure that anyone stuck in a traffic jam on a hot day in London or New York has ample reserves of air-conditioning capability.'

An example of the kind of detailed attention that was lavished on the project involved the introduction of a humidity control in the air-conditioning system. The control needed a clear symbol accurately representing the concept of 'humidity', so the project team assembled 'creativity groups' comprising people with experience of humid climates and asked them to make suggestions. Their ideas were translated into symbol form and then tested on further groups of people. The best symbol to emerge was a simple water droplet. But should it be one droplet or several? The project managers undertook control tests to discover which best communicated the concept of humidity. They then tested different forms of instrument to discover whether drivers preferred a push-button control or a graduated sliding mechanism. No stone was left unturned in the attempt to achieve perfection.

Even more attention was given to major concerns like body shape. Here the company's requirements were relatively simple. The new car had to be elegant and graceful in the best Jaguar tradition – feedback from the clinics had indicated a preference for traditional bodywork as well as traditional interior styling. For their part, Jaguar felt the new car also had to be more aerodynamic. The aim was to achieve a lower drag coefficient than that achieved by either the XJ6 or the cars produced by Jaguar's competitors. The XJ6 was tested in a wind tunnel and the company discovered to its horror that the feature which added most to the car's drag was the very feature that most obviously made it a Jaguar. The front end of the car had very poor aerodynamics: the corners were too sharp, the slope of the radiator acted as a windbreak and the lips above the headlamps trapped air. All these features were tackled by the XJ40 project team and several further improvements were made. A discreet spoiler was added at the front to reduce front-end lift and although it would have been aesthetically unattractive for a Jaguar to be fitted with a rear spoiler, as seen on sports and racing cars, a gentle lip was built into the boot lid to help reduce rear-end lift. When all the bodywork design changes had been made the XJ40 was deemed a major improvement on both its predecessor and the opposition. The drag coefficient was dramatically reduced, the car was lighter in weight which meant it was more fuel-efficient and with 25 per cent fewer body panels it would be a lot easier to build.

By the time the XJ40 was on the road the project had cost not just the initial £75 million allocation from BL but a further £125 million. The most expensive element of the project was the engine: about half the total development costs were spent on it. Jaguar engineers had begun work on a wholly new engine in the mid-1970s. Their brief was to develop a replacement for the XK engine which had been the basic Jaguar power unit since the end of the Second World War. Two things were absolutely essential. The new engine had to show an improved power output and it had to be 20 per cent lighter than the XK. Here Jaguar's racing experience paid off. It was suggested that a four-valve engine would offer the best compromise on power output, fuel efficiency and low exhaust emissions and so a new four-valve, 3.6-litre engine was designed. The power unit for the bottom of the range XJ40 derivative had to be smaller so a 2.9-litre version was developed that could be built cheaply to enable the car to compete in the executive car sector against cars like the Rover Sterling and the Ford Scorpio. To be competitve the smallest Jaguar had to be priced at less than £20,000 and in order to appear a little more fuel-efficient it had to have an engine capacity of less than three litres. The new engine was called the AJ6, the Advanced Jaguar six-cylinder. It was made of aluminium castings to reduce weight and it first appeared in the autumn of 1983 when it was introduced into Jaguar's grand tourer, the XJS.

For a time, in the late 1970s, it had looked as if the AJ6 might be stillborn. One of the problems never adequately tackled within BL was the fact that the group made too many different models and too many different engines. The whole point of bringing a host of medium- and small-sized car companies under the BL umbrella was that there might be some savings of scale. This would not be achieved if each of the separate companies continued to make its own models and its own engines, and this formed the basis for much of the friction between BL and marques like Jaguar. It was the reason why BL considered the option of putting a Rover V8 engine into the Jaguar XJ40. This met with total hostility at Jaguar. Pride in the Jaguar marque, combined with growing resentment at what was thought to be BL incompetence, interference and lack of sensitivity, made the Jaguar engineering department in particular bitterly resist any plans for the incorporation of a Rover engine. They wanted a Jaguar engine for a Jaguar car and they intended to have their way.

Some of the arguments and methods they used might be considered sharp practice. People at Jaguar saw the issue as a matter of life and death. Certainly a major power battle took place between executives at Jaguar and their bosses at BL. The convolutions that resulted even had Jaguar agreeing, at one stage, that its own 5.3-litre V12 engine would not be used in the new XJ40, because it was heavy and not fuel-efficient. But once that decision had been taken the Jaguar designers used it as an excuse to devise an engine compartment that would not accept *any* V-shaped engines. This, of course, ruled out the Rover V8. They achieved this by designing support structures for the 'crush tubes' in the front of the new car that ran back into the engine tunnel. This had the valuable effect of making the XJ40 a very safe car and the equally valuable side effect of making it impossible to squeeze in the Rover engine. No holds were barred in what had become open warfare between executives at Jaguar and their opposite numbers at BL. While other marques became absorbed into the BL structure Jaguar managed to retain its integrity and its identity. Whatever other engines might be scrapped it would certainly not be the Jaguar engine. Asked if, at the time, he had not been working against the best interests of his parent company, BL, Jim Randle replies, 'Yes, I'm sure that's true. I guess I would have got the sack if they'd known what we were up to. But history is written by the winners, isn't it?'

Apart from the fierce loyalty of those who worked for the company Jaguar's other great asset was its increasingly efficient production methods. John Egan was convinced that the way to make cars efficiently and effectively was to ensure that the development people who designed them and the manufacturing people who made them really worked together. The way to achieve that was to provide them with a common, agreed database of information about the product. CADCAM, computer-aided design and manufacturing, provided the technology to establish that database. It is a relatively new technology that allows design engineers to draw their blueprints on a computer screen and then store them in an electronic memory. The blueprints can then be retrieved by other interested engineers.

When the basic three-dimensional shape of the XJ40 had been agreed it was electronically measured and the measurements were recorded on the common database. Alterations were agreed and entered on to the computer blueprint, any implications of those alterations being dealt with by the computer. Hundreds of Jaguar engineers were trained in the use of this new technology and everyone began working off the same basic information. Between them the two essential departments, Product Engineering and Manufacturing Engineering, installed almost 100 CADCAM terminals. There were no silly arguments over the length of a line or the angle of a corner; the computer became the final arbiter of who was right and who was wrong. Precision and speed were improved and everyone throughout the company, indeed throughout the supply network, had access to the information they needed.

The XJ40 was designed to be built with fewer body panels, fewer welds and more robots. This made it cheaper and easier to produce. Egan also decided to install a pilot assembly line for the new model. The one-off track was a full-scale try-out of what would later be introduced

throughout the Jaguar assembly plant; it was used to build the prototypes tested in Canada and around the world. It was also used to train
assembly line workers before the XJ40 went into full production. It
helped to iron out early production-line teething problems and it was
valuable in avoiding disruption of the existing model production while
the XJ40 was under development. For all these reasons the installation
of the pilot assembly track proved to be a particularly smart idea. It was
one Egan had borrowed from his German competitors.

The most complicated element of the new car was undoubtedly its
electronics, the vehicle's cardiac system that kept everything going,
from the lights to the air conditioning, from the engine management
system to the central computer. Hundreds of micro-electronic
components were linked together with well over half a mile of wire.
The car's electrical and electronic systems involved a thousand man-
years of development. At different stages of development cable insu-
lation was found to be cracking at low temperatures, switches stopped
working and faults were even caused by radio interference. Some
components were designed, tested, redesigned and retested no fewer
than four times.

It soon became clear that the new Jaguar could not be serviced in the
traditional manner by a half-trained mechanic with a handful of spanners. For its new, largely electronic car Jaguar had to develop a new
electronic servicing system that relied heavily on computer technology
and avoided mechanical servicing techniques. In conjunction with
GenRad, a test equipment company, and Cirrus, a computer software
company, Jaguar developed a computer on wheels called the JDS or
Jaguar Diagnostic System. It consisted of a terminal and a selection of
electronic probes that were simply inserted into control points around
the car to test the status of different systems or components. Every
Jaguar dealer was required to invest in a JDS, thus ensuring that every
dealer could offer the same high standard of customer service. The
software can be rewritten to take account of updating and even of new
models. The JDS is the most sophisticated piece of service equipment
ever produced and it can be programmed to operate in any one of six
languages.

10

A legend up for sale

ON THURSDAY, 22 October 1987 the Right Honourable John Moore MP, then Secretary of State for Health and Social Security, did not have time for his regular lunchtime swim. The minister had two appointments in his diary for the late morning, one rather more pressing than the other. The lesser of the two was a lunch engagement with journalists from the Channel Four Television current affairs programme *A Week In Politics*; the more important was a cabinet meeting with Mrs Thatcher. Three days earlier the London stock market had suffered its biggest single-day fall ever. Fortunes built on the great bull market of the 1980s vanished from the screens of a thousand City computers. The Big Bang had given way to the Big Crash as a hundred billion pounds was wiped off the value of British companies. On that Thursday the cabinet had its first collective opportunity to discuss the matter.

It is not clear precisely what Mrs Thatcher had to say about the stock market. It is clear, however, that by the time John Moore had been driven from Downing Street to his lunch appointment in the private dining room at Frith's restaurant in London's Soho any concern he may have had that this was a crisis had certainly dissipated. Over the first course he explained that the crash was merely a market readjustment. Over the main course he held forth on the blessings of popular capitalism, his enthusiasm undented by the recent fall in share prices. By the time the cheese and the chocolate truffles had arrived, Mr Moore was convinced that the stock market collapse would not divert Mrs Thatcher's government from its historic course.

John Moore had to make his own way in the world. Born on 26 November 1937 to a family far from affluent, he progressed to national service with the Royal Sussex Regiment and afterwards studied at the London School of Economics, where he became chairman of the Conservative Society and president of the Students Union. In 1960 he went to America where he was bitten by the 'free market' bug; he became an investment banker and stockbroker. He also developed an interest in politics, becoming a precinct captain and ward chairman of the Democratic Party. On returning to Britain in the late 1960s Moore continued both his financial and political careers. In 1974 he was elected to Parliament and when Mrs Thatcher swept to power in 1979 he was appointed Undersecretary of State at the Department of Energy. He was something of a Thatcher favourite. As she and Sir Keith Joseph were developing the policies of the New Right, he was waiting in the wings ready and willing to put them into practice.

Perhaps the most far-reaching of all the policies that Thatcher and Joseph developed was the scheme to take many of Britain's nationalised industries into the private sector. Until the early 1980s the concept of privatisation was barely thought of but in John Moore Mrs Thatcher found a faithful enthusiast who was prepared to think the unthinkable. In 1983 Moore was appointed Financial Secretary to the Treasury which made him, in effect, the minister with responsibility for taxation policy and privatisation. His civil servants assumed that the bulk of their work would involve taxation. How wrong they were. Moore set about the privatisation side of his brief with the zeal and fervour of a religious fundamentalist. He visited every government department and asked quite bluntly what could be sold off, noting later: 'In many cases I was greeted with a marked lack of enthusiasm.'

Moore's eagerness was born of his family circumstances. While Thatcherite Conservatives from a middle-class background framed their politics in terms of 'market forces', John Moore believed in 'ownership'. Intellectually, of course, he understood the arguments about free market competition but instinctively it was the concept of personal property rights that really captivated him. Speaking to an

American audience in 1987 he explained, 'I have an advantage that some might call a disadvantage: my family did not own anything until, late in life, they bought a tiny terraced house in the back streets of Brighton. So I know at first hand the fascination, and the fear, that ownership exerts on those who do not have it . . . I know, not in academic terms, but in very personal terms, that when you own something you feel independent and when you do not you feel vulnerable.'

Moore's straightforward analysis of ownership cut right through the complex New Conservative theory and political ideology and his views had a simple appeal for all those 'ordinary people' who, when Mrs Thatcher came to power in 1979, knew little about share ownership and less about the enigmatic workings of the City of London. Moore spotted what many Conservatives had missed, namely that politicians generally come from a background where the ownership of property, shares, even wealth, is often taken for granted. He also recognised the paternalism and snobbery within his own party as evinced by the many members who felt that ordinary people should not be encouraged to 'play' the financial markets.

It took, in political terms, a long time for views like Moore's to gain ascendency even after Mrs Thatcher was elected. In 1979 the Conservatives had had a vague and ill-defined sense of concern about the performance of the nationalised industries, but there was no cogent policy of privatisation. There was certainly a desire to reduce public sector borrowing but few ministers seriously felt that that could be achieved by selling off national assets. The government's preferred option, which it believed would be less unpopular, was to cut public sector spending. It was only when, despite its best endeavours, the government failed to reduce public expenditure that it was forced to consider privatisation as an option. The policy was arrived at almost by a process of elimination.

According to its advocates, privatisation offered many advantages above and beyond that of reducing the scale of the public sector. Privatised companies became more competitive as they began to operate in the free market; in turn that led to greater efficiency and a more responsive attitude towards the customer; and once employees owned shares in a company they felt a greater involvement and were less likely to go on strike. There were other advantages, too. The sale of public companies raised a great deal of money for the government which meant that tax cuts became feasible. The wider ownership of shares meant that more people had a stake in the stock market. This in turn meant that more people felt their interests would be protected by the Conservatives. The privatisation programme was social engineering on a grand scale and, as John Moore acknowledged, it was a policy that was skilfully administered. 'We have managed the programme to ensure that progress is made in a number of key areas,' he said later. 'I have no doubt, however, that when the final history of privatisation comes to be written, its effect on the patterns of ownership in the United Kingdom will be reckoned as its greatest achievement.'

Perhaps the biggest shock the government had in store was the discovery that privatisation could be made popular. On the face of it, selling the nation's assets seemed a remarkably unpopular thing to do but as the privatisation policy was stepped up such negative thoughts were swept aside. The programme became positively celebrated. The public began to see government share flotations, attractively priced, as the sort of gamble on which you could not lose. Each time a company was sold off those who were lucky enough to get some shares saw them jump up in price as soon as trading started, thereby guaranteeing an immediate profit. Privatisation became known as Mrs Thatcher's 'Big Idea', an idea that had apparently found its time. Other countries soon followed the Thatcherite lead, even non-capitalist countries. In the wake of the free market flood came massive deregulation, especially of the financial markets. Consequently, privatisation was perceived to be such a central plank of the Thatcher revolution that her supporters began to fear that any failure affecting share ownership would lead to rapid disenchantment and a collapse of popular support.

Yet it was only after four years in office that Mrs Thatcher decided to invest her entire political future in the policy of privatisation. Her appointment, in 1983, of John Moore as minister with special responsibility for privatisation was the turning point. His driving forcefulness gave the policy a special impetus and by January 1984 he had developed a strategy for its implementation.

His strategy was to attack the state sector with all his might and to establish a long-term privatisation programme involving every government department and every government minister. He called the public industries 'large remote monoliths that may be strong on paper but are weak on actual performance'. He declared that 'Less government is good government,' and said that industry needed the competition that came only with the free market: 'Competition is an extraordinarily efficient mechanism. It does not require politicians or civil servants to make it work.' He insisted that privatisation was the route to competition and that it 'hands back, to the people of this country, industries that have no place in the public sector'. His message was summed up in the simple assertion that 'Governments are not very good at owning or controlling businesses.' With views like that it was not surprising that Moore became the champion of popular capitalism, the man who brought share ownership to the masses. Within the year he would privatise British Telecom, the largest share sale ever to take place anywhere in the world. But before that, almost as a curtain raiser, he privatised the Jaguar Car Company.

Mrs Thatcher had been pressing for some form of private sector involvement at BL ever since she gained office. To begin with, she felt the private sector was the natural place for a car company especially since successful car companies in many other parts of the world were in private hands. What made the BL case more urgent was the fact that the company was a serious drain on government resources. What made it absolutely imperative was the fact that Mrs Thatcher was not supposed to support lame ducks. Mrs Thatcher, however, had not reckoned with the substantial personality of Sir Michael Edwardes. Her desire to strike a quick blow for privatisation was thwarted by his desire to get BL back on its feet. Mrs Thatcher suggested that a gesture would help. If BL was in no fit state to be privatised as a whole, why not privatise parts of it? Sir Michael insisted that piecemeal privatisation would damage what remained of the company and further weaken the group's balance sheet. If the profitable parts of the company were sold off, he feared the unprofitable rump would be doomed to extinction or perpetual government subsidy. To make absolutely certain his message got home he told Mrs Thatcher's supporters on the Conservative backbench Industry Committee: 'It is the [BL] board's overriding objective to reduce and eventually be free of State funding. But piecemeal, ill-timed sell-offs are not the way.'

Further conflict lay in the fact that by 1982 Mrs Thatcher was keen to demonstrate before the next general election that she was doing something other than pour money into BL. The Prime Minister was operating in a timespan dictated by parliamentary democracy but Sir Michael was operating in the international market place and the revival of BL could not be arranged in time for an election.

Sir Michael Edwardes left BL at the end of 1982 when his five-year contract expired. The group's mainstream business was still in one piece but government pressure for selective sell-offs at BL was becoming irresistible. The 1983 general election returned Mrs Thatcher to a second term of office a few months later and John Moore increased the pressure for the sale of BL's assets. At first it seemed that Land Rover might be an appropriate candidate but its performance did not inspire the requisite confidence for a successful flotation. It was then that the public spotlight fell on Jaguar.

When he first arrived at Jaguar, John Egan had barely considered the possibility of privatisation. He was rather more preoccupied with what he described as one of Sir Michael Edwardes's regular 'shoot-outs', an industrial dispute over pay and conditions. 'I didn't realise it was even feasible that Jaguar could be floated off separately. That idea started to really form amongst our team here within about six to nine months after I'd actually arrived. It began from the question of what we would do if the whole corporation blew up in one of the Edwardes shoot-outs. After about twelve months of me being here we began to understand that this was a "goer". We could actually put together a financially capable company and we thought it would be a damn shame if one of these shoot-outs left us high and dry. So each time there was a shoot-out we would make sure that, if necessary, we could borrow the money actually to pick up the company if it fell.' Eventually Egan came to believe that privatisation was not just a useful bonus that came with survival but an absolute prerequisite of that survival. Without privatisation, 'We probably would have sunk without trace.'

That was the view John Egan inculcated in his top management team, who saw privatisation as a means of escaping from the BL straitjacket. David Boole says, 'I think we saw full escape, full flotation, privatisation, as very much the end point in our survival programme.' Jaguar executives were still concerned that BL would not allow the company to operate as an independent profit centre within the group, and that Jaguar profits would be creamed off to cover losses in other parts of the organisation. The only way to make certain that did not happen was to establish Jaguar as a wholly separate company.

Egan also recognised that the prospect of a stock market quotation meant that Jaguar would be better able to attract top managers: 'I am not quite sure that it [the Jaguar company] would have attracted the right kind of senior management if indeed the possibility of independence had not been there.' Privatisation meant better rewards, especially for senior managers: 'A lot of the rewards for . . . all of our people in the company are connected to our share price and the better we do the more financially rewarding the whole thing is to everyone in the company.'

Perhaps the most important single business factor that made Egan and his management team favour privatisation was the belief that operating independently would enable them to invest precisely as they saw fit. As part of BL, Jaguar had had to fit in with wider corporate investment policies and, of course, BL itself operated under the fiscal straitjacket imposed by its largest shareholder, the British Government. Freedom to invest always rests, of course, on the assumption that a company has the means to invest and there, too, John Egan believed that privatisation would be advantageous for Jaguar. It is, as he sees it, a question of business attitudes. 'We have to make any money that we require for our capital investment programme from the customer. The only person who can possibly pay us is the customer . . . that is never the way that nationalised concerns ever looked at it. They wanted money? They asked the government for it. And everybody, including the workforce, believed that the whole purpose was to see how much money you could get from government invested in the forward development programmes. Here [at Jaguar] everybody understands the only way to get money is to create it.'

At the heart of John Egan's support for privatisation was a firmly held political conviction that the private sector encouraged higher standards of excellence in almost every conceivable sphere. 'I've always been absolutely clear', he said, 'that the government had no right to own a luxury car maker. It's better off in the market place working out its own salvation in its own way.' His political belief in the free market was unswerving and extended well beyond manufacturing industry. 'Let's see people standing on their own feet. Let's see people owning their own houses. Let's see people spending their own money and not having it all taken away in tax and being spent for them by the nation.' And if people came to expect a great deal from privatised companies, well, in John Egan's view that was fine: 'It's a jolly good thing that people are demanding excellence. It's a good job people think it [privatisation] is a panacea because that doesn't half put the spark into managers to start to improve.'

While Egan advanced the wider political arguments for privatisation he never lost sight of the immediate practical advantages that could be drawn from greater freedom of manoeuvre. Not surprisingly his managers, the people who had to deal with BL on a day-to-day basis, focused almost exclusively on these practical implications. They were particularly keen to escape what they saw as the dead hand of BL bureaucracy. According to David Boole, attempted integration within BL, such as the plan to put a Rover engine into a Jaguar car, meant that 'Jaguar was not really in search of excellence. It was being compromised potentially at every corner . . . and that happened throughout the whole design process. It also happened through the manufacturing process as well.'

Michael Beasley, John Egan's number two, says the problem with the Jaguar-BL relationship was that the two organisations were in very different businesses. Jaguar managers 'were suffering because we were subject to volume car-style management, volume car-style marketing, volume car-style pressures within a luxury car facility'. Privatisation would provide a way out of the BL relationship and a move towards the very different industrial culture of luxury car manufacutring.

Jaguar's finance director, John Edwards, had some sympathy for BL: 'They didn't want to get rid of something that was making money but obviously in political terms they had to do something.' In other words the main BL shareholder, the government, was forcing the corporation to sell off its most valuable asset. As Edwards saw it, even if Jaguar's reputation had improved out of all recognition, its image was still suffering because BL was attracting so much bad publicity. In his view successful people liked to buy successful cars from successful companies; it was all about the reinforcement of personal achievement.

'Buying a car for £25,000 is a symbol of it. If you're in a company that's losing £500 million a year and everybody talks about it in a negative way, then that rubs off on the company image.'

As it became increasingly clear that BL would not be able to fend off the pressure to sell Jaguar, the parent company tried to press Jaguar into an early launch of the new XJ40 saloon and when that failed persuaded the Department of Trade and Industry that Leyland should be allowed to retain a 25 per cent stake in Jaguar. The hope was that by retaining a major shareholding BL would still get a share of Jaguar's profits and would have some restraining influence if Jaguar ever decided to compete with BL's new model, the Rover Sterling. Not surprisingly that was precisely what Jaguar intended to do. Egan was far from happy that BL should be allowed a substantial say in his business. As David Boole explained: 'If they [BL] had seen us [Jaguar] going for a particular niche in the market that they had plans for, it could have been a conflict of interest.' Yet in the face of Department of Trade and Industry agreement there seemed little Jaguar could do about it. Gloomily, John Edwards set to work on the preparation of an official 'Offer For Sale' document, indicating that 75 per cent of Jaguar's shares would be placed on the market.

It was Norman Tebbit, Secretary of State for Trade and Industry, who early in 1984 took the proposal to cabinet – only to have it roundly rejected. Tebbit's colleagues were keen to extract every ounce of political advantage from the Jaguar sell-off and they felt that a complete break from BL would best underline Jaguar's new status as the rising star of the private sector. David Boole has little doubt about the Prime Minister's role in the affair: 'I've got no firm evidence to confirm this but I think it was the Prime Minister herself who insisted – with the assistance of a couple of ministers that we heard about – that it would be a total flotation, that there would be no retained shareholding by BL.' John Edwards also believes it was the Prime Minister herself who questioned BL's right to a retained shareholding. Norman Tebbit's discomfiture over BL's stake in Jaguar was one of many disagreements he was to have with Mrs Thatcher over the next few years.

The BL board was bitterly disappointed but it was getting used to interference from a government that claimed not to interfere in the running of industry. In the early 1980s talks had taken place between the British Government and a number of car companies about the purchase of some part of BL, and on each occasion the company concerned had hoped the government's desire to be rid of the trouble-some car giant would enable it to pick up a bargain. On each occasion BL had had to fight off the predator.

Between 1979 and 1981 BL poured the best part of £150 million into Jaguar. In the run-up to privatisation growing Jaguar profits meant that much, though not all, of that money had been repaid. The last that BL was to recover was in the form of a special dividend paid by Jaguar just before privatisation. BL's risk investment had proved unfortunate from their point of view. Not only did they fail to get all the money back but just as the investment was about to mature Jaguar was floated off and went its own way – as a competitor, too.

John Egan's success in leading Jaguar from the brink of disaster to unparalleled commercial success had been lauded as the great industrial turnaround of the Thatcher era. His general political views were largely Thatcherite and not surprisingly his specific views on privatisation had a staunchly Thatcherite ring to them as well. The public sector was 'a rather flaccid, bureaucratic, low-performance sector', he said. If Britain wanted a strong, thrusting economy then it needed to get companies out into the private sector 'fending for themselves, defending their record to people who expect good service'. In early 1984 such views were particu-larly pleasing to John Moore. The two men saw eye-to-eye over Jaguar's problems; indeed in time they even told the same anecdotes. In a speech in 1986 John Moore was describing Jaguar under BL manage-ment as 'merely "Large Car Assembly Plant Number Two". And this loss of identity – crushing for the prestige of the company and for the morale of its employees – was accompanied by an equally serious loss of managerial independence and initiative.'

So it was that Jaguar became a prime privatisation prospect early in 1984. The big question that remained was how precisely the sale would take place. There were three broad options: the company could be sold lock, stock and barrel to a single buyer; John Egan and his management colleagues could organise a staff buy-out; or the company could be floated on the stock exchange with the shares being offered for sale to the public and to the financial institutions.

The attractions of Jaguar to a single buyer were many and varied. Clearly the Jaguar name and the company's superb image were very valuable assets; the company's distribution network might also be deemed to have some intrinsic value. Certainly the removal of a competitor from the market place could have attracted interest from Jaguar's main rivals in West Germany.

The advantages to the government of a sale to a single buyer were substantial. Such a sale would be simple, straightforward, relatively quick and possibly more lucrative. Faced with the choice of purchasing the company from the British Government or mounting a takeover bid on the London Stock Exchange most potential buyers would have preferred to do an orderly deal with the government and would have been prepared to pay a premium for that privilege. There was certainly a great deal of interest in the idea of purchasing Jaguar. As long ago as the early 1970s the world's motor manufacturers were beating a path to the factory gates at Browns Lane, Coventry. Geoffrey Robinson recalls that 'In my day, I think it is fairly well known now, I had two or three approaches from companies, and the most realistic, I think, from General Motors, for a takeover.' General Motors' interest made perfect business sense. GM is a large conglomerate of different motor companies brought together, very successfully, under one banner. Jaguar would have made a brilliant addition to the range and represented an excellent financial hedge. As the dollar weakened against the pound so GM's export profitability would go up. As the dollar strengthened against the pound Jaguar's export profitability would go up. Whatever happened to the pound/dollar exchange rate, General Motors would win.

A decade later General Motors had still not given up hope, but now they were joined by a host of other interested car companies. According to John Edwards, 'BMW, General Motors and Ford were the three companies that expressed some interest in talking about the situation.' Ultimately it was Ford that pushed events beyond the talking stage by announcing, in September 1989, its intention of acquiring 15 per cent of Jaguar's shares, despite opposition from the Jaguar management. The attraction for Jaguar of a large and profitable parent company (as opposed to a large and then unprofitable parent company, like BL) was that during the inevitable 'hard times' of the highly cyclical motor industry the parent company would be able to shelter Jaguar, and ensure that forward development programmes for new models did not suffer unduly. But, on the whole, 'We were not enamoured . . . we saw that we would gain very little benefit from being part of a large car company.' Whatever value was to be found in an arrangement with a big car company, there was always more in it for the purchaser than there was for Jaguar.

The one thing these various approaches did achieve was to confirm the government in its belief that Jaguar was a saleable concern. In the end two factors combined to persuade the government not to sell Jaguar to a single corporate buyer. The first involved John Moore's faith in the public's desire to own shares. While others vacillated, wondering whether it was really possible to persuade tens of thousands of ordinary people to pay cash for a piece of company 'image', Moore had no such doubts. The second factor concerned the nature of the prospective buyers: none of them was British and the prospect of a protracted political battle, if Jaguar passed into foreign hands, European or otherwise, was not something the government relished.

The second option, the possibility of selling Jaguar to its management with or without a substantial stake for the workforce, did have certain attractions for the government, not least of which was that the management team clearly knew what it was doing and the company that had become known as the Thatcherite success story would continue to be run by one of her greatest supporters. For John Egan and his colleagues it would have offered a tremendous opportunity – to own the company they ran and to make a fortune into the bargain. Sadly for them, it was not to be. A merchant bank valued Jaguar on behalf of the BL board and when John Edwards heard what that value was he could scarcely believe his ears. 'The first valuation of the company was £50 million and we said, "That is ridiculous." We probably shouldn't have said, "That is ridiculous." We should have said, "Right, there is £100 million on the table" . . . We could have actually done that. In financial terms . . . we had several offers with very good practical propositions . . . for a management-type buy-out.' But the BL board opposed such an option and that, combined with the opportunity of promoting wider share ownership and the spread of popular capitalism, was enough to persuade the government to opt for a public share offer.

11

The stag party

'BL ANNOUNCES that it intends to proceed with the sale of the whole of its interest in Jaguar Cars Holdings Limited, to be renamed Jaguar plc.' With that stark press announcement on 14 June 1984, Hill Samuel, the merchant bank that offered Jaguar's shares for sale, proclaimed the company's privatisation.

Privatisation had become the principal focus of management attention at Jaguar Cars. The management team spent many long hours preparing the company for flotation. Top executives split themselves into two groups; one, including John Edwards and the company secretary, Ken Edwards, took principal responsibility for privatisation, while the other, under Michael Beasley and Jim Randle, continued to run the company. For John Edwards, in particular, privatisation meant burning the midnight oil. 'I spent hours – massive periods – intense concentration periods – pulling together the basic agreements and fabrics of the Offer For Sale document in conjunction with the merchant bank and BL . . . I spent a lot of time in Wood Street [Hill Samuel's London head office] but we used to do it in concentrated bursts. We used to start early in the morning and work very, very late at night and I would stay overnight and then do it the next day. Then I would come back [to Coventry] for a couple of days.'

In order for Jaguar to be privatised every single element of the manufacturing operation had to be extricated from the BL business and reassembled into a single integrated company. When Egan had arrived at Browns Lane in 1980 Jaguar had no legal existence at all; it endured as a luxury car marque in name only. By 1982, as privatisation became more of a certainty, Jaguar was taking full control of its own sales operation, particularly in the key North American market, but there remained many aspects of the business that needed to be separated from BL before Jaguar could be sold off.

One of the most difficult problems that had to be tackled was the problem of recreating a balance sheet for the years when Jaguar had been part of BL. The arcane complexities of British Leyland's accounting procedures meant that for several years no separate audited accounts were prepared for Jaguar: the Jaguar operation was part of BL Cars and the accounting records were not designed to give separate trading results. With careful and painstaking research John Edwards and his finance team, assisted by a group of auditors from the accountants Coopers and Lybrand, recreated the missing results as best they could. Their estimate for 1980 was that the company had made a £47 million loss on a turnover of £166 million, but their figures were not capable of detailed verification. The results for 1981 and 1982 were more reliable but still included certain irrelevant items that could not be eradicated from the BL figures. Edwards reckoned that in 1981 Jaguar had made a £32 million pre-tax loss and in 1982 had gone into the black for the first time since Egan's arrival with a £9 million pre-tax profit. By 1983, however, it was possible to construct a full Jaguar balance sheet which showed that the company turnaround had been achieved. With a turnover of £473 million Jaguar made a 1983 pre-tax profit of £50 million. It was a far cry from 1979. Jaguar's official Stock Exchange Offer For Sale document said, 'No meaningful accounts can be prepared for 1979 and the best estimates that can now be made indicate that, for the continuing activities of the Jaguar Group, the value of turnover in 1979 was similar to that of 1980 and that the operating losses incurred in 1979 were slightly below those of 1980.'

Splitting Jaguar off from BL meant that the new company had to enter into 'arm's length' contracts for a number of services that had hitherto been provided by BL on a simple corporate basis. In 1984 Jaguar contracted BL's Unipart to provide a parts service throughout the world and contracted Austin Rover to continue the supply of body panels. Computer services and software maintenance were supplied by BL's subsidiary, Istel, and BL Technology was contracted to provide certain research and development services. Jaguar also had to extricate itself from the BL distribution network. This had largely been achieved by the time of privatisation but for a period after flotation Austin Rover distributors continued to handle Jaguar cars in France, Spain and Italy.

Even the freehold of the Jaguar factories had to be transferred to the new company. In 1983 Jaguar acquired the Browns Lane assembly works and 100 acres of land from BL for £3.5 million. Later it bought the Radford engine plant for just under £1 million and the Castle Bromwich paint and body shop for £7 million. Jaguar was also given a deed of indemnity by BL guaranteeing the new company 'that not less than £77.9 million of tax losses were available to Jaguar Cars at 1 January 1983 . . . and that such losses are available against subsequent trading profits'. Nothing was overlooked. John Edwards even agreed to pay a nominal sum for certain trade marks that belonged to BL and when it became clear that both Jaguar and Austin Rover wanted to use the name 'Vanden Plas' they signed an agreement which, in effect, allowed both companies to use it.

The myriad service agreements that had to be drawn up required an enormous amount of detailed work. Edwards co-ordinated the effort but as it would have been physically impossible for one office to draft and negotiate every contract he appointed deputies to sort out specialist contracts involving things like panel supply and computers. Edwards explained, 'There were about twenty people who were actually dedicated to a point in the process and spent, I would say, 55 per cent of the time [working on the contracts] . . . and it was not 55 per cent of their normal work, it was 55 per cent of their working hours and their working hours increased a lot.'

While BL continued to provide some corporate services on a sub-contract basis, many others passed into Jaguar's direct control. The company soon discovered that it could run many of them more economically than BL, which seemed odd since BL was providing the service not just for Jaguar but for several other car makers as well, and it should therefore have been able to do so more cheaply. David Boole says, 'I can't think of a single area where we didn't actually save money. It sounds odd but we were able to do things much more cheaply doing them ourselves than [when] we were paying for a corporate service.' Boole believes the problem was largely that BL was an inefficient bureaucracy. 'There were several hundred people based in a big office in Marylebone Road, the BL corporate staff. Then there was another headquarters building in Coventry for Leyland Cars and then beneath Leyland Cars you had the individual companies. So there were many tiers of bureaucracy and there was conflict between them because, on many occasions, they were doing the same thing and there were tussles to see who would be dominant within that bureaucratic structure.'

As privatisation became a certainty Jaguar was forced to address a difficult problem that had been assuming greater proportions the closer the company came to flotation. Since the company was a subsidiary of state-owned BL its directors had had little collective experience of working on the board of a publicly quoted company. Although they had undoubted talents as industrial executives, it was felt in some quarters that when Jaguar was floated it would need additional non-executive directors with a reputation and credibility in the City of London. It was with this in mind that Hamish Orr-Ewing was approached to become non-executive chairman.

Orr-Ewing had been the chairman of Rank Xerox since 1979, having joined that company almost twenty years earlier from the motor industry. In the 1960s he had been product planning manager for the Ford Motor Company, in charge of the Cortina development project. He had even spent some time working for British Leyland. A few months before Jaguar was privatised Sir Austin Bide, BL's chairman, had invited Orr-Ewing to consider becoming non-executive chairman of Jaguar. Orr-Ewing recalls that 'It struck me as an enormously exciting thing to be able to do and if I could help the full-time executives to make a success of the privatisation it appealed to me enormously. After a very brief period of reflection I accepted the invitation.'

Orr-Ewing was, in his own words, a man 'who had no ambition' in the sense that he had nothing to prove. He was not trying to 'earn his spurs' and it seemed, therefore, that he provided a perfect foil for John Egan's thrusting management style. But Jaguar executives felt Orr-Ewing had been imposed on them by BL which was not keen to sell

Jaguar anyway. In due course, the appointment led to a rare boardroom battle at Jaguar Cars.

Orr-Ewing was joined on the Jaguar board by Edward Bond, finance director of the Beecham Group and, significantly, a member of the City Take-Overs and Mergers Panel. In the same way that Orr-Ewing was intended to provide weight and credibility for the new public company so Bond provided additional support for John Edwards who, though widely considered an able and talented finance director had been litle more than 30 years old when he had taken up his senior post at Jaguar in 1980. Both Edward Bond and Hamish Orr-Ewing were appointed non-executive directors of Jaguar on 1 May 1984, increasing the size of the main Jaguar board to six: John Egan, John Edwards, Edward Bond, Hamish Orr-Ewing, Ray Horrocks from BL and Graham Whitehead, president of Jaguar's North American subsidiary. Egan, Edwards and Whitehead, the three executive directors, all signed service agreements that bound them to Jaguar after flotation. On Monday, 30 July 1984, the official Jaguar Offer For Sale document was finally published, with Jaguar employees, along with other BL employees and BL's small shareholders, being given preferential rights to apply for shares in the company.

In March the number of ordinary shares to be issued by Jaguar had been increased from 100 million to 180 million, and all 180 million were sold to the public when Jaguar was privatised. On 3 July, Jaguar had been re-registered as a public limited company and John Egan had begun a promotional tour of City institutions. Late that month an Extraordinary General Meeting of BL shareholders approved the Jaguar sale. Since 99.7 per cent of BL's shares were held by the Secretary of State for Trade and Industry, this technical requirement was something of a formality but it served to underline who was making the running on the Jaguar privatisation.

The Offer For Sale document detailed certain controls that the government would retain over Jaguar. In June 1984 the company had created a single Special Rights Redeemable share to be held by the Secretary of State for Trade and Industry which gave the minister certain rights, the most important of which concerned the size of shareholdings. Under the Jaguar Company's official Articles of Association no shareholder could own more than 15 per cent of the company's shares and the Articles of Association could not be changed without the consent of the Special Shareholder. The point of this complex arrangement was to ensure that when Jaguar had been floated it did not become the immediate subject of a takeover bid. Having decided not to sell Jaguar direct to an overseas company, the government did not want one of the foreign companies that had expressed an interest in buying Jaguar simply to step in and purchase a majority of Jaguar's shares as soon as they were available on the open market. The solution was to create this special 'Golden Share'. There was, however, a problem with the golden share: it offered Jaguar a degree of protection that was unavailable to other publicly listed companies. It gave the company an unfair advantage, in that it could plan for the future without fear of takeover, while other car companies operating in the private sector had to be constantly aware of the threat from predators.

There followed lengthy discussion between the government, BL, Hill Samuel and the Stock Exchange. John Edwards takes up the story. 'What was a reasonable time for us to establish ourselves in terms of what we needed to do in capital expenditure? . . . The Stock Exchange said, "Three years, no more than that, because that is not fair." We said, "Three years in the motor industry is nothing, it is not even a half product cycle. So you can't expect that." So then they said, "Five years." We said, "Five years is not enough."' In the end Jaguar was given six years in which to become self-supporting. The golden share was to continue in existence until 31 December 1990, at which time Jaguar would be expected to stand on its own feet and to fend off any predators as best it could.

In the weeks before the flotation, press coverage of Jaguar and its cars reached new peaks. The combination of an exceptional history and a reinvigorated reputation proved irresistible to the feature writers and the City editors, but the marketing of the Jaguar share sale was far from straightforward. Should the PR people concentrate on the cars or the company? What was the company really worth? While the cars themselves could be compared with the competition, and the company's assets could be accurately valued by accountants, it was impossible to place a price on the Jaguar brand name and image. There had been plans for a major advertising campaign but the Jaguar management

team had serious reservations. They felt some of the advertising proposals were too 'down-market' and they tried to persuade BL to drop the
campaign. Fortunately for David Boole, BL executives were already
beginning to blanch at the cost of a major advertising campaign so
when he was able to demonstrate that the substantial press interest
meant there was no need for the campaign, they swiftly agreed.

Despite the fact that Jaguar's reputation could be made or marred by
the way in which the flotation was handled, David Boole and Jaguar
had little influence over the selling of the company. 'We didn't really
have too much formal access to the way in which we'd be marketed,' he
explained. BL and the government made the running which meant
Jaguar 'had to try very hard to use informal ways of trying to represent
what our wishes were in all of this'. Senior BL executives thought Sir
John Egan was in regular contact with Mrs Thatcher, undermining the
parent company and ensuring the newly privatised Jaguar would be
established just as he wanted it. John Edwards explains that 'The BL
board thought that John was talking to the government quite regularly.
In fact he wasn't but the BL board thought he was so they were
suspicious of our motives.' But if Egan was not actually meeting the
Prime Minister on a regular basis his views were certainly being made
known to her. As Edwards acknowledges, Sir John is 'a high-profile
person. He has been a high-profile person for many years and so he has
always had regular contact with very senior people in every walk of life,
including the government.' Egan had become identified with Jaguar
and Jaguar with him. David Boole says,'When it came to privatisation it
was quite useful to have someone like that who had the ear of
government – of ministers – who could actually represent our position
. . . It helped our lobbying in terms of achieving what we wanted out of
the privatisation process.'

Eight a.m., 3 August 1984. A seething mass of people crushed through
the doors of the Barclays Bank office in Fleetway House, Farringdon
Street on the western edge of the City of London, carrying last-minute
share applications for the Jaguar flotation. Some bore single application
documents, others were loaded down with armfuls of forms. Each
application was accompanied by a large cheque. The lobby of Fleetway
House looked more like the setting for a local parish jumble sale than

the foyer of a major London bank. A long trestle table had been set up and upon it were piled box after box of applications; pink ones as published in the *Financial Times*, white ones from the form in the *Daily Telegraph*, and glossy ones from the company prospectus. But the hand-delivered forms were a mere trifle compared with the hundred sacks full of applications that arrived with the post. As the stampede of human bodies surged forward policemen and bank staff looked on helplessly. Outside the scrum had spilled into the road, bringing rush-hour traffic to a standstill.

It was soon apparent that the Jaguar share offer was wildly oversub-scribed. More than 300,000 applications had been received, cheques written for some £2.5 billion. Individuals and institutions had applied for eight times as many shares as were being sold. In the media coverage that followed, a host of new words and phrases gained common cur-rency. Everyone became an overnight expert in 'stagging', 'bulls and bears', 'the aftermarket' and how to devour a 'red herring prospectus'.

The stags are the most interesting creatures in the new privatisation farmyard. These are the speculators who apply for shares with the sole intention of immediately selling them in the aftermarket to make a quick profit. Privatisation share issues are their speciality. They work on the assumption that if a share is advertised at a certain price it will almost certainly be undervalued and will therefore rise in price once dealing begins. There is nothing the stags like more than a bull market, a market in which share prices are constantly rising. It is still possible to stag during a bear market, when share prices are falling, but the risks are much greater. Stags apply for as many shares as possible and then quickly sell whatever shares they are allocated. In the case of Jaguar they expected a bonanza because the offer price of 165 pence a share was almost 10 per cent lower than most City analysts had expected. Professional stags always wait until the last minute before putting in their applications, just in case the stock market falls before they are able to take delivery of their shares to resell them. They often apply for shares under a host of different names. They know the government sometimes encourages wider share ownership by reducing the number of shares allotted to the large institutions and allowing small investors to buy all the shares they want. By using the multiple application tactic stags hope to maximise their ultimate shareholding and thus their profit. When Jaguar was floated, multiple applications were not illegal, they were simply discouraged. By the time former Conservative MP Keith Best used different versions of his name to purchase shares in British Telecom he was breaking the law.

On the top floors of Fleetway House bank staff worked feverishly to weed out the multiple share applications. Instead of favouring a large number of small shareholders, Hill Samuel tried to create a balanced shareholders' register for Jaguar comprising a number of big institutions that would become long-term investors in the company and a number of smaller shareholders who might sell more quickly, thereby creating a liquid market. Despite their best efforts to reject applications from stags, many got through. Jaguar began its new life with well over 100,000 shareholders. Within a year that number had been reduced by two thirds as many people sold for quick profits.

The stags were not the only people to make a substantial gain on the Jaguar flotation. BL hit upon the novel idea of cashing all the large cheques that had been sent in before allocating any Jaguar shares. The money sat in a deposit account for several days earning half a million pounds in interest every 24 hours before BL finally sent out the shares. But the underwriters made the biggest killing. Underwriters are merchant banks that, in effect, insure share sales by promising to buy whatever shares are not purchased by the public; in return they are paid a fee by the company selling the shares. The chances of the Jaguar flotation being a flop were negligible but the merchant banks underwriting the issue earned more than £5 million for insuring against the remote possibility that few people would wish to buy a piece of British motoring history.

A week after share applications closed the shares were allotted and trading began on the London Stock Exchange. The Jaguar sale was one of the last colourful sell-offs to take place before the City was revolutionised by the computerisation of share dealing known as the Big Bang. On the old Stock Exchange trading floor jobbers' pitches were decked out with company posters and small statues of the leaping Jaguar and the exchange opened ten minutes early to allow brokers to make an orderly market in Jaguar shares. The price rose rapidly from 165 pence – at which level the new company was worth some £300 million – to close the day at 179 pence. The volume of Jaguar shares traded was enormous. In just a few hours almost 50 million shares changed hands.

On the basis of the share price at the end of that first day's trading, Jaguar had been undervalued by about £25 million, a relatively modest sum in comparison with the hundreds of millions of pounds that were lost to the Exchequer when British Telecom was privatised. Those responsible for the pricing of the Jaguar issue took some solace from the fact that while the shares may have been undervalued by about eight per cent the stock market had risen by about the same amount in the period between the fixing of the share price and the sale itself. Overall the City felt the Jaguar flotation was a great success.

But one group of people was not rushing to buy Jaguar shares: the Jaguar workers. Fewer than one in five exercised their preferential rights to purchase the company's stock. Between them they bought little more than one per cent of the company.

Part of the thinking behind the government's privatisation programme had been that workers should be encouraged to own shares in the companies they worked for. Through such ownership workers would feel a greater commitment to their company and would work harder – or so the theory went. However, even Sir John Egan felt that this was an optimistic oversimplification. 'I think these things mean something over the longer term,' he said. 'They don't actually, I believe, influence the day-to-day activity so much. I don't think just because a person's got a stake in the company he'll be involved in frenzied activity for eight hours a day.'

In the months after privatisation the Jaguar workforce made it clear that shares alone were not enough. They were looking for something more tangible than pieces of paper: they wanted substantial pay increases. Three months after privatisation they went on strike and secured a 20 per cent pay rise over two years. It became very clear that share ownership was not an alternative to collective bargaining. Aware that his employees might need a little encouragement, Egan ensured that when Jaguar was sold off there was a workers' non-contributory share scheme based on a proportion of the company's profits. Each year five per cent of Jaguar's profits are placed in a trust fund and fund managers use the money to buy Jaguar shares on behalf of the entire workforce. Whether they like it or not, almost all Jaguar's workers own a small slice of the company. The shares are held in trust for two years and then if they so choose individual employees can withdraw their shares and sell them. The scheme enables Sir John to say that 'practically all of our employees are shareholders in the company. I don't think it changes the day-to-day behaviour but I think it does change the long-term view that people take of the company, and all of the decisions at the margins are probably influenced by the fact that the employee does have a stake in the company.'

At the time of privatisation certain senior executives at Jaguar could earn bonuses of up to 50 per cent of their annual salary depending on their performance in meeting pre-determined targets. On top of his bonus, Egan and several of his senior colleagues had been granted options to buy the company's shares at discounted prices; the higher the share price went the more valuable the options became. These various incentives had added up to a strong inducement to make the company more successful but their value depended on the company being privatised and having a publicly quoted share price. Now, Egan had a powerful incentive to succeed and he was keen to give the Jaguar workforce an incentive too. In 1986 he introduced another workers' share scheme based on the Save-As-You-Earn principle. Each month Jaguar employees can save a regular sum of between £10 and £100 which is placed on deposit in a building society. On joining the scheme each employee is granted a special Jaguar share option which gives the holder the right to buy shares at a particular time in the future at a particular fixed price. If the share price rises beyond the fixed price specified in the option the holder will make a profit. If the share price falls the holder will simply not exercise his or her right to purchase the shares. In the case of the Jaguar scheme, the option is to buy Jaguar shares at slightly less than the quoted share price on the day of joining the scheme. The option can be exercised after a set number of years. The plan is very attractive because if the share price rises the options become more valuable and if the share price falls the workers are at least left with the full value of their savings in the building society plus, of course, some interest. The scheme was so appealing that 40 per cent of Jaguar workers signed up for it.

With a maximum saving of £100 a month nobody was going to make a fortune – at best workers could hope to make a few thousand pounds

– but ironically, by the end of 1988, the workers' share option scheme appeared to be more attractive than the senior executives' scheme. Directors and senior executives held options on just over 1.5 million shares but many of the options had been granted when Jaguar's share price was almost 600p and they were therefore correspondingly expensive. Many of the workers' share options had been granted when the Jaguar share price was well under 300p and were consequently very cheap. Options on almost 5 million shares had been granted to Jaguar employees which, by the summer of 1989, represented a paper profit of around £3 million.

Share options give workers and executives financial incentives to make their company as successful as possible. There is some debate over just how effective such options really are but they do achieve one thing: they act as an inducement to stop executives from flitting, like soccer managers, from one company to another for rapidly spiralling salaries. Such schemes are often called the 'golden handcuffs' of British industry.

12

Risk and opportunity

In 1980, when John Egan arrived at Jaguar, he had gambled on not introducing a new car straight away, staking the future of the company instead on an improvement in quality and the reputation of the existing model range. In 1984 he had gambled on privatising Jaguar before the launch of the XJ40: with a new, unproven model just around the corner there had been a serious risk that investors might fail to take up the share issue. By 1986 Egan was ready to gamble on the XJ40 itself. Within a year the car was scheduled to represent 80 per cent of Jaguar's sales. If it was well received it would carry the company almost into the 21st century. If it failed, Jaguar's vulnerability as a virtual one-product company would be cruelly exposed and John Egan could expect no quarter from his competitors, from his shareholders, from the public or from the government.

With privatisation had come a new-found freedom to invest some of the company's profits in technology and infrastructure and some in advanced products like the new convertible version of the XJS grand tourer. Egan says privatisation 'allowed us to invest in the long-term requirements of a luxury car company in terms of the distribution, in terms of the equipment and in terms of the new model programmes. I'm sure that a new convertible XJS would have been seen as highly frivolous by a car company strapped for cash [BL] and yet, of course, it will be an extremely good return on investment for a luxury car company.'

As an investment Jaguar had certainly represented a spectrum of risk and opportunity. The opportunity was a rare chance to buy into a prestigious and glamorous company that was clearly doing well, but the risks were substantial. In the months that followed privatisation the dangers that littered the road ahead for Jaguar became of increasing concern for the company chairman, Hamish Orr-Ewing. He thought Jaguar was over-reliant on the US market; it was practically a single-product company and it was far too small, making it susceptible to eventual takeover. As Orr-Ewing saw it, 'However brave and courageous, however excellent the product . . . Jaguar was David versus Goliath. That may occasionally work but there are always tremendous risks.' Orr-Ewing was concerned that those risks were not being taken seriously. He felt the problem of Jaguar's size could be tackled by acquiring other businesses but he recalls that the problem 'was very seldom discussed adequately at the time'. Jaguar executives saw it rather differently. They thought that Orr-Ewing and another non-executive director, Ray Horrocks, were secretly planning to shift the direction in which the company was heading. Whether or not this was true, Orr-Ewing was on a direct collision course with Egan, who strongly believed that diversification and acquisition would be a mistake. According to a senior Jaguar executive, 'They [Orr-Ewing and Horrocks] seemed to have plans to do things with the business which were not discussed with the executive directors first – which we didn't take too kindly to. And it was becoming divisive so we decided that it would be a sensible thing to get rid of them.'

Failing to dissuade Orr-Ewing from pursuing what he saw as his brief at the head of a publicly quoted company, Egan decided to act. He mounted a boardroom coup to oust Orr-Ewing as non-executive chairman. It was not easy. Although the Jaguar board was balanced between the three executive and the three non-executive directors – the latter being Orr-Ewing, Horrocks and Edward Bond – in the event of a tied vote Orr-Ewing also had a chairman's casting vote.

Egan waited until Ray Horrocks was out of the country to call a snap vote of confidence. The other two executive directors, John Edwards and Graham Whitehead, both supported Egan and without the support of Horrocks, Orr-Ewing was voted out as chairman. His enigmatic response to questions about the episode was: 'Never explain and never complain.'

Orr-Ewing's tenure of office had lasted barely seven months. Egan assumed the mantle of chairman as well as that of chief executive. Two more Jaguar executives, Michael Beasley and Ken Edwards, were appointed to the board to ensure that Egan had total control over the non-executive directors and after a decent period both Orr-Ewing and Horrocks resigned from the Jaguar board.

By the autumn of 1984, detailed planning for the launch of the XJ40 had been well under way. The car would not be released to the public for another two years but an auditorium, new reception facilities and a museum display area were completed at Jaguar's Coventry headquarters. By the autumn of 1985 Jaguar executives were shortlisting advertising concepts. By the spring of 1986 it was finally decided to launch the new car that autumn and the publicity hype began in earnest.

Introducing a new car to the public is an increasingly complex marketing exercise. Potential customers need to be persuaded that the car has acceptable technical specifications, a particular maximum speed, a certain fuel consumption and so on. But just as important as the technical detail is the overall impression a car launch creates. Motor manufacturers spend millions ensuring that opinion formers at all levels see their new cars presented in the best possible surroundings. Journalists, politicians, brokers and city analysts are given every opportunity to appreciate new vehicles, something never more important than with a new luxury car for which the cachet of image and style are so much more significant. For the launch of the XJ40, presentation was of supreme importance.

For Jaguar the XJ40 launch signified the end of one era and the beginning of another. It was the culmination of many years' work and the foundations upon which Jaguar's future was to be built. It was quite simply the most important launch the company had ever undertaken. In the sense that Jaguar represented the renaissance of the British motor industry, it was perhaps the most important British car launch ever.

One thing marked it out as particularly unusual, indeed unique. The normal practice when launching a new car is to suggest that it is completely different from the model it is replacing – usually the old model has become outdated or unpopular and its image has suffered accordingly. The XJ40, however, was following in the tracks of the highly popular XJ6. Precisely because the XJ6 was still selling so well Jaguar decided to introduce an element of continuity, even though the XJ40 was a wholly new car. As far back as spring 1985, Egan had decided the car would be known and sold as the new XJ6.

In the spring of 1986 the company set up a special committee to take control of the launch operation, meeting weekly throughout the spring and summer. At the end of March the UK and US Jaguar Dealer Councils, the bodies representing Jaguar dealers in the principal markets, were given the first preview at the Gaydon test centre in the Midlands: a measure of the importance Jaguar attaches to dealers and their opinions. Their response to the car was very positive. Until that moment there had been a nagging fear that with sales of the Series III XJ6 still booming, the US dealers might have preferred the old car. Such fears proved groundless. Three months later the launch shows began to follow each other in rapid succession. On 24 June, Jaguar's suppliers were given a preview; executives from over 100 component supply companies saw the complete new car for the first time. The following month Jaguar's main assembly line was switched from production of the Series III XJ6 to production of the new XJ40. The changeover took just eight days and was achieved with the sort of speed and efficiency that would have surprised Sir William Lyons. In August, Jaguar held a preview for national, regional and local trades union officials. Through-out August and September groups of Jaguar dealers were flown into Coventry from all over the world for a series of highly theatrical unveilings. Lights, lasers and music were combined to dramatic effect, as if this Midlands car factory had become the latest set in a Star Wars movie. Speakers, videotapes and live transmission from each of Jaguar's three factories were linked to create an atmosphere of solid teamwork and great style. In the auditorium at Browns Lane three video screens dominated the main stage. 'The future is here. The future is now,' announced a disembodied voice. The script may have been obscure but the message was clear. Preliminaries over, the lights dimmed, the dry ice poured across the stage and the central video screen began to descend from the wall – it had been mounted on a three-ton hydraulic platform and as it dropped to the stage it was bathed in light. The misty dry ice cleared slightly to give a glimpse of the new car mounted on the back of the platform. Two more cars emerged from beneath the side screens. Another breath of dry ice and the new model was revealed in all its glory. As with earlier previews the reception was clamorous, indeed so rapturous that the whole launch show, including the three-ton hydraulic platform, was transported round the country for all the subsequent 'official' launches.

The car's most important audition was the one made to the motoring press. The opinions of journalists from the national newspapers and motoring magazines could sink the XJ40 straight away. It was imperative that they should be allowed an opportunity to examine the car comprehensively in conditions that were both pleasant and yet quite testing. Jaguar could not have journalists saying they had been given a 'soft' route over which to test drive the new car, but at the same time the company wanted the press launch to be relatively close to the civilised facilities that would make it a memorable affair.

Eventually they settled on a luxury hotel at Dunkeld in Scotland. Throughout September journalists were flown up to Edinburgh, driven to Dunkeld and allowed to drive the car over some of the most beautiful but most difficult roads in Britain. When they arrived at the hotel they were shown a video presentation and during a champagne reception were given an opportunity to examine the XJ40 in fine detail. After dinner and a good night's sleep it was off for a drive on a route that took them past Balmoral Castle and up into the Cairngorm Mountains. There was also a visit to a distillery and a traditional haggis dinner before the journalists were chauffeured back to Edinburgh and flown thence to London. Over 400 reporters were entertained at Dunkeld; it was a very expensive operation. Egan and his executives commuted between Scotland and Coventry, ensuring that the journalists did not lack any snippet of information that might add to their positive appreciation of the new car. In return journalists had to agree to hold their copy until the day on which the car was publicly launched.

Towards the end of September, Jaguar employees were invited to one of four 'J-Days' at the National Exhibition Centre in Birmingham. They were the people who had made the car and Sir John felt it appropriate that they should have a launch of their own. The three-ton hydraulic platform was pressed into action once more and with funfairs, playgrounds and exhibitions, the company underwrote a comprehensive family day out. Almost 30,000 people went along over the four-day period. In late September the car was also shown to the police and to government officials. On 1 October it was 'revealed' to the City of London and 7 October saw dozens of smaller parties up and down the country as dealers presented the car to their valued existing and potential customers.

It was 8 October 1986. John Egan had spent six years working towards this day, the UK public launch of the XJ40, henceforth to be known as the new XJ6. Egan held his breath as he waited for the first editions of the national newspapers. He need not have worried. The reception for his new car was universally ecstatic. The *Daily Mail*'s motoring correspondent, Michael Kemp, summed up the new Jaguar like this: 'The engine will run even with major electrical failures, tyres will seal punctures as you drive, paint has a double depth shine, dashboard messages warn you before things go wrong – and the automatic is also a manual.' He called it the 'car of the decade'.

The official launch day had been deliberately timed to fall in the middle of the Paris Motor Show. Overnight Jaguar technicians had removed the old XJ6 and replaced it with the new XJ6. It was finally and officially introduced to the public at a press conference in Paris in the middle of the morning. A few days later the car was unveiled yet again at the Birmingham Motor Show. With this simple dual-launch device Jaguar significantly increased its press coverage. Over the next few months the car was gradually introduced into the European and Middle East markets. It did not start selling in the US until May 1987, partly because the company needed time to build up stocks and partly because a later US launch gave Jaguar one last chance to correct any faults that might have appeared in Britain before the car's introduction in the all-important US market.

Sales of the old XJ6 had been so buoyant that just weeks before the XJ40 launch stocks of the old car had been reduced to under 100, a remarkable marketing achievement, given that customers who waited could have purchased a completely new model. Within a week of being launched in Britain the first six months' production of the new car had been sold out. A black market soon developed, with the new XJ6 changing hands for £3000 more than the list price of around £20,000.

Such an obvious success meant that Jaguar could cut back on its planned advertising but in every other respect their sophisticated marketing operation continued unabated, especially in North America. Even if sales were sky-high, the continual reinforcement of the Jaguar reputation remained a priority. The key marketing theme was 'evolution' as opposed to 'revolution'. According to the marketing literature Jaguar sent out to its US dealers, the new XJ6 was to be presented as 'The New Breed Jaguar . . . an evolutionary leap forward . . . a world-class car in every respect.' The advice was to 'present the XJ6 as a totally new, state-of-the-art automobile, but we also associate this car with the great Jaguar traditions of the past'. Dealers were told that the company's new roadside assistance scheme called 'Service-On-Site' would help them sell the new XJ6 more easily. 'Service-On-Site will send a strong message to the public about our confidence in the [new] Jaguar range. It will be one of the most powerful closing tools you have ever had.' In dealer parlance, a closing tool is a device to persuade a wavering customer to buy a car, thereby 'closing the deal'. Dealers were provided with videos, local advertising support, sales promotion material and attractive sales brochures. Nothing was left to chance.

Jaguar estimated that the launch of the new XJ6 would cost around £9 million. In fact, when the financial results were published for the first half of 1987, it became clear that despite the cutback in advertising the cost had been much higher, around £15 million. According to Sir John the changeover to production of the new XJ6 had put 'a considerable strain on our resources . . . The demands of producing a completely new car, using all new parts, utilising much new equipment and establishing necessary training programmes resulted in higher than expected launch costs.' Jaguar's problem was that the company had not launched a new car for so long that it was out of practice. Despite the much-vaunted eight-day changeover, the company ran into problems as it tried to step up production from an early level of 200 cars a week. When the XJ40 project had begun, the intention had been to ensure that productivity doubled with the new car. By the time it was launched that target had become redundant because Egan had already improved productivity by two and a half times while still making the old XJ6 model. Nonetheless, new manufacturing methods meant that further substantial savings could be made and once teething problems had been sorted out the new XJ6 was found to be a lot easier to build. It was designed to be manufactured at the rate of 1300 a week but Jaguar tried to raise the volume too quickly. Suppliers fell behind with component orders and the pace proved too fast for the workforce, who had only just been retrained to cope with the new production line. In Jaguar's 1987 annual report Sir John wrote that the changeover to production of the new XJ6 had involved 'more disruption and less productivity than was expected . . . There is no doubt that our new model introduction costs were higher than expected as a consequence of our failure to achieve the improvements in productivity our new car offers as quickly as we would have liked.' He insisted that the lessons had been learned but the continuing costs were to dog him for almost two years. It was not until June 1988 that Jaguar finally achieved the new productivity targets set at the time of the XJ40 launch.

Even so, by international standards the XJ40 was not an expensive car to develop and launch. The total cost of £200 million looks positively frugal against the sums of money spent by Mercedes and BMW on developing their new models. Research and development on the BMW 7-series, which was also unveiled in 1986, cost £700 million and BMW has never revealed the total launch costs. In the case of the new Jaguar the money was particularly well spent because it served two wholly separate purposes. The new car would, of course, represent a large slice of Jaguar's production for many years to come but the investment in building infrastructure, in quality control, in design hardware, in a new engineering centre, in robotics, in a new engine – all would be of value as Jaguar moved on to develop a sports car and other new models. The stake in Project XJ40 yielded not just a new car but an investment platform from which the company could build for the future. If Sir John Egan was to realise his ten-year dream of taking Jaguar from the edge of extinction through survival on to profit and up towards a place with the world-class car makers, he would need that platform very badly indeed.

13

The dollars and the Deutsche marques

THE SAVOY HOTEL, in the heart of London's theatreland, is a strange setting for a public crucifixion, but as journalists and city analysts gathered there on the morning of 26 August 1988 they expected nothing less. The press leaks had been clear enough. Jaguar Cars, the one-time glamour stock of both London and New York, was to announce a massive drop in profits. Of itself the announcement might have created adverse comment in the financial pages of the national press, even a hint of nervous excitement in the City; but the Jaguar results were being published the day after the British Government had announced the worst-ever balance of payments figures, and that meant that Jaguar was big news. Ten months earlier John Moore had been convinced the crash in world share prices was just a market readjustment, but since the crash Jaguar's US sales had been badly hit and the trade figures seemed to pose a question. Were the chickens coming home to roost for Mrs Thatcher and her economic policies? Sir John Egan, one of the Prime Minister's most steadfast supporters, seemed about to provide an answer and as the Jaguar success story faltered and stumbled, the City, the press and almost everyone else was ready to pounce on him.

The press conference started late. Sir John had agreed to give television interviews to both the BBC and ITN. They took longer than expected. In a conference room in the bowels of the Savoy, Jaguar executives sipped coffee and chatted with journalists and City analysts in small, hushed groups as they awaited his arrival. Eventually Sir John strode in. It rapidly became clear that the results were far worse than even the most pessimistic analysts had expected. Gone was Egan's natural, buoyant optimism. In its place was a sombre recognition that the party was over and that a radical shift of emphasis was needed if Jaguar was to survive.

He began by admitting that the results for the first six months of 1988 were 'much worse than we expected'. He said the problem stemmed from a 'softening' of the American market following the crash on world stock markets in October 1987 and a rapidly strengthening pound. The press moved in for the kill. He was asked if the Jaguar success story had simply been overblown; if it was not, in effect, a fraud. A spark of the combative Egan returned. 'The fact that we have grown from 14,000 to 53,000 [cars produced each year] is itself an enormous story,' he said. 'I never promised short-term profits. I have made our prime goal satisfy-ing customers.' But the upbeat optimism was difficult to sustain amid news of such a dramatic slump in profits. Egan, a fitness fanatic, was tempted into a sporting metaphor. 'Sometimes it feels as if you are jogging along and the road is going very rapidly backwards,' he mused.

As Sir John Egan had been taking over at Jaguar in the spring of 1980, Ronald Reagan was emerging as a formidable Republican candidate in that year's race for the Presidency of the United States. The incumbent Democrat, Jimmy Carter, had been for long dogged by the Iran hostage crisis, a crisis which showed him to be impotent in the face of the Islamic Republic's religious fundamentalists. In November 1980, Reagan was elected President and from that apparently unrelated event had stemmed many of Sir John's problems.

Ronald Reagan was the 40th President of the United States. His economic policies were wholly unlike those of any of his predecessors. In a period of 200 years the first 39 US Presidents had amassed, between them, a total national debt of $1000 billion. In less than eight years Reagan had more than doubled their combined borrowing. He did it by embarking upon the most expensive build-up of arms ever undertaken while at the same time fulfilling his promise to cut taxes. Vast government expenditure helped keep the economy buoyant but the gap between US government income and US government expenditure – the budget deficit – yawned wider and wider.

Reaganomics was based on the assumption that the economy would grow faster than the national debt. Since such an assumption was, by its very nature, incapable of proof, it required an act of faith or at least a certain degree of confidence. For seven years faith held up but in October 1987 it finally gave way to scepticism and fear. Wall Street decided that America's ability to pay its debts was not such a foregone conclusion. The New York Stock Exchange reacted by marking prices down. A slide became a tumble and turned into a crash which engulfed other stock markets around the world.

The immediate consequences of that share price collapse were not cataclysmic. For most people life went on much the same as before. The world did not immediately stagger into an economic recession as it had done in 1929. Indeed Sir John Egan was moved to say that the US economy was continuing to grow and that 'People who said the lights were going to turn out will be proved incorrect.' There were some immediate effects, however. Sales of luxury cars in America, especially in the financial centres of New York and Chicago, slumped dramatically. For Jaguar, as for every other luxury car maker, that was bad news indeed. Every year about 750,000 new luxury cars are sold round the world. Three out of every four of them are sold in the United States. As Jaguar's finance director, John Edwards, explains: 'Most of the folks who are rich and have got disposable incomes live in the States . . . it's always going to be the biggest luxury car market.' In fact America's ultra-rich spend almost $15 billion annually on new luxury cars. A measure of the country's predominant position in the market place can be gleaned from the fact that in 1984 a single Los Angeles Jaguar dealer sold over 900 vehicles. Outside the USA, in that same year, Jaguar only managed to sell the equivalent number of cars in a handful of countries.

From its low point in 1980, when Jaguar had sold just 3000 cars in the USA, the company had by 1986 built up to a high point of almost 25,000 US car sales. Fears were expressed that the company was becoming over-reliant on the US market; indeed Sir John's critics accused him of running a single-product, single-market operation. His response was typically pragmatic. With a strong dollar a Jaguar car that was sold in America earned significantly more profit for the company when the proceeds were converted into pounds sterling than an identical car sold in Britain or elsewhere. The alternative to massive sales in America was to divert cars to less profitable markets. Had he done so Egan would have been accused of squandering the opportunity for big windfall profits while the pound was weak.

In the last three months of 1987 luxury car sales plummeted. The sales of Porsche cars, particularly popular with the Wall Street yuppies, dropped by over 60 per cent. Jaguar fared less badly in the immediate aftermath but over the next year did suffer from depleted sales. Sir John Egan responded by accelerating a trend that had started before the crash. Jaguar keeps most of its markets under-supplied and in many parts of the world Jaguar dealers operate a waiting list. Egan began diverting cars away from the weak American market towards other parts of the world, with the result that the balance of Jaguar's markets was transformed. Instead of selling 60 per cent of production in the US and 40 per cent in other world markets, the company was now selling 40 per cent in America and 60 per cent elsewhere.

The American interest in Jaguar had been firmly built on the company's US sales boom, a boom that was itself based on a four-year slump in the value of the pound against the dollar. In 1980 the pound had been worth almost $2.50. Over the next four years it dropped in value to something much closer to parity. In 1988 the new XJ6 was selling in America for around $45,000, of which about $30,000 went to Jaguar in the UK. At an exchange rate of $1.80 to the pound, $30,000 translated into £16,500. Had the exchange rate been, say, $1.20, that same $30,000 would have produced a sterling equivalent of £25,000. The weaker the pound the greater the profit and the greater the incentive for Jaguar to sell as many cars as possible on the American market, and in order to keep the sales curve climbing, Sir John ensured that his cars remained very competitively priced, especially by comparison with the Germans'.

The main reason for the pound's weakness was an international belief that in the early 1980s the British economy was underperforming. Manufacturing capacity was being closed down, unemployment was rising rapidly and output was falling. At the same time, interest rates were dropping, from over 16 per cent in 1980 to half that in 1984. Naturally, low interest rates offered little encouragement for foreign investors to buy sterling and that too helped to drive down the value of the currency. But in 1984 interest rates began to climb again as British industry clawed its way out of the recession, and with overseas investors being offered higher interest rates in Britain the pound became a popular, and therefore a more expensive, currency. Para- doxically, it may seem, a strong pound – which sounds so positive – had an adverse effect on major exporters, including Jaguar.

Egan had been the first to admit that as Britain pulled out of the early 1980s recession the pound would strengthen: 'As our nation becomes more competent the pound will rise. It is absolutely inevitable,' he said. But that did not stop him from criticising the government for keeping the exchange rate at a level that was crippling exports. Announcing Jaguar's 1987 results Sir John had said that interest rates were keeping the pound '. . . unnecessarily high. I hope there will be an interest rate reduction.'

By the middle of 1988, Egan was complaining that part of the problem was the speed with which exchange rates moved. Such swift movements could spell disaster. A fall in the dollar of just one cent wipes £3 million off Jaguar's paper profits. Between 1987 and 1988 the dollar fell by 40 cents.

The exchange rate was at the heart of the bitter row that rumbled on throughout 1988 between Mrs Thatcher and the Chancellor of the Exchequer, Nigel Lawson. Though he never said so publicly it often seemed that Sir John Egan's support for the Prime Minister was wear- ing very thin. Like the Chancellor, he certainly favoured a more inter- ventionist policy to stop the pound rising. As it climbed towards $1.90 alarm bells were ringing at Jaguar's Coventry headquarters. 'It's very simple,' said John Edwards. 'We can't live easily at a $1.85 exchange rate. No "ifs and buts"! . . . It does actually put a great squeeze on us in a way that we cannot easily react to.' Well before the squeeze had begun, however, Egan and Edwards had seen the writing on the wall and in 1984 they had embarked upon another extraordinary gamble. Their aim was to beat the money markets and to obtain for Jaguar a better exchange rate than the so-called 'spot', that is, the rate quoted by a foreign exchange dealer for an immediate currency transaction. Their gamble involved the buying and selling of colossal sums on the inter- national finance markets.

The gamble was essentially quite a simple one but it was all the more incredible in that they had seen the need for it before many exporters had even recognised there was a looming problem. Egan could predict with some accuracy the total dollar income his company expected in any particular year. He knew what his car prices would be over a particular twelve-month period; he knew what his realistic production targets were; and, since there was an excess demand for Jaguar cars in the United States, it was a fair bet that the dealers there would sell all the cars Jaguar could deliver to them. This made it relatively easy to work out, in advance, what the company's dollar receipts would be. But instead of waiting until the income had been generated before converting it into sterling and repatriating the money to the UK, Egan entered into contracts to buy 'forward currency'. He promised, in effect, to buy hundreds of millions of pounds at a set date in the future. The exchange rate for these transactions was set at the time the deal was struck and was invariably a rate close to whatever the spot rate was at that time. If in the interim the pound rose against the dollar, Jaguar would end up making a killing.

Within the Jaguar headquarters at Coventry these foreign exchange deals were called the 'hedging operation' and the small team involved worked out of an office known as 'the Treasury'. From small beginnings it grew into one of the largest foreign exchange operations ever undertaken by a British company. During the 1980s Jaguar had taken over from the Scotch whisky industry as Britain's largest non-oil dollar earner and in 1987 the company had a turnover of more than £1 billion, half of which was generated in the USA. Between 1984 and 1989 Jaguar entered into forward currency deals worth around £2 billion and year after year the gamble paid off. In 1986 the company achieved an incredible average exchange rate of $1.28 while the spot rate for the pound hovered between $1.40 and $1.60. In 1987 Jaguar secured an average rate of $1.44 as the pound soared from $1.45 to almost $1.90. By 1988 the upward surge of the pound was halted and it became more difficult to obtain advantageous hedging rates but Jaguar still managed to achieve an average rate of $1.55. 1989 saw an average rate of $1.70, but a weakening of the pound and a strengthening of the dollar towards the end of the year meant that Jaguar was once again able to step into the currency markets and secure average exchange rates for 1990 of around $1.60.

However, as the pound rose it became increasingly difficult for Jaguar to make substantial profits even with the hedging operation. The 'Treasury team' began to adopt more sophisticated foreign exchange measures. At one stage Jaguar began buying 'cylinder options'. These are not actual purchases of currency, but complex contracts that give the purchaser the right to buy currency at a fixed rate on a specified date in the future. If, on the date in question, the fixed rate turns out to be better than the spot rate, the purchaser obviously exercises the option to buy, but if the spot rate is better than the fixed rate, the option is simply allowed to expire. Cylinder options offer a no-lose solution to the problem of fluctuating exchange rates but they are very expensive. Depending on the precise rates being offered such an option could cost £1 million for a £100 million contract.

Nevertheless, the advantages of the hedging operation were substantial. Jaguar was able to inject a degree of predictability into the business that would otherwise have been impossible and when it felt the dollar exchange rate was favourable, the company was able to fix its future income at that rate. Generally Jaguar sold its predicted dollar earnings about nine months ahead, but when particularly favourable rates were available John Edwards and his lieutenants sometimes sold much more of their predicted income. Of course, there was a risk involved in this massive gamble: if the pound suddenly weakened below the average exchange rate that Jaguar had achieved through its currency dealings, the company would have lost a giant cash windfall. But Egan and Edwards judged that even so this would not make the company uncompetitive because there was some evidence that their German rivals were involved in similar operations involving the dollar and the Deutschmark. If the dollar suddenly strengthened they too would make a loss. There was another important factor. The scheme was essentially a gamble that presumed bad trading conditions. In a sense, nothing would have pleased John Egan more than a sudden, and unexpected, improvement in trading conditions like a strengthening of the dollar. Such an improvement would simply have allowed him to 'lock in' bigger profits for the company with even more forward currency deals.

It seemed like a system that could not go wrong. But with every gamble there is a risk and the risk for Jaguar was a major one. If the house of cards was not to come tumbling down Jaguar had to come up with substantial quantities of US dollars as each currency contract fell due and such sums were wholly dependent on the continued production and sale of Jaguar cars in the United States of America. A major downturn in US sales or a protracted production stoppage, such as a long strike, would have been catastrophic for the company. Egan judged that the risk was worth the gain and as the pound continued its long climb from a low point of near-parity with the dollar it gradually became clear just how handsomely his gamble had paid off. In 1987, Jaguar made £97 million profit, of which it is estimated that a staggering £80 million came from the dollar hedging operation. In 1988 the company would almost certainly have made a loss but for the currency deals.

One of the factors that makes the luxury car market a particularly difficult one in which to operate is the complex thinking that lies behind the decision to buy a specialist car. In the USA, for example, with its stringent exhaust emission regulations and a speed limit of 55 mph it makes absolutely no economic sense to buy a five-litre car that generates 300 horsepower and has a top speed of three times the legal limit. But such cars are not purchased principally as means of transport. They are bought in order to make subtle (and not so subtle) statements about the status, power, class, wealth, lifestyle and even the sexuality of their owners. This makes the marketing of luxury cars highly complex and means that quite often, especially when they are buying a second, third or even fourth car, potential buyers may feel that their choice is not between, say, a Jaguar and a Mercedes but between a Jaguar and a yacht, or a Jaguar and a second home. Sometimes a US buyer might judge that by buying a cheaper American luxury car he or she could afford some other luxury as well. For the marketing men, it means that fad or fashion often determines which marque is in vogue and which is not. The selling of luxury cars is more like the marketing of entertainment than the marketing of motor transport. In the late 1970s, German hi-tech and superb engineering had been the fashion of the moment among US luxury car buyers. In the early 1980s, as more people became aware of Jaguar's industrial resurgence and the improvement in the cars' quality, the trend shifted. By comparison with Mercedes and BMW, Jaguar cars were still something of a rarity and suddenly, as with clothes and the Ralph Lauren clothing outfits, their traditional, English appeal became fashionable. The cars, like the clothes, conveyed the impression of old-established money. Following the company's privatisation in 1984, American interest in Jaguar became more intense: as well as owning a Jaguar car Americans could also own Jaguar shares and lay claim to a thoroughbred portfolio.

Jaguar shares are traded in the US as American Depositary Receipts, or ADRs. An ADR is a so-called substitute document that confers upon the holder the right to own a particular share without actually taking possession of it. The share itself is held on deposit at a British bank. If American citizens wanted to deal directly in UK shares they would need to meet a wide range of Securities and Exchange Commission regulations. An ADR is a simple mechanism for by-passing that red tape.

Jaguar shares started trading as ADRs early in 1985 when the company's share price was hovering around 250p. Over the next year or so American interest in the company pushed the share price up to over 500p. The main reason the Americans suddenly started buying Jaguar was that Wall Street analysts felt that their opposite numbers in the City of London had undervalued the company.

The traditional way of measuring a company's worth is to examine its price/earnings ratio or P/E. The P/E is simply the company's current share price divided by the annual earnings per share: a company with a share price of 300p and earnings per share of 30p would have a P/E of 10. In 1984 British financial analysts felt that Jaguar should have a P/E of around 8 to 10, in line with the engineering sector. Wall Street analysts felt that Jaguar was something more than a simple 'metal bashing' firm. They thought it was a very special company with an aura of quality and a name that was part of motoring history. In their view, that marked the company out as rather superior to the general run of engineering firms and they felt the shares should be trading on a P/E ratio of nearer 12. Accordingly, the New York analysts advised their clients to buy. In 1985 there was practically a stampede into Jaguar shares on Wall Street and the share price soared.

By 1986 over half Jaguar's shares were held by Americans in the form of ADRs. British analysts continued to warn that the company was vulnerable to exchange rate oscillations, but the American love affair with Jaguar continued and the share price broke 600p. When the crash finally came in October 1987 Jaguar suffered more than most. While shares quoted on the London market dropped by an average of 25 per cent, the Jaguar share price was cut in half.

John Edwards was the first to admit that the hedging operation had never been intended to solve the problem of hostile exchange rates; it was simply a way of buying a little time. 'As we do our forward hedging we push the problem away from us,' he said, 'but it is still there, creeping up on the horizon. From my point of view you have got to learn to live by a mixture of pricing, productivity and producing more cars with whatever exchange rate comes your way.'

As Egan saw it in the summer of 1988, there was only one way out of the company's problem, a strategic corporate switch from increased production to decreased unit costs. 'We have shifted the emphasis away from growth in the short term towards efficiency,' he announced. Egan's new policy marked a major turning point, a tacit acceptance that the seven-year boom in Jaguar's American sales was now over. It had been based on the weakness of the pound sterling and now – for the moment at least – the pound was weak no more. There was little Egan could do about that but he could learn a lesson from his competitors.

Two years earlier Japanese car makers had faced a similar problem when the yen suddenly strengthened. Instead of sitting back and meekly accepting the fact they put all their efforts into countering the effect of sluggish sales by increasing profitability through greater efficiency. Small productivity gains were gratefully harvested and when added together made the difference between success and failure. The Japanese had weathered the economic storm. Egan said Jaguar would do the same. He was looking for a five per cent annual productivity improvement. For each such improvement, he said, Jaguar would be £50 million better off. 'Cost effectiveness', he said, 'has to go right to the top of the list.' Every area of expenditure would be examined, even the capital investment programme which Egan knew represented the company's future prosperity. There was reluctance to cut investment but some expenditure would be deferred and every effort made to ensure that Jaguar got everything it could from new plant already installed. One thing was clear: Jaguar was moving into a period of severely limited growth.

Perhaps the silver lining in the grey cloud of exchange rates is that Jaguar is now making greater productivity savings. As David Boole observed, 'We are facing really quite remarkably hostile economic conditions. But they are forcing us to do all the right things in terms of the long-term interests of the company. We've got to find £120 million out of the business in order to maintain margins and we're trying to do precisely that. It is hard and it is tough but it is a discipline that I think companies have to face up to from time to time.' Jaguar has faced up to it before and then, as now, it adopted typically assertive tactics.

The technique of a few years ago conveys the company's determination. An assembly line is temporarily closed down. A group of 200 workers is taken off the track and ushered into a large conference room to be shown one of Jaguar's occasional in-house video productions, made by a London production company specialising in corporate communication through video. The lights dim and across the screen leaps a cartoon Jaguar. The production is called *Recognise the Enemy*. It is about Jaguar's international competition, which primarily consists of three companies, all based in West Germany: Daimler-Benz, the makers of Mercedes automobiles; BMW; and Porsche. Between them these three, plus Jaguar, have 98 per cent of the world market for cars costing more than £20,000.

The corporate message contained within the video is very simple. The Germans used to dismiss Jaguar as a serious luxury car maker but now they are taking the British company more seriously. Jaguar has made major strides towards greater productivity and improved quality and the Germans are beginning to look over their shoulders. They are desperately trying to beat off the Jaguar challenge, and if the Germans are to be outpaced Jaguar's employees will have to fight alongside the company management. The workforce will have to recognise that the common enemy is not management but the car makers of Regensburg, Bremen and Stuttgart. A German Jaguar dealer gives the workforce a stark warning: 'Never forget, the competitors are always there.' Beneath the major message is a subtext. As well as the European competition, Jaguar perceives a growing threat from the Japanese, so they too are drawn into the company video. It may be coincidence but the image of the patriotic British car maker fighting off the powerful Germans and Japanese evokes powerful memories. The meaning is not stated explicitly in the video but it is clear enough. This is war.

The feeling of constant rivalry, of the battle against the opposition, the passion for the fight, are emotions which are encouraged at Jaguar from the very highest levels of management to the shop floor. 'Your competition never gives up,' explains Michael Beasley. 'You can't ever give up either. We have made tremendous strides on quality but you are never satisfied with what you have achieved. You can always get better . . . and you have got to have an environment in which everyone is trying to do better. The same is true of productivity. We have made tremendous steps in productivity but we have not done anything like enough yet. You can never stop. Our business is not a business in which you can reach a goal and then sit back on your laurels.'

The company that offers John Egan the principal model upon which so many of his plans are based is the giant Daimler-Benz AG, pride of Germany's manufacturing industry. It is the largest manufacturing company in Europe. It manufactures the Mercedes S-class motor car, the luxury automobile that already attains the level of quality to which Jaguar aspires. It is the benchmark against which all other luxury cars are measured. The Daimler-Benz success story has been based upon a policy of building supreme cars and selling them at very high prices; substantial revenue has then been used to fund the next generation of luxury motor cars. The company also makes commercial vehicles and it has built up a cash mountain with which it is now diversifying into the new fields of aerospace and electronics. But, like Jaguar, Daimler-Benz faces problems. The difficulties associated with a weak dollar and a softening US market have been exacerbated by a decline in the company's share of the European market. And while diversification may seem sensible, it can also distract management from the job of running the core business.

The other great German luxury car maker is BMW and in many ways it provides a direct contrast to Daimler-Benz. While the Mercedes manufacturer has concentrated on engineering excellence and supreme quality, BMW has placed greater emphasis on the need for sophisticated marketing.

The history of BMW is the history of a battle against adversity. The company was established at the time of the First World War to manufacture aircraft engines. With the ending of hostilities German companies were not allowed to make such products and BMW was forced to adopt a new direction. It went into automobiles but by the end of the Second World War it was making arms. That too was now forbidden. A new change of direction into the motorcycle market was less than entirely successful and in the early 1960s the company came close to being taken over by its arch rival, Daimler-Benz. At the last minute a substantial proportion of the company was acquired by one man, Herbert Quandt, and over the next 25 years a highly successful family of automobiles was developed.

In the 1970s and 1980s BMW's success was assured through a sustained marketing campaign that saw the emotional appeal of its cars enhanced and polished until they had an irresistible cult attraction. BMW executives elevated marketing to the level of a precise science. They embarked upon a thorough analysis of demographics and market trends, they identified specific market niches and targeted their products very precisely on those niches. They watched their competitors closely and made sure that wherever and whenever possible the BMW owner was offered reassurance that he or she had made the right choice of car. No specific aspect was singled out as being exceptional, the marque was sold as a whole. Quality, reliability and performance were implied rather than stated, such features were almost taken for granted. The BMW had no special strength but neither did it have a single weakness. It was marketed as a modern, status-conscious, luxury package and traded heavily on the benefit of being 'made in Germany'. The strategy worked and was refined through the development of the complementary Series 3 (smaller, executive cars) and Series 7 (larger, pure luxury cars). It was made clear that technological improvements at the top end of the market were being incorporated into the less expensive cars. The strong implication was that the owner of a cheaper Series 3 BMW was part of the company 'family' and would one day graduate to the top of the range.

It seemed nothing could stop the onward march of BMW until Mercedes introduced a competitor to the smaller Series 3 car, the Mercedes 190. At the same time other European and Japanese manufacturers began to move into the crowded executive market and BMW was forced to change direction. The company moved up-market, relying more on its top range of luxury cars and significantly improving the performance of the lower range Series 3. After losing ground for a while, BMW recovered and re-established its position with the help of a new engineering research centre and a range of innovative high-technology developments. BMW scientists began looking at ways of using alternative fuels to power cars; they experimented with in-car navigation systems; and they began work on a 'smart chassis' that would adapt to changing road conditions.

The difference between Jaguar and its two main German rivals is twofold: the Germans have a diversity of interests and at the bottom of their range they make volume cars for the 'executive' market. Jaguar, by contrast, is a specialist car company, pure and simple, and in this respect is more akin to its third German rival, the firm of Porsche. At first glance Jaguar and Porsche may not seem to be in compeition at all: Jaguar's cars are mainly high-performance saloons while a Porsche is an unashamed sports car. The reason why the two companies are in fact competitors has more to do with image and market appeal: both cars sell as status symbols. For the self-made, successful entrepreneur it can be a difficult choice between the racy German car and the more conservative British model.

The story of the Porsche car company is almost as intriguing as the story of Jaguar's growth under Sir William Lyons. It began at the start of the century with the innovative designs of one Ferdinand Porsche. In the early 1900s he developed electric cars, petrol engines and vehicles that ran on both electricity and petrol. His work was well ahead of its time and shortly before the Second World War he was commissioned by the Archduke Ferdinand to transform the Austro-Hungarian Army into a modern motorised fighting unit. He was later appointed an occasional chauffeur to the Archduke but by good fortune Porsche was not driving his mentor when, in 1914, Ferdinand was assassinated while sitting in the back seat of his limousine during a trip to Sarajevo. By 1931 he had started his own consultancy and manufacturing operation. He won a contract to develop early Grand Prix racing cars and eventually 'graduated' to open-top sports cars. Porsche died in 1951 and his company passed into the hands of his son, his daughter and his eight grandchildren.

In the years after Porsche's death the company did not perform well. During the 1960s growing tension and disputes between different Porsche family members had resulted in an agreement that they should all withdraw from the day-to-day management of the company and this they had done in 1972. Despite their departure and despite the highly acclaimed Porsche 911 model the hoped-for turnaround in company fortunes did not materialise. It was as if the Porsche sports car was out of place in the austere 1970s; the company seemed to have lost its corporate direction.

For another decade the Porsche family continued to own a large slice of the company, but family frictions and tempting offers eventually persuaded them to float part of the company on the German stock market. In the same year that Jaguar was privatised, 30 per cent of Porsche's shares were also sold. They were all non-voting shares but they were eagerly snapped up by the German public.

A few years earlier, as John Egan was taking over at Jaguar, a new chief executive was being appointed at Porsche. Peter Schutz was a German who had spent much of his life in the USA. Like Egan, he was a swashbuckling free marketeer who wanted to place greater emphasis on marketing and who felt it was important to re-establish a strong marque image. One of the ways he did this for Porsche was to found a major research consultancy at Weissach, near Stuttgart. This became, in some respects, a model for Jaguar's research and development facility built at Whitley near Coventry. The Weissach centre undertook development work for a wide range of companies and became a valuable currency earner. Typically it developed new models for low-technology car manufacturers like the Soviet Lada firm and the Yugoslav Zastava concern. At home it added to Porsche's impressive reputation for producing high-performance technology and that, of course, was no bad thing. Further diversification followed and car sales picked up, but Porsche too was badly hit by the 1987 crash.

By the spring of 1988 all four of the world's major luxury car makers, Jaguar and its three German competitors, were finding it difficult selling cars in the US market. As the Deutschmark strengthened in the months after the crash the Germans tried to raise their prices to compensate for the loss of revenue but then the market weakened and suddenly monthly sales were down by 20 and 30 per cent. The

European companies embarked on a price war, Mercedes and BMW offering discounts to protect their market share, which left Jaguar with little scope to raise its generally lower prices. In order at least to maintain the status quo and its own market share, Jaguar had to freeze its prices and accept lower profits on each car sold in the United States. Even so, pressure on the Coventry firm remained intense because clever buyers recognised that the German discounts would only be available temporarily, until European firms had brought their production levels into line with demand. The discounts offered a one-off opportunity to buy a Mercedes or a BMW at below the official price.

The winners in the price war were the American companies, Ford and General Motors. Their Lincoln and Cadillac models encroached further into the US luxury car markets as their prices held steady against the rising prices of the German models. In the first nine months of 1988 Jaguar's US sales dropped by around ten per cent. The company was only saved from disaster by the fact that this was more than offset by sales increases in other parts of the world.

In fact Jaguar could hold its prices steady and still make a variable profit on the cars it sold at any exchange rate up to $2.40, but at those exchange rates the company would not raise enough revenue to fund the research and development programme for future models that represented Jaguar's lifeblood. In just a few months the stock market crash had shaken the belief that the specialist car sector was recession-proof; the collapse of world oil prices had confounded market forecasts; and oscillating exchange rates were playing havoc with revenue forecasts and investment plans. And just over the horizon was another problem. European dominance of the luxury car market was being seriously threatened by new entrants.

The Japanese first hit upon the idea of moving into the world luxury car market in the early 1980s. Following the oil crisis of 1979 the Japanese had entered into voluntary agreements with the Americans by which they promised to limit the total number of cars that each Japanese manufacturer could export to the US. It was not long before the Japanese realised that the profit on one luxury car could be ten times the profit on one small volume car without using up any more of the export quota. The race to produce a top-class Japanese luxury car was on.

Equally quickly the Japanese realised that they would need more than their undoubted skill at manufacturing in order to compete: they would need to build an exclusive image and a distinctive style. And, as sales of the new luxury models built up, they would need to protect and enhance their new growing reputation with top-class service and back-up. One Japanese car maker hired an Italian styling house to help design a new luxury model and Honda decided to sell its first up-market car, the Legend, through a separate dealer network, thus helping to establish the vehicle as rather special by comparison with Honda's other products.

The Japanese march towards the luxury sector has involved a step-by-step approach, from the sports car market and the top end of the executive car market. It will not be long before a fully fledged luxury car is available. Toyota and Nissan are developing top-quality luxury models and even Subaru has ambitions in the luxury sector. The Japanese models will almost certainly be sold at a lower price than their European rivals and that will inevitably restrict the ability of Jaguar, Mercedes and BMW to push their own prices up. Profits will be squeezed. Just as significantly, the Japanese experience of building volume cars with shorter life spans will probably speed up the product cycle in the luxury sector as well. Instead of a life expectancy of eight years or more, with an update after four years, the new Japanese luxury cars may have a life span of just five or six years. Such a rapid turnaround will force the European manufacturers to follow suit or face the prospect of competing with outdated models. If they adopt the same strategy their research and development costs will escalate dramatically. It costs hundreds of millions of pounds to develop a new luxury car; if these costs have to be recouped over a very short period profits will inevitably be squeezed once again.

One thing is absolutely clear: Japanese fascination for and expertise in electronic wizardry will lead to substantial improvements in specification. Automatic air conditioning, sophisticated on-board computers and electronic engine management systems are now standard features. The Japanese are now working on voice-operated windows, keyless car entry, electronic systems that warn drivers when they are becoming tired, and a host of navigation and communication systems. If features like these are developed for the top end of the market and gradually fed down to mid-range Japanese cars, there could even be a reversal of the industry maxim which says there is always a greater profit margin on luxury cars than on volume cars.

The Japanese will not break through suddenly and destroy the power of the European luxury car makers with one mighty blow. There is too much brand loyalty at the top of the market for that to happen. But the first effects of the Japanese move into this lucrative, though fragile, market place are already being felt. With the twin threat of difficulties in North America and increased competition from the Japanese, John Egan decided there was only one thing to be done. He would carry the battle into the heart of the enemy camp. He would open up a second front and take on the competition in its home territory.

About ten miles from Frankfurt, on the busy main road to Bonn, is the town of Kronberg. It is one of the most affluent places in one of the most prosperous parts of Europe's wealthiest country. As you drive through Kronberg it is difficult to miss an elegant, if somewhat futuristic, glass-fronted building decked in British racing green. This is the headquarters of Jaguar Deutschland GmbH, the company that distributes Jaguar cars in West Germany. The building also houses the company's spare parts operation and a main Jaguar dealer. It is located on the route from Frankfurt to Bonn because at some time just about every top businessman in Germany drives along this road. They never fail to spot the Jaguar presence.

West Germany is the second most important specialist car market in the world after the United States. About 50,000 luxury cars are sold there every year. Early in 1984 Jaguar had joined forces with the Swiss car importer, Emil Frey, to launch Jaguar Deutschland as a sales company for Jaguar cars. The firm was launched with less than £2 million capital and was owned 35 per cent by Jaguar and 65 per cent by the Swiss. Frey had been associated with Jaguar for almost 60 years; his company had first started selling William Lyons's Swallow sidecars in the 1920s. In 1984 Prince Otto of Sayn-Wittgenstein was hired as Jaguar Deutschland's colourful chief executive and the company began a major shake-up of the West German dealer network. As in the United States, a number of dealers had to go.

The task of building up Jaguar sales was not easy. The German driving public is undoubtedly the most discerning group of car buyers in the world. The national tendency for German firms to buy German company cars makes this market even more difficult to penetrate. Their own reputation for engineering excellence and built-in quality is second to none. It means that any importer has to beat the best in the world in order to succeed and the lack of a maximum speed limit on German autobahns makes them the most testing public environment for fast cars. But Jaguar was willing to take on the challenge and sales began to creep up slowly. In 1987 progress was hindered by a domestic price war between Mercedes and BMW but the Coventry firm stuck doggedly to its task, its long-term aim to secure an ambitious ten per cent of the West German market. It will be a difficult target to achieve but simply by making the effort Jaguar forces German manufacturers to try harder on their home patch – and while they are doing that they are not concentrating their efforts on other export markets.

Sir John Egan also decided to sink a great deal of time and energy into the Japanese market, traditionally one of the most difficult in the world for foreign car importers. Vehicles produced by domestic manufacturers had taken up all but a tiny fraction of the market. In the early 1980s Japanese car imports from all sources amounted to just a few thousand cars a year, but in the mid-1980s several economic factors combined to trigger a substantial growth in Japanese automobile imports. The first was a strengthening of the yen against most other currencies, which had the effect of making imported cars somewhat cheaper. At the same time the Japanese Government was keen to reduce international trade friction and therefore happy to allow imports to rise. A great deal of red tape that had hindered British, American and German car makers was gradually removed and taxation on luxury cars became less punitive.

All these factors, combined with the effects of the buoyant Japanese economy and readily available consumer credit, led to an annual growth in car imports of some 30 per cent – total imports of well over 100,000 cars a year. However, only a small proportion of these imported cars were genuine luxury models. The Japanese luxury sector is relatively small and although it is growing rapidly it still accounts for only a few thousand vehicles a year. In 1987 Jaguar launched a major Japanese initiative similar to the Jaguar Deutschland venture, setting up a distribution and sales company called Jaguar Japan KK in conjunction with the Japanese department store, Seibu. It is 40 per cent owned by Jaguar and 60 per cent owned by Seibu and has a plush headquarters in one of the most exclusive locations in Japan. A department store may seem to be an odd partner for a car company, but Seibu is the Harrods of the Far East. It has the right image for Jaguar and an unrivalled reputation for selling quality imported luxury goods. Sales of Jaguar cars in Japan are now rising steadily. They could be forced up more quickly but Egan is aware that if the sales curve rises too quickly the number of dealers will need to grow just as quickly, and if that happens problems of quality and poor service could easily creep in. With a dozen or so dealers in 1988 it sold around a thousand cars, twice the number sold in 1987. Jaguar needs to make a balanced judgement between stagnation and growth.

Around the world, then, Jaguar is doing battle with Mercedes and BMW and with the US corporate giants like Ford and General Motors, all large corporations with a diversity of interests ranged against a single company concentrating on a small niche in a large market, all with a safety net to save them from the vagaries of currency fluctuations and the cyclical nature of the motor industry. Jaguar has no such safety net, no major diversification, no plans for any major acquisitions. But Egan believes that if Jaguar diversified, management effort might be diverted from the business of building the most beautiful, the most exquisite cars in the world. He believes in the purity of the Jaguar product, the clarity of the Jaguar image. But as he does battle with the leviathans of the motor industry the words of Hamish Orr-Ewing must increasingly ring in his ears: 'However brave and courageous, however excellent the product,' said Orr-Ewing, 'Jaguar is David versus Goliath.'

14

Racing certainty

GUY EDWARDS belongs to that rare breed of people who feel completely at ease in the opulent boardrooms of multi-national corporations, explaining to hard-nosed businessmen why they should spend millions of pounds on pure frivolity. In the early part of 1987 he spent a month in the United States on behalf of Jaguar's racing team doing little else. Unusually, for him, it did not prove to be a particularly successful exercise – until he visited the US headquarters of the Castrol oil company in Hackensack, New Jersey. There the jet-setting superstar of the sponsorship business met an executive who oversaw a small drag racing programme that Castrol sponsored. Edwards explained that he was proposing something rather more substantial . . .

There is a debate within the motor racing fraternity as to whether Le Mans is principally a race for drivers or principally a race for cars. Some top drivers refuse to take part in what they concede is the world's greatest race because, they say, it is simply too dangerous. They question where control really lies. Is it with the driver or with the machine?

The opposition with which Jaguar does battle at Le Mans is almost a carbon copy of the opposition the company faces in high street showrooms: Mercedes, Porsche and soon, perhaps, the Japanese. Le Mans is the gentlemanly battlefield for corporate warfare. The weapons of this war are marketing expertise and engineering skills, and the winner takes all.

Until recently racing cars had to be 'nursed' round the Le Mans circuit simply because they would not survive being driven at top speed continuously for a day and a night. Now cars are designed and engineered not just to survive but to race flat out for 24 gruelling hours. They are held back only by the rules of international motor racing. World motor sport is governed by the Fédération Internationale du Sport Automobile, the FIA, responsible for organising and regulating all forms of motor racing from top Formula One Grand Prix through to rallying.

The sport that attracts the manufacturers of luxury cars is Group C, or prototype sports car racing. Group C does not receive as much coverage as Formula One but then polo does not receive as much coverage as soccer. For Jaguar, Porsche and Mercedes the image of Group C racing is perfect: prototype sports cars built solely for competition. Under FIA rules they must be two-seaters, though the second seat is wholly superfluous. The cars can use any petrol engine of any size but it must be fuel-efficient – under the FIA's most controversial Group C rule, cars are restricted to just 2550 litres of petrol for the entire Le Mans race.

The FIA also insists that for safety reasons the rate of flow at which fuel is pumped into the car's fuel tanks during pit stops should be restricted to 60 litres per minute. No driver can drive for more than four hours in any one continuous stretch, nor for more than fourteen hours during the entire race. No more than four mechanics, two fuel attendants and one tyre technician can work on a car in the pits. And if the car breaks down on the circuit only the driver can work to repair it, and then only with tools, parts or fuel carried in the car.

All of which means that Le Mans is a race of compromises. Team managers need to maximise speed while minimising fuel consumption. They must build in enough downforce to stop the car leaving the ground at 250 mph at the same time they must ensure that it is not too difficult to handle through the slow corners.

Despite the complex rules, prototype sports car racing has become remarkably popular in recent years, attracting vast interest from sponsors, manufacturers and the public. The development of shorter, sprint races has made it even more attractive to television companies and the introduction of races in four different continents has given Group C a glamorous international appeal. The decision to make the World Sports Car Championship a team event rather than simply a manufacturers' trophy has attracted more participants. As for the racing drivers – they welcome the resurgence of sports car racing, but they have a 'love-hate' relationship with Le Mans. For the 200,000 trackside spectators there is no such equivocation. For them Le Mans is quite simply one of the three most exciting events in the motor racing calendar. In terms of prestige, image and status it ranks alongside the Monaco Grand Prix and the Indianapolis 500, but of the three Le Mans has a special attraction all its own.

Motor racing came to Le Mans in 1906 when the first race ever to use the title 'Grand Prix' was set over a 63-mile course centred on the town. Competitors had to complete six laps of the course on each of two consecutive days. It was popular enough but after the First World War the French decided that to make motor racing more attractive to the general public they would stage an endurance race for genuine production cars and hold it at Le Mans.

Over the next 30 years Le Mans had a limited appeal for British race enthusiasts, despite a number of victories for Bentley in the late 1920s. Real interest developed in the 1950s, when the Jaguar Car Company began to take an active part in the race.

Jaguar's involvement at Le Mans was not undertaken simply on the whim or fancy of Sir William Lyons. In the 1950s, Jaguar, like all British engineering companies, needed to export to survive. In the years following the Second World War government steel allocations were based on export performance and victory at Le Mans helped Jaguar to sell abroad. Consequently 1950 saw three Jaguar XK120 coupés entered privately for the race. They were each prepared by the Jaguar factory but they failed to perform well: one finished twelfth, another fifteenth and the third dropped out after fifteen hours.

Throughout 1950 and 1951, however, Jaguar had been developing a purpose-built racing version of its legendary XK120 sports car, engineers and aerodynamicists borrowing design techniques from the aircraft industry to produce a Le Mans-winning car. They entered a team of three XK120Cs for the 1951 race. Stirling Moss was hired to drive one of them and the development work paid off. Moss was the frontrunner for much of the race and when he was eventually forced to drop out, because of an oil pipe fracture, the lead was taken up by Peter Whitehead and Peter Walker who drove the second Jaguar 'C-type' to victory.

In 1952 the Jaguar team was up against stiff opposition from Mercedes. That aside, the Jaguar 'C-types' suffered serious overheating problems and all three cars retired before the race was four hours old. 1953 saw a second Jaguar victory when the works team reverted to its 1951 aerodynamics in order to avoid the overheating problems. Superior disc brakes, used at Le Mans for the first time, enabled the winning car to brake into corners much later and thereby increase its average race speed to more than 100 mph. Jaguar works cars took first, second and fourth places.

Determined to go even faster, Jaguar had by 1954 developed a successor to the XK120C called the 'D-type'. At the end of that year's Le Mans race little separated the new Jaguar from a Ferrari, but the British car had to make do with second place. There followed Jaguar's most successful racing era to date. In 1955 the British team won but the event was marred by a tragic accident in which more than 80 people died when a Mercedes car crashed. The German team, Jaguar's main opposition, was withdrawn from the race. In 1956 the three official works cars failed to finish but a Jaguar entered privately by the Scottish Ecurie Ecosse racing team fought off an Aston Martin to claim victory. Then, in 1957, Jaguar achieved a clean sweep: despite a mighty effort from the Italians, who threw no fewer than fifteen Maseratis and Ferraris into the race, privately entered Jaguars were placed first, second, third, fourth and sixth.

There is a certain irony in Jaguar's 1957 victory. It took place in the very year in which the official factory team withdrew from motor racing altogether. At that time racing cars were prepared by the same works engineers whose job it was to develop the company's range of production models and Jaguar's patrician boss, Sir William Lyons, decided that the company should concentrate its efforts on the development of a new production sports car. This was the age of rock 'n roll and with the swinging 'sixties just around the corner the market was ready and waiting for the E-type Jag.

Still, between 1951 and 1957 Jaguar had won Le Mans five times and the company name became a household word. Racing success added lustre to the Jaguar marque's image and prestige, and the value of high-profile racing achievement as an aid to selling luxury cars was something Jaguar managers would remember almost 30 years later. In the mid-1980s, as the Jaguar revival began to take shape, the company was gripped by an obsession to win the Le Mans 24-hour race once again, to win at almost any cost because Porsche, Jaguar's arch rival in the sports car market, now dominated Le Mans, with twelve victories in eighteen years, and seven consecutive wins since 1981.

The TWR Group is a disparate collection of over twenty companies with a total annual turnover of around £100 million. The group has interests in manufacturing, agriculture, plastics, industrial equipment and electronics. It is best known, however, for its activities in the field of motor sport. TWR is the brainchild of Tom Walkinshaw, the most successful international saloon car racing driver Britain has ever produced.

He was born in Scotland in 1948 and was first attracted to motor racing because a local garage in his home town of Mauldslie used to race Minis. At the age of twenty he began racing his own car, a Formula Ford Lotus that his father had encouraged him to buy, and it was not long before he was winning races north and south of the border. In the 1970s he graduated to Formula Three racing, then Formula Two, before he was talent-spotted by Ford and invited to develop and race Ford cars in Britain and Europe. A three-year relationship with the company was crowned with several significant victories but in 1976 Walkinshaw switched allegiance to BMW for whom he would drive the racing team cars and carry out technical development work. The following year he won the coveted Tourist Trophy for the Germans. 1976 was also the year in which he established TWR, Tom Walkinshaw Racing, as a company through which he could channel his competition car development work. By the early 1980s the company was preparing racing cars for BMW, Mazda and Rover and its proprietor was gaining a reputation not just as a talented driver but also as an experienced engineer and shrewd businessman.

Tom Walkinshaw puts part of his success down to the fact that during his career as a racing driver he developed very swift reactions. Those reactions were taken with him into the business world. 'If you are used to motor sport reaction times . . . you tend to start things up and get them going fairly quickly,' he says. This flexible approach, this ability to see an opportunity and react to it immediately, proved particularly valuable in 1981. A change in the rules governing international touring car races meant that Jaguar's XJ-S grand tourer became a potential race winner overnight.

Walkinshaw could see a golden opportunity and he guessed that if the proposition were framed carefully, John Egan would see that opportunity too. He approached Egan and suggested that TWR prepare and race the XJ-S in the European Touring Car Championship. Egan was keen on the idea but in 1981 Jaguar was still fighting for survival and the company could ill afford an investment in anything as apparently frivolous as motor racing. Egan was also keen to ensure that when Jaguar returned to racing it would be with the greatest possible chance of success. He was not interested in some half-hearted attempt to regain past glories and he certainly did not want his company associated with unmitigated failure. In the end Egan was persuaded that Walkinshaw could do a professional job and agreed, in the first instance, to give TWR some technical support. A sponsor – the French oil company Motul – was found to underwrite the venture and the TWR Jaguar team was in business.

Driving the Jaguar himself, Tom Walkinshaw scored four victories in the 1982 season, enough to persuade Egan into a closer relationship. In 1983 he managed five victories and came second in the European Touring Car drivers' championship. In 1984 Walkinshaw registered six victories, still in the Jaguar XJ-S, and won the drivers' championship outright.

On the other side of the Atlantic, Jaguar was engaged in a similar racing arrangement with an American team, based in Virginia, called Group 44. The team's founder, Bob Tullius, had been racing E-Types and XJ-Ss since the 1970s, but Jaguar's rapidly declining fortunes in the BL years put a considerable financial strain upon the relationship with Group 44. The arrival of John Egan provided an opportunity to revive it and the result was a brand new car called the XJR-5, incorporating a Jaguar V12 engine. The car was designed and built in America but was nonetheless called a Jaguar and in 1982 it began racing in the

International Motor Sports Association (IMSA) prototype sports car championship.

The IMSA championship is the US equivalent of the European-based Group C sports prototype circuit, the championship which includes the Le Mans 24-hour race. When Jaguar decided upon a return to Le Mans in 1984 it was Bob Tullius and Group 44 who provided the two cars, Tom Walkinshaw's efforts then being directed towards the lower division of touring car races. Neither car finished. In 1985 they tried again. One car struggled in thirteenth with a broken valve, the other dropped out after twelve hours. Group 44 was also having trouble winning races in North America, and without a major North American sponsor Jaguar was left to pay a large proportion of the ever-mounting costs. Egan decided to end the company's relationship with Group 44, but public interest in Jaguar's return to Le Mans was so great he decided he could not pull out of racing altogether. Indeed, what the company needed, to achieve racing success, was an *increased* dedication to the sport. Egan decided to give Tom Walkinshaw control over all Jaguar's racing activities, and to make a full commitment to prototype sports car racing.

As John Egan was coming to the conclusion that Jaguar should co-operate with TWR so too was Tom Walkinshaw, and in fact by early 1985 TWR was already working on the provisional design of a new car for Jaguar. Walkinshaw had engaged Tony Southgate, one of the most experienced racing car designers in the world, and together they developed a new Jaguar, the XJR-6. Southgate's strategy was very clear. 'To win Le Mans you have got to dominate the [Mulsanne] straight,' he said. That meant designing a car that would be faster than the opposition without sacrificing downforce: in a racing car the power that is not used to generate speed is converted into downforce which gives the car added grip. The more grip the car has, the later the driver can brake into a corner and the earlier he can accelerate away from it. At Le Mans the downforce on cars at the end of the Mulsanne straight can be two or three times their total weight.

Southgate worked throughout 1985 to perfect his new design and towards the end of the season the car was unveiled. It was clearly a potential winner and Jaguar asked TWR to help them evaluate whether a full three-year racing programme would be worthwhile for the company. Walkinshaw said he could not guarantee results but he felt there was a good chance of success. He worked out how much the racing programme would cost and submitted his budget to John Egan. Once again Jaguar decided to take a gamble. Walkinshaw raced the XJR-6 at Le Mans in 1986. It failed to finish. In 1987 he developed the XJR-8. It proved to be a world beater, winning eight of the ten races in the World Sportscar Championship, but still victory eluded Jaguar at Le Mans. That year the race went to Porsche once again.

When Egan first met Walkinshaw he soon recognised a kindred spirit, an entrepreneurial spirit that the Jaguar chairman admires. 'We understand each other,' says Walkinshaw, 'I think both of us are fairly hard-headed. We define our objective and then we go for it . . . We are pretty similar in a lot of ways.' Walkinshaw is undoubtedly the best in his business, which is why Jaguar decided to use him.

In the spring of 1985 Jaguar was not yet formally committed to racing but even at that early stage it was clear that if Jaguar and TWR worked together they would need a sponsor to underwrite a substantial proportion of the very high costs. In March 1985 Egan's sales and marketing director, Neil Johnson, approached the man who knew more than anyone else about motor racing sponsorship, Guy Edwards.

Guy Edwards was born in Macclesfield, near Liverpool, towards the end of the Second World War. He spent his childhood in Fleetwood and the family later moved to Liverpool. Edwards studied psychology and geography at Durham University and at the age of 21 arrived in London. He desperately wanted to be a racing driver and in 1965 began his journey on the long road to the top by racing a Ford Anglia and later a Mini Cooper S. But his racing career was hampered by the fact that he had no money, a problem exacerbated by the fact that he spent so much time preparing his car for race meetings that he could not hold down a steady job. In an attempt to break out of this vicious circle Edwards took a direct sales job, selling china to US service personnel in France and Germany. It was not long before he was back in Britain, having saved some money, ready to launch himself once again into the racing scene. He bought himself a racing car, crashed it several times, ran out of money and had to begin the whole painful process again. This time he became a central heating salesman, a job he stuck for three gruelling years. 'It was a pretty black time but I learned a lot about people. People aren't really different whether they are multi-millionaires or scratching for a few bob.' Edwards was certainly in the latter category. His central heating job was not providing enough money to make any serious impact in the world of racing and his career looked doomed.

In 1969 his forturnes were at their lowest point when he hit upon the idea of finding a sponsor to underwrite his racing plans. Today, with sports sponsorship so prevalent, such an idea might seem somewhat obvious but at the time there was only one sponsorship contract in the whole of motor racing, the deal that brought Gold Leaf and Team Lotus together. Guy Edwards organised the second sponsorship deal. He persuaded the Tor Line Shipping Company to pay for a racing car and thus he became a professional racing driver.

Today Guy Edwards is such a successful businessman it must be tempting for him to suggest that he always knew sponsorship would take over from racing as his principal source of income. If so he certainly resists the temptation. He is quite clear about the matter. He sought a sponsor because he passionately wanted to drive racing cars and in order to do that he needed money. The money certainly transformed his prospects. It was not long before he had graduated to Formula One and was driving Grand Prix cars. In the mid-1970s he drove the most memorable race of his life.

The Nurburgring is a very long and winding circuit and in 1976 it was the scene of the West German Grand Prix. The race started in pouring rain with most of the drivers opting for wet-weather tyres. By the end of Lap 2, however, the circuit was rapidly drying and several drivers, including Niki Lauda, stopped at the pits in order to switch to dry-weather tyres. To stop or not to stop? It was a difficult decision. On a damp circuit wet-weather tyres give better control on corners but as the circuit dries they overheat and begin to disintegrate. Edwards decided to go on and as he passed the pits area Lauda emerged from the pit lane immediately behind him. Edwards was soon overtaken and Lauda built up a lead of almost a hundred yards. But as he accelerated through a corner at 125 mph Lauda lost control and crashed through some catch fencing into a bank. The car burst into flames and careered back across the track, towards the oncoming Edwards, who remembers the moment with horror. 'I thought, "He's going to take me with him."'

Edwards clipped Lauda's front wheel but just managed to scrape past. As he glanced into his mirror he could see Lauda's car blazing and the driver clearly trapped inside. Edwards stopped his car and sprinted back. Two other cars had by now collided with the wreckage of Lauda's Ferrari but fortunately neither driver was hurt. One of them seized a small fire extinguisher from a race marshal and began playing it round the cockpit area of Lauda's car. The flames, which had been leaping fifteen feet into the air, were temporarily cut back a little and Edwards dashed forward to grab Lauda and drag him free. He recalls, 'It was a big old bonfire. I remember thinking, "Oh, my God, I can't stay here much longer. If nothing happens in the next couple of seconds, you're dead."' But luck was with Niki Lauda. Edwards just managed to pull him out of the burning wreck. The British driver received serious burns to his arms and legs and though Lauda was very seriously injured he did at least survive, thanks to Guy Edwards's bravery. Edwards was later awarded the Queen's Gallantry Medal.

Edwards continued to race professionally until 1984 when he finally decided to quit. He did come out of retirement to take part in one further race, claiming fourth place at Le Mans in 1985, but found that his rapidly developing interest in sports sponsorship was beginning to offer him more stimulation. He had been steadily increasing his involvement in sponsorship over a number of years. One of the most important contacts he had made was with a man called Peter Gilpin, former marketing director of the giant Rothmans tobacco company. The two men had become close friends following a trip to South Africa. Edwards had been trying to persuade Gilpin that Rothmans should sponsor the March Formula One racing team and the deal was finally agreed at the South African Grand Prix. A couple of days later Edwards was waiting in the airport lounge for a return flight to London when he spotted Peter Gilpin, also flying home. Gilpin was travelling first class. Edwards was not. The two men began chatting to each other and Edwards decided to upgrade his ticket in order that they might continue their conversation during the journey to London.

As the flight got underway they inevitably discussed motor racing. Their companion in the first-class lounge was an elderly man who was clearly very ill, being tended by a nurse. Somewhere over Africa the old man died. Undeterred, Gilpin and Edwards continued to avail themselves of the airline's hospitality. At some point in the conversation Gilpin asked if Edwards knew of any other sponsorship opportunities coming up. Edwards said there might be an interesting possibility with Porsche and the result of that chance remark was that Rothmans ended up sponsoring not one but two Grand Prix teams. Gilpin later left Rothmans to join the rival firm of Gallaher International but he and Edwards remained in contact.

Edwards had gained his grounding as a salesman in the toughest selling environment there is, selling face-to-face on the doorstep. Gradually those skills were refined and polished until he became the supersalesman of motor racing sponsorship. He developed a gut feeling for why sponsors were prepared to pay large sums of money in order to have their corporate logo emblazoned across a racing car. 'If you did not understand why they sponsored you,' he said, 'they were not going to sponsor you.'

The key to his early success was the development of packages that helped sponsors to achieve their aim in a manner that was at least as effective as the promotional areas they knew and trusted, like press and television advertising. He quickly discovered that clinching a sponsorship deal is invariably time-consuming and always expensive. The risk factor is whether to take on the project in the first place. Today Edwards rejects many more proposals than he becomes involved with. 'You need to have a real belief in it,' he says.

The two most important factors in determining whether a sponsorship deal will work are the image of the product to be sponsored, and the ability to help the sponsoring company achieve what it wants to achieve from the deal. Edwards sees 'image' in a very wide sense, as a matter not just of how the public sees a company but of how the business community and very often of how government perceives it.

When it comes to persuading companies to sponsor a racing team Edwards is the first to admit that it is not a scientific process. It involves trial and error, an instinctive feeling. Corporate egos vie with practical financial considerations as companies decide whether they should be a major sponsor or a minor one. The major sponsor gets the lion's share of the publicity and its company logo is placed in the most prominent position on the racing car – but in return that sponsor must pay the lion's share of the sponsorship fee. The alternative is to become a minor sponsor, which is financially attractive but which can leave corporate pride somewhat bruised, playing second fiddle. No company ever takes the full sponsorship risk.

If Guy Edwards has not turned sports sponsorship into a science, he has certainly elevated it to a fine art and in the process he has made himself a very rich man. He admits to being a sterling millionaire; he may well be a multi-millionaire. His clients have included Barclays Bank International, ICI, Gillette, the Encyclopaedia Britannica and Guinness. Since first finding himself a sponsor in 1969, Edwards has introduced almost 50 companies to motor racing sponsorship. He, like Tom Walkinshaw, is undoubtedly the best in his business, which is why Jaguar decided to use him as well.

Neil Johnson met Edwards at his London home and explained that Jaguar were ready to take on Porsche, the dominant force in sports prototype racing. It did not take Edwards long to decide that Jaguar had one of the top brand names in the world, an image and status out of all proportion to the company's relatively small size. 'There are companies in America that are twenty, thirty, forty times that size that nobody has ever heard of. The value of that brand name is substantial,' he says. He wrote a letter to Sir John Egan explaining what information he needed from the company and what strategy he felt would be effective. He then spent a month at the Jaguar headquarters in Coventry learning about the company and what it could offer a sponsor. When he had marshalled his thoughts, he asked Egan for a letter of authority and he asked Neil Johnson to provide him with the most important document of all. 'I want you, in your own words,' he told Johnson, 'to encapsulate in one page why Jaguar is going racing and what you think you have to offer the sponsor.'

Johnson wrote that successful motor sport was a basic ingredient in the Jaguar product mix. 'I believe we should be looking for a partner with wide horizons, ambitions and energy. We can bring a great deal to the party . . . The "Legend Grows" [advertising] campaign has been very successful. I am confident that with the right partner we can make the legend grow faster and bigger than ever before.' Armed with the letter from Johnson and another from Egan, Edwards set about the task of extracting all the appealing elements from the project, teasing out every single advantage a sponsor could expect for its money. He then simplified these advantages and represented them in a very accessible fashion as part of his glossy presentation. 'Why should someone spend millions and millions of pounds with Jaguar?' he asked himself. 'You have got to think there is a very good reason for that.' Edwards drew up a 'hit list' of 99 potential sponsors and then began the gruelling job of 'cold calling' every one of them. Of course his impressive list of contacts made the job a little easier, but often he had to spend a great deal of time ensuring that he was talking to the right person within the target company.

At the very top of Edwards's hit list was the name Peter Gilpin. What put him at the head of Edwards's list was the fact that he was now chairman of Gallaher International, the worldwide marketing company for Silk Cut cigarettes. Gallaher is owned by the giant American Brands Inc.; and among its UK subsidiaries are such household names as Dollond and Aitchison, Prestige and the office equipment firm Rexel. Edwards invited Gilpin to his home for Sunday lunch and it soon emerged that the new Gallaher chairman was keen to mark his arrival by doing something spectacular to put his company firmly on the map. Edwards told him about the Jaguar sponsorship deal but suggested that before he seriously contemplated spending a great deal of money on that, he might like to consider a rather smaller contract, Edwards's own out-of-retirement final drive in the 1985 Le Mans. Gilpin agreed to sponsor Edwards in a Porsche 956 prototype sports car and this small sponsorship deal proved to be the sprat that caught the mackerel. Gilpin travelled to France to watch 'his' car perform and while he was there Edwards introduced him to John Egan, at Le Mans to see the Group 44 Jaguars in what proved to be their final Le Mans appearance. Edwards explained to Egan that Gilpin was considering the Jaguar sponsorship deal. With typical bluntness Egan asked Gilpin if he had enough money.

Throughout the summer of 1985 Guy Edwards's life was one long round of meetings. Persuading Peter Gilpin that the Jaguar deal was right for Gallaher International proved relatively easy, but Edwards then had to convince many other Gallaher executives. He had agreed with Gilpin that the package would not be offered to any other tobacco firms but time was pressing and if Gallaher could not reach a decision

Top: Jaguar Chairman Hamish Orr-Ewing *(left)* and Chief Executive John Egan watch the hectic trading on the Stock Exchange floor *(below left)* as Jaguar's shares go on sale for the first time. *Below right:* August 1984. At Barclays Bank New Issue Department a seething mass of people scramble for Jaguar shares as the deadline for applications approaches. The Jaguar privatisation was eight times oversubscribed.

Top: the Nurburgring, 1976. Racing driver Guy Edwards *(far left)* battles to drag Niki Lauda from the blazing wreck of his Ferrari, an act for which he won the Queen's Gallantry Medal. Retiring from Grand Prix racing to concentrate on business, he later raised millions of pounds for Jaguar's racing programme. *Below left:* the Jaguar XJR-8 on its way to victory in the final 1987 World Sportscar Championship race at Fuji, Japan. Jaguar took both the team and driver's championships. *Below right:* Tom Walkinshaw, the brains behind the Jaguar racing team.

The Jaguar XJ40 was the most rigorously tested car ever to come off a British production line; 90 prototypes were driven a total of more than 5½ million miles. Much of the testing was carried out in the searing heat of the Arizona desert and up on the Colorado Plateau south of Grand Canyon, the true shape of the new car disguised with specially made camouflage panels.

Top: Le Mans, 1988. Tom Walkinshaw and Jaguar threw everything into winning this classic 24-hour race; well over 100 mechanics and other support staff were needed to sustain the team's five racing cars. *Below:* 3 p.m., Sunday, 12 June 1988: Jan Lammers, victorious in car number 2, leads a convoy of Jaguars to the Le Mans finishing line. It was 31 years since a Jaguar had won at Le Mans.

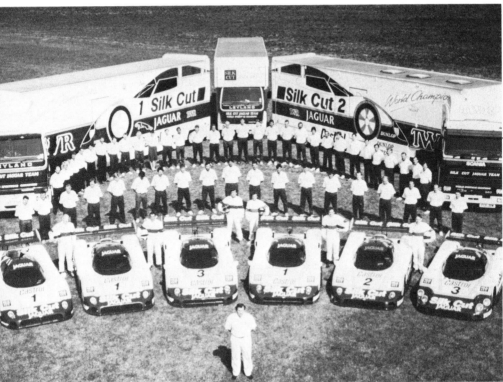

Top: Lammers saluting the crowd in the traditional manner – with champagne. Behind him Tom Walkinshaw looks on. *Below:* the 1989 Jaguar racing team.

A Jaguar car – like the Jaguar Company – is a subtle blend of the old and the new. The fascia is crafted from burr walnut veneer and the leather upholstery is matched for both grain and colour. But behind the traditional materials is the very latest in high technology, and increasingly the cars are built by robots.

op: Sir John Egan, Chairman and Chief Executive of Jaguar plc. *Below:* the board of Jaguar Cars, the main operating company of
aguar plc. *From left to right:* David Boole, Ken Edwards*, Pat Audrain, Mike Beasley*, Egan*, Graham Whitehead*, David Fielden,
John Edwards*, Jim Randle and Roger Putnam. (*denotes a director of both Jaguar Cars and Jaguar plc.)

Top: the USA is Jaguar's largest single market. The company's new US headquarters is being built in New Jersey at a cost of $25 million. *Below:* the headquarters in Japan. The Japanese market for imported cars has been expanding and Jaguar is making a determined push for the rapidly growing luxury sector.

immediately Edwards would need at least to open negotiations with other prospective sponsors. In fact he came close to signing a deal with British Caledonian before Gallaher made its decision. The American Express company were also very keen to sponsor Jaguar, but Edwards felt that Gilpin was a man of vision who could see the potential of the deal and would know how to exploit it to the full. In August a deal was agreed in principle. Gallaher had to rewrite its marketing budgets in order to accommodate the immense cost of the project but the company was prepared to gamble that it would pay off. In September the lawyers drew up the formal contract, which ran to dozens of pages, and in October it was signed.

Once he had set up the main sponsorship deal Edwards turned his attention to the minor deals. He wanted to offer the secondary sponsors an attractive package but he also wanted to ensure the car had a clear, simple identity like the Rothmans Porsche and the Marlboro MacLaren teams. 'I wanted a clean look for the cars,' he says. 'It should be quite clear it is a Silk Cut Jaguar . . . rather than what I call a sticker special – lots of little ones which don't do anything for anyone.' Once the secondary deals had been done Edwards turned his attention to the other side of his business. When he has arranged a sponsorship deal Guy Edwards can then offer his services to help the sponsoring company. His company, Guy Edwards Racing, has offices in Britain, France and the US and has associate agreements with public relations companies, experts in VIP entertainment and exhibition specialists. Edwards sees the arrangement of sponsorship as an intellectual challenge. But even with a highly saleable image like Jaguar's, it still cost him well over £100,000 to find the right sponsor. As he looks back at the Jaguar–Gallaher deal Edwards can see why it works so well. 'There are no weak links in the chain. That is the beauty of this project. The Jaguar people are good. Tom [Walkinshaw] is good. I have done my job. The sponsors have done their job.'

The only real problem that arose concerned the nature of the main sponsor. There was some debate within Jaguar as to whether the company should associate itself with a tobacco company. In the mid-1980s smoking was becoming to many an increasingly distasteful habit, progressively banned from cinemas, public transport and even the workplace. In the end John Egan took a pragmatic position and decreed that tobacco sponsorship was a fact of life in motor sport and that Jaguar was prepared to take Gallaher's money. But he had to live with a good deal of bad publicity in the local Coventry press, and local laws or voluntary agreements in different parts of Europe meant that the Silk Cut Jaguars sometimes had to run their distinctive purple and white colouring without the Silk Cut insignia.

All of which raises the question: who gains what from the Silk Cut Jaguar racing programme? For Gallaher International the answer involves a complex combination of several factors. There is the publicity factor, the amount of press coverage a sponsorship deal generates. There are the sales figures: in due course a sponsor will want to see increased brand awareness translated into increased sales. There is also intuition. A sponsor may sometimes 'feel' that a sponsorship deal is working simply because there is no real evidence to the contrary. Specifically, Gallaher wanted to make its Silk Cut brand of cigarettes more attractive to men without making it less attractive to women. Motor racing was clearly a male-oriented activity and that appealed to the sponsors, but as Guy Edwards recalls, 'They were terrified of doing something overtly masculine.' This was where the Jaguar deal was particularly attractive. Jaguar has a precise niche in the car market, a niche that clearly appeals to women: in the United States half of those who buy Jaguar cars are women. Put crudely, Gallaher International hoped the motor racing would attract male smokers while the Jaguar profile would help counter the alienation of female smokers. The scheme certainly seemed to work because the brand awareness of Silk Cut has risen dramatically.

Similarly press and television coverage can help build a successful company profile for the motor manufacturer which in turn helps to sell cars, a lesson not lost on the Japanese. Jaguar has calculated that if the press and television coverage of its motor sport activities was company advertising, the cost would be approximately the same as for the racing programme itself. In fact the coverage is far more valuable than that precisely because it is not advertising. Editorial coverage helps build the corporate image in a way that no amount of advertising can and that is the principal reason why Jaguar has been involved in motor racing for over 50 years.

There are, however, further valuable spin-offs, perhaps the most important of which is engineering innovation. When Jaguar was a regular winner at Le Mans in the 1950s the team had been experimenting with disc brakes and fuel injection. It was not long before these revolutionary refinements were fed down into the company's production cars. Today sophisticated engine management systems undreamt of even in the early 1980s have been developed for racing cars and are already standard features on luxury production models. Within five years they will be standard on many volume cars too. Such systems have evolved at ten times the pace they would have done without motor racing. In the field of engine design, components like the combustion chamber have been radically improved because the motor racing authorities have introduced strict new fuel limits. Racing car designers have had to find ways of generating more power from less fuel and this has led to the development of 'lean burn' engines. In years to come these, too, will find their way into production models. New materials are being tested, aerodynamics are being improved, weight is being reduced: in fact each Jaguar racing car is a working laboratory where new ideas are analysed and where production components can be tested to destruction.

There is a host of beneficial peripheral activities involved in racing, too. Both the sponsor and the manufacturer can bring customers and dealers along to the racing circuit; they can energise their sales teams in an atmosphere of competition and success; they can use racing to raise morale amongst the workforce; they can use victory as a great motivating force. The ambience of the race meeting can be valuable for anything from entertaining to specialist advertising. The sponsorship industry is one which feeds off its own success, too. Advertising agencies, public relations firms, marketing consultancies and media analysts are all drawn into the web and they duly extract their share of the profits. It is difficult to see how anyone can prove the cost effectiveness of the strategy but they all seem to think it works.

Certainly the cost of operating a major racing team runs into many millions of pounds a year. Guy Edwards says coyly, 'I have been asked not to reveal the numbers.' Tom Walkinshaw is a little more forthcoming. He knows the total operating cost because that is the figure for which he invoices Jaguar which in turn recoups part of the cost from the sponsors. 'You are obviously talking about several million pounds a year but you are not talking about tens of millions of pounds a year,' says Walkinshaw. Within motor sport it is assumed that running a top-class Grand Prix team costs about twice as much as running a top-class prototype sports car team. At that rate the Jaguar racing team would cost about £15 million a year, of which sponsors would provide about half. Jaguar, running two such teams, one in Europe and one in America, faces a total cost for its racing programme of around £30 million a year.

When Tom Walkinshaw took control of Jaguar's North American racing team as well as its European-based team, the company decided to intensify its search for a US sponsor and asked Edwards to help. In October 1986 he began drawing up a North American version of his 'hit list'. It consisted of well over 100 companies that might be prepared to sponsor Jaguar, many of them British exporters that could use the sponsorship to increase their market share in the United States. Throughout the autumn Edwards talked to these companies, trying to convince them of the value of an arrangement with Jaguar. By January 1987 he was depressed and frustrated. He was not making progress. 'To me it was a marvellous Trojan horse into the underbelly of America,' he recalls. But he encountered a great deal of complacency.

In a new initiative Edwards decided to cast his net wider and to seek sponsorship from an American firm. He travelled to the US, allowing himself a month to find the sponsor. At the end of the month he had arranged to meet his wife for a holiday in Jamaica, so he felt he was working to a deadline. He travelled all over the country, making his presentation to 30 companies, meeting oil industry executives in Texas, food industry executives in the Midwest and computer industry executives in Silicon Valley. He worked sixteen hours a day for almost four weeks without finding the right company. Then one evening, just four days before he was due to leave for Jamaica, he met up with an old friend from university. They went out for dinner and after the meal went into a bar for a drink. They fell into conversation with a group of people, one of whom mentioned that his father had just sold the family oil business to Castrol. Edwards suddenly recognised a name that had been missed off his hit list.

Castrol is a British company but it has a substantial US presence. Edwards rang an old friend who worked for Castrol in Britain and discovered who he should talk to at Castrol in the United States. Eventually he made his Jaguar presentation to a group of British and American Castrol directors.

'We are talking about a marketing partnership with Jaguar,' explained Edwards. 'Egan has rebuilt the dream ... Jaguar are in pursuit of perfection.' Infectious enthusiasm took him through his 80-slide audio-visual show in record time, covering the company's history, its motor racing record, the industrial turnaround, owner research, promotional opportunities, plans for the future and, crucially, how much Jaguar was looking for from its racing sponsors. 'It was a short sharp presentation,' Edwards recalls. When it was over he was left waiting in the boardroom while the directors went outside to discuss their response. Edwards thought the American directors opposed the deal while the British directors supported it. 'For me, sitting back there in the boardroom alone, it was going to be quite interesting to see how that was resolved.'

On the face of it the deal he was offering was not a particularly attractive one; indeed Edwards had given the same pitch to dozens of companies around the US and the response had been negative. He was asking for several million pounds and in return he was offering a slice of publicity. Before backing Jaguar's North American racing team it would be natural to look at the results of the company's European racing team. They were not good, and neither Edwards nor his audience could know that they were just about to improve beyond all measure. That day, however, Guy Edwards had found a company that was prepared to take a gamble.

Castrol decided to back the project. The deal was finalised and a contract was signed in October 1987. In Europe Edwards had persuaded the first company on his hit list to sponsor Jaguar; in America it was the last.

The party to celebrate the signing of the US sponsorship contract was lavish even by the standards of motor racing. It was held on a fine Monday morning in the Boat House Café, on the lake in New York's Central Park. Edwards recalls, 'It was one of those gorgeous October days, brilliant sunshine, blue sky and a little crisp.' Waiters in white livery dispensed champagne to 120 guests. As he looked at the gleaming Castrol Jaguar, Edwards felt an inner glow. He was blissfully ignorant of what else was happening in New York that day. Had the party taken place a little later the Castrol-Jaguar contract might not have been signed at all. Five miles from Central Park, down the Avenue of the Americas, Wall Street was going into free fall and Jaguar's share price was plummeting like a stone. It was 19 October 1987, Black Monday, the day the stock markets crashed.

15

Win on Sunday . . .

NINETEEN EIGHTY-EIGHT saw the Porsche works cars in their new distinctive red and yellow livery. Their team was sponsored by Shell and Dunlop; the year before it had been Rothmans. In Hans Stuck, Derek Bell and Klaus Ludwig, Porsche had the most successful driving team in the history of Le Mans; between them these three drivers had won it ten times. In their third car Porsche combined maturity with youthful vigour: the veteran Grand Prix driver Mario Andretti was teamed up with his son Michael and his nephew John. Porsche also had a secret weapon, a new engine management system which they hoped would help their cars match Jaguar's fuel economy and Mercedes's power.

The great German Daimler-Benz company had joined forces with the Swiss-based Sauber racing team. Mercedes's turbo-charged, V8, 5-litre engine developed 30 per cent more power than the Jaguar but there were questions over the car's reliability. During testing it burst a tyre. Nobody was hurt but the mechanics could not be sure what caused the blowout. Ever mindful of the terrible accident of 1955, Mercedes decided to pull out of the race, leaving Jaguar to do battle with Porsche and the Japanese, represented by Nissan, Toyota and Mazda. The Japanese did not expect to win Le Mans but they are serious about breaking into the luxury car market and, like the specialist car companies, see the value of spending time and money enhancing their image as purveyors of high-performance, prestige motor vehicles. A victory at Le Mans, some time in the future, is an increasingly important priority for Japanese manufacturers. For Jaguar the equation is very simple. If they can keep the Japanese at bay in the world of motor sport the company stands a better chance of keeping them at bay in the sales showroom.

As the cars speed round the track the world's press report their progress. Le Mans is a media event. High above the pit grandstand is the private press gallery with telephone, telex, copying and even photo-laboratory facilities. Behind the pit paddock is the official press room, with giant TV monitors relaying the closed-circuit race coverage and replaying important race incidents. A series of computer terminals outlines the position of every car in the race, along with information about drivers, mechanical problems, latest fuel consumption and a wealth of other considerations. News bulletins summarise race retirements and new lap records, the number of laps covered and the average speed of the leaders; press releases are used to cover anything that may have been missed. A line of telephone kiosks keeps the outside world in touch as the clatter of mechanical typewriters mingles with the gentle tap-tap of portable word processors. A hundred and thirty people work at Le Mans to support the press team – and then there is television.

TV networks from five continents transmit pictures of the Le Mans race; six separate satellite paths are used to carry the television signal for live transmission in fifteen countries. In 1988 the Japanese Asahi TV network took a 30-man technical team to Le Mans and transmitted eight hours of live coverage. The European satellite channel Screen Sport carried almost half the race live, with simultaneous translation into English, French and German. An international independent sports programme carried edited highlights to 43 countries from Australia to Zimbabwe and from Iceland to Malaysia. Almost 50 TV cameras were registered at Le Mans; the American CBS network had no fewer than six camera crews working to compile a 'behind the scenes' look at Le Mans for broadcast to an estimated audience of fifteen million. Success and failure at Le Mans will be seen by tens of millions of people.

In the dead of night the first Jaguar succumbs: the XJR-9LM driven by Pescarolo, Watson and Boesel retires with transmission problems.

The Porsche of Stuck, Ludwig and Bell has clawed its way into second place after losing several minutes with a fuel tank problem. The Porsche team's tactics seem to be to push its cars to the limit. It wants Jaguar to do the same in the hope that most, if not all, of the works cars will crack under the pressure. Porsche knows that if it can break the heart of the Jaguar team, even at the cost of its own challenge, there will be privately entered Porsches to take up the running.

In the pitch darkness it is difficult to identify the leading vehicles. Some, like the whining Japanese Mazda, can be distinguished by their sound. Others cough and spit flame from exhaust pipes barely hidden beneath the belly of the car. All of them emit ear-shattering explosions as they slow to steer around the chicanes and corners, vicious cracks that erupt from the engine, caused by the explosive combustion of fuel the engine has failed to burn. It sounds as if they are not precisely tuned. In fact they are tuned to perfection and operating at the very limit of their capabilities.

As the sun rises over the Sarthe countryside rain begins to fall. For Jaguar this is particularly bad news. In Hans Stuck, Porsche have the best wet-weather driver anywhere in the world. What's more, the rain is slowing the pace, effectively reducing the distance that can be covered in 24 hours. Further bad news for Jaguar. In his attempt to break the Coventry challenge Stuck has been driving flat out and is now running ahead of his fuel limit. Unless the distance to be covered is reduced he will be forced to stop before the end of the race. Jaguar's advantage is being washed away by the rain. To make matters worse, another Jaguar has retired, leaving Jan Lammers in a slender lead with the remaining two Jaguars several laps adrift.

As the exhausted drivers move into the final hour the leading British car is being pressed by no fewer than nine Porsches. It will need to make two more pit stops. The Porsche in second place will need to make only one.

Two fifty p.m., Sunday, 12 June. With three laps to go Lammers's Jaguar is still in the lead, just 90 seconds ahead of the second placed car. There have been other close finishes at Le Mans but no race has been so evenly contested over its entire duration. It is as if two runners had raced each other over the distance of a marathon and finished neck and neck.

[189]

As the leading Jaguar turns into the home straight and heads past the chequered flag the British contingent in the crowd surge on to the circuit and engulf the car. Race marshals are powerless to intervene and simply flag the following cars into a safety enclosure. Jaguar has won at Le Mans for the first time in 31 years and the winning car comes to a halt in front of the pits, directly opposite the giant Jaguar advertising hoardings. Corporate forethought has paid off.

One of the first people to congratulate the Jaguar team was the Porsche team manager, Peter Falk. On the rostrum there were predictable scenes of congratulation and spilt champagne. Afterwards Sir John and his communications director, David Boole, were driven around the tented camp on the back of an open-top car. This was as much a victory for Jaguar's marketing department as it was a sporting victory for the three racing drivers. As Sir John spotted his colleagues he leant down from his perch and exchanged congratulations, a handshake for Jaguar's chief engineer, Jim Randle, a word with company secretary, Ken Edwards.

Jaguar's victory was a proud one for British style, British elegance, British engineering and British craftsmanship over Germany's Porsche, but the euphoria disguised for most of the spectators a carefully organised, painstakingly planned, very expensive victory in a corporate battle between two leading car makers. It was, of course, a victory for image and a victory for engineering, but more than anything else it was a victory for modern management techniques, professionalism and corporate work rate over amateurism and the 'make do' mentality.

When future motor racing enthusiasts look back on the late 1980s and early 1990s they will almost certainly remember it as the period when the mechanic carrying a bag of spanners finally gave way to a technician armed with a computer keypad, and when greasy overalls were exchanged for a smart tracksuit emblazoned with the manufacturer's logo and finished in the sponsor's corporate colours. Guesswork and instinct will be gone for ever, replaced by wind tunnel analysis and computer-aided design. The cars will go faster than ever, the rules will become ever more complex, the drivers will combine the brains of mathematicians with the bodies of athletes and 'building the corporate image' will be the name of the game.

When Guy Edwards first set about the task of persuading a sponsor to back Jaguar he deliberately decided to underplay the chances of success. He was aiming for a three-year contract in order to give Tom Walkinshaw a season or two in which to perfect the new Jaguar prototype sports car. He told potential sponsors the team was unlikely to win a race in 1986, the first year of the contract. It might win a single race in the second year and if Jaguar was lucky it could perhaps secure the World Championship in 1988. As for Le Mans, Edwards would only say it was a lottery. In fact in 1986 Jaguar took a creditable third place as it settled into the World Championship and in 1987 it won eight out of ten races and ran away with the championship itself. That same year Jaguar's four regular drivers filled the top four places in the World Championship drivers' listings. In 1988 Jaguar won Le Mans for the first time in 31 years. The TWR team also retained the World Championship for a second year and a Jaguar driver, Martin Brundle, headed the drivers' table.

It is difficult to overestimate what winning really means in motor racing sponsorship. It is important that the race should be close enough to be entertaining but few sponsors are ever satisfied with a creditable second place. Even the reserved Tom Walkinshaw is moved to say, 'Winning sure as hell beats getting beaten!' When Jaguar wins a race abroad sales in that country immediately peak. Within three weeks of the TWR team winning an important race in Australia, dealers had sold their allocation of cars for the next five months. Market research shows that following a Jaguar victory people who own the company's cars feel a glow of satisfaction. Of course, the racing car bears no resemblance to a production model but association with success is enough.

The key to Jaguar's racing success has been the relationship between John Egan, Tom Walkinshaw and Guy Edwards. Without Egan's vision it would have been stillborn, without Walkinshaw's will to win it would have failed and without Edwards's sponsor it would have been too expensive. At first glance they may seem three very different characters: Walkinshaw, the dour Scot who rarely uses two words when one will do; Edwards, the flamboyant ex-racing driver; Egan, the committed modern manager. But something unites them: a tenacious belief in their own judgement and the nerve to back that judgement with everything at their disposal. Of Egan, Edwards says he is 'a doer

not a talker. He understands the basic ingredients of how to be successful. He cuts the crap away.' Of Walkinshaw he says, 'Tom is utterly
professional in everything he does. He will give you a a straight evaluation if something can be done or if it can't be done. And if he says it can
be done, it will be done. You know precisely where you are with Tom.'
On his own success Edwards is particularly candid. 'I tend to go in for
projects that I really emotionally believe in. The more grand the scale
the more I am excited about them. Jaguar was grand scale, heroic in its
concept. I go for projects that excite me personally, turn me on, if you
like.'

Elkhart Lake is one of the most scenic and most spectacular racing
circuits in North America. A month after Jaguar's 1988 success at Le
Mans the prototype sports car circus had shifted continent and at
Elkhart Lake it was about to render another performance to an
expectant public, the ninth race in the IMSA Championship. While
Jaguar racing cars had been achieving unparalleled success in Europe
they were running up against a new and fearsome competitor on the
circuits of North America. The V6-powered Electramotive Nissan GTP
ZX-Turbo, to give the car its full name, was proving unbeatable and the
frustration this caused its competitors was about to explode.

Heavy rain during the pre-race practice and qualifying sessions
meant that the Nissan could not perform at its best, but the weather
brightened for the race itself and the Japanese car was soon using its
superior power advantage to good effect. The pattern of the race was
rapidly established. A Porsche and a Jaguar stormed off into first and
second place leaving Jan Lammers in another Jaguar and Geoff Brabham in the Nissan fighting for third place. Lammers was determined
that Brabham should be given no quarter, especially as his car had been
damaged on the warm-up lap when he and Brabham made contact
jostling for position. There had been some confusion over positions on
the starting grid and Lammers, the victor of Le Mans, was trying to force
Brabham out of his way. The result was that Lammers lost a rear wheel
spat and the dispute between the two drivers smouldered on into the
race itself.

The Nissan was significantly faster than the Jaguar and Brabham
pressed Lammers harder than ever. As the two frontrunners extended

their lead Lammers, in third place, doggedly refused to let Brabham pass. At every corner he hugged the inside of the bend, forcing the Nissan to the outside of the circuit. Brabham's frustration built up as he sensed the two leading cars drawing further away. They were gaining three seconds for every lap that Lammers kept Brabham in fourth place. Eventually Brabham tried to overtake Lammers on the inside, the two cars collided and they both spun out of control. Neither driver was hurt but both the Nissan and the Jaguar were damaged. The Japanese car limped into the pits where a new nose section was swiftly fitted and it resumed the chase. The Jaguar was effectively out of contention.

In normal circumstances a crash would be enough to put a prototype sports car out of a major circuit race but these were not normal circumstances and the Nissan was no ordinary car. A fortnight earlier, at Watkins Glen, Geoff Brabham had become the first driver ever to win five consecutive victories in the IMSA Championship. At Elkhart Lake he was hoping to extend that winning run. It seemed he would fail but luck was with him and as the race drew towards its close the distance between the Nissan and the leaders was dramatically reduced when another crash forced the course marshals to slow down the entire field. Brabham soon seized the lead and held on to it to score his sixth consecutive victory. Later the Nissan's remarkable winning streak would be extended to seven and then eight races before it was finally defeated by a Porsche. Nevertheless, its sudden appearance and high success rate sent shock waves through the ranks of the world's luxury car makers.

There is speculation within the motor racing industry that Jaguar would like to move up into the very top level of motor sport, Formula One Grand Prix racing, something Sir John Egan denies. But the rules of motor racing are constantly evolving and may one day force Jaguar to reconsider its place in motor sport. Having conquered the challenge of sports car racing in the 1980s, Formula One could offer a new challenge for the 1990s – but Jaguar would only take up the challenge if it stood a realistic chance of wining. The cost would be astronomic. If the company were to move up into Formula One it would need to ask Guy Edwards to find a sponsor with very substantial reserves of cash. Edwards for his part does not deny that Jaguar has made such a request.

[193]

There would be good reason for the company to have done so. After all, the American advertising industry coined the phrase 'Win on Sunday, sell on Monday,' and neither Jaguar nor its competitors would contradict that.

16

Tomorrow is another day – or is it?

THE GLOBALISATION of international finance and the deregulation of Britain's money markets has turned the City of London into a haven for corporate raiders, the adventurers who now threaten international business like pirates on the high seas. 1988 was the first year of the mega-bid. With stock markets in the doldrums; many companies in Britain and elsewhere looked relatively cheap. As the volume of share dealing came down dramatically after the crash of 1987 financial institutions began to make money by encouraging larger and larger takeover deals. There were almost a dozen UK takeover bids in 1988 worth more than £1 billion, half of them involving foreign 'investors'. The banks everywhere, of course, are on a percentage but in America the best-known corporate raiders are also household names now.

Predators talk of 'industrial logic', claiming that takeovers are essential to replace weak managements and to maximise return on capital. Critics say predators are often nothing more than asset strippers and point to the time and energy managements spend on repelling them – time and energy which could be better spent running the business efficiently. They also point to the enormous debts some companies are forced to take on in order to defeat a hostile takeover bid. 'Greenmail' – cash paid over for a predator's shareholding on condition that he drop a takeover bid – is now commonplace.

In Britain the Confederation of British Industry has been trying to persuade the government and the Bank of England to tighten up the rules on takeovers. The CBI wants to slow down the bid process, to stop speculators from making windfall gains, to introduce a greater emphasis on local factors like employment considerations and to make more difficult bids that involve vast borrowing. The CBI's concern is that the present system is unfair: Britain's companies are wide open to takeover while those in many other countries are effectively bid-proof. There is particular concern that in the run-up to 1992 and the introduction of a single market throughout the European Community, British companies are prime targets for overseas corporations wanting a foothold on the Continent. Despite the CBI's protests, the government remains unmoved. The Department of Trade and Industry points to the many acquisitions that British companies make abroad and insists there will be no change of policy.

Shortly after privatisation in 1984 Jaguar executives realised that they had about six years before the government's golden share – the share that stops any person or company owning more than 15 per cent of Jaguar's total equity – ran out. Not long in which to secure the future of the company and ensure that it was bid-proof but nonetheless they felt there were several reasons to be optimistic about their chances of remaining independent. To begin with, there is no history of hostile takeover bids in the motor industry: companies are taken over but generally by agreement between the two parties. What is more, Jaguar would not appear to be a particularly tempting target for an asset stripper: the factory and plant are good for building cars and little else, so Jaguar would have to be bought as a going concern or not at all. Then there is the price. Some Jaguar executives and City analysts talk of the share price rising to £10 a share in the event of a takeover bid. Company executives estimate that it would cost £1.5 billion to replicate the Jaguar design and manufacturing operation and another £500 million for the value of the Jaguar brand name – all of which would certainly make the company a very costly purchase. Finally, Jaguar believes it can disregard the possibility of a takeover by a non-car maker: car making is a specialised business and the Jaguar brand name has a specialised appeal, so that only other car companies will be interested in bidding.

All the same, with no indication of whether or not the government intends to allow its golden share to lapse, the possibility of a takeover remains and the Jaguar board intends to use several discouraging tactics. To begin with, executives are prepared to offer anyone who will listen a frank explanation of the company's position, and their message is clear: Jaguar does not have any significant need to borrow money, as all its capital investment needs are covered by revenue. If the company should need assistance at some point in the future it would not be slow to ask for it but in the meantime Jaguar directors believe it is best for the company to remain independent. By constant repetition of this message Jaguar hopes to create a public climate in which takeover is seen as unnecessary and in which any such approach must be interpreted as hostile. Certainly the announcement by Ford that it intended to acquire 15 per cent of Jaguar's shares was widely interpreted as marking the end of the 'phoney war'. Jaguar now hopes to create a permanent 'stand-off' in which each of the predators would prefer to control Jaguar but would settle for none of them doing so. According to David Boole, 'The last thing they want is for their rivals to get the company.'

If Jaguar's first defence tactic should fail and a hostile bid were made, the company's second tactic could be to encourage a public furore. Jaguar is currently mounting a major publicity campaign to explain why they should remain independent. Not only are journalists and City analysts being given the Jaguar line but, as David Boole explains, 'We are trying to encourage people who believe that Jaguar should remain independent to purchase equity.' The outcry against the sale of such a prestigious slice of British industrial heritage into what would almost certainly be foreign hands would be very loud indeed.

Jaguar's third option could be to persuade a friendly corporation to acquire a large but minority stake in the company, say 30 or 40 per cent of the equity. Such a move would be impossible before the golden share runs out unless the government agreed and unless shareholders voted by 75 per cent to approve changes in the company's Articles of Association. Government approval would almost certainly be forthcoming – after all, this third option would forestall an embarrassing political row in what could be election year. But the support of shareholders would be less certain. Many Jaguar shareholders are in fact hoping for a contested bid in order to make a quick profit as the share price jumps. This is a very real possibility, for if the government were to allow the golden share to lapse, some predators might see it as their only opportunity to acquire Jaguar before a large blocking shareholder made takeover impossible. The government could effectively trigger the very situation Jaguar is trying to avoid.

Part of the reason why Jaguar is such a tempting takeover target is that the company does not have a stable, long-term shareholder base. When the company was privatised, the government was keen to encourage wider share ownership and that led to a shareholders register with a large number of small holdings. Today 4 out of 5 Jaguar shareholders own 500 or fewer shares and a quarter of the company's equity is owned by 13,000 Americans. Such a profile clearly includes a large number of people who would take a relatively short-term view of the company's future and might well accept an inflated offer for their shares rather than hold on to them as a long-term investment.

While its shareholders may have short-term horizons, a luxury car maker like Jaguar inevitably plans on a much longer timescale. By contrast, German luxury car companies tend to have a much more stable, long-term shareholder base: half the shares in Mercedes-Benz, for example, are owned by just two shareholders, Deutsche Bank and an investment club.

There are three types of car company in the luxury sector – those that make around 500,000 cars a year, those that make 50,000 cars a year and those that make fewer than 5000 cars a year. Over the past few years many of the smaller, independent, specialist car makers have been taken over by large multi-nationals. In 1984 Chrysler took a minority interest in Maserati of Italy; 1986 saw Lotus snapped up by General Motors; in 1987 Aston Martin fell to Ford, and Chrysler bought Lamborghini; Ferrari is now largely owned and controlled by the Fiat Group.

The advantages to a small business of having a large, multi-national parent company would seem clear: in a rapidly changing world and a highly cyclical industry like the motor industry, a company with access to substantial reserves of cash can help it to survive the occasional period of economic downturn. It can also help it to strike a better deal on component supplies, and there are certain areas – like keeping track of legislative changes around the world – where two companies working together can avoid duplication of effort. Perhaps the most important advantage, however, involves technology. Developments in automobile technology now happen so quickly that sometimes even the multi-nationals get left behind. Consequently the support of a large car maker's research and development division can make all the difference between survival and bankruptcy. It is nevertheless true that the specialist car makers do much of the research at the leading edge of automobile development, so the large multi-nationals can, to an extent, benefit there. But the biggest advantage to the volume car firms in taking over small ones lies in the area of image-building. Through its association with Aston Martin, Ford expects to enhance its long-term image and thus to increase sales. Fiat owns Ferrari because the name is worth owning, and for General Motors the cachet of living with Lotus is something that has real value.

Each one of these luxury car makers represents a golden goose that can lay golden eggs for its owner, but the goose must be allowed to grow and prosper as an independent being – if it is placed in a pen with many other geese it will neither look nor feel very special and before long the golden eggs will cease to be.

Jaguar is not among that group of tiny manufacturers who make a handful of cars each week. It is in the next size up, making about 50,000 cars a year and behind its almost desperate desire to remain independent lies the fear of a return to the past. The spectre of British Leyland haunts the corridors of Browns Lane. The very idea of again becoming one goose among many, of becoming a small part of a large corporation, reminds workers and managers alike that they have been there once before. Michael Beasley makes the point: 'I think we'll have better standards and values as a company if we remain independent. We've seen what happens when a company like Jaguar gets sucked into a big organisation – it becomes sloppy and fat.'

Yet the Jaguar management cannot afford to be complacent or blind to the commercial possibilities offered by a takeover. David Boole says, 'We can't rule out the possibility – in the future – of needing help. It would be stupid and terribly arrogant for us to say that. I think the crunch would come if ever we thought that we could not maintain our ambitious capital expenditure and research-and-development programmes.' But for the moment, Jaguar insists, such programmes can be maintained and 'help' can be politely rejected.

Perhaps the most productive thing that Jaguar could do to forestall a takeover would be to become closely involved with another company in some sort of merger or complex joint-venture. Such an operation would almost certainly involve a high-technology co-operation deal. In the view of Jim Randle, Jaguar's director of engineering, it would be 'complicated and difficult and it's not made any easier by Jaguar's present profit circumstances'. Nonetheless, Jaguar is investigating such possibilities. In 1988, together with GKN, a major component supplier, it set up a new jointly owned company called Venture Pressings to manufacture and supply all Jaguar body panels from 1991, rather than continue the present Austin Rover contract. This new, part-owned company may offer the kind of co-operative model Jaguar could build upon to deter a takeover. If such plans ever come to fruition Randle is likely to play a central role in whatever proposals emerge. For him, the battle to keep Jaguar independent is a very personal crusade: 'I've spent the last twenty-three years trying to maintain this company's independence. The last thing I personally would want to see is the company going back to a situation where that independence is lost. I would feel that in some way I had failed . . . I feel a tremendous emotional interest in keeping the company independent.'

Any company contemplating a takeover of Jaguar Cars would do well to consider why it wanted to own the company. It would be very easy to take over Jaguar and fall into the golden goose trap by destroying its brand image almost unwittingly. If another car company were forced to pay a high price for Jaguar it would inevitably face pressure to start recouping its investment. 'The one way it could benefit immediately', explains David Boole, 'is by using the marque name to enhance the balance of its business. That is a commercially sensible thing for a car company to do because it gives instant return.' To give golden geese another name, Boole is talking about 'badge engineering', the practice of putting a desirable marque name on a less desirable car. A standard family saloon could be sold for an extra £250–£500 if it bore the name Jaguar – fine for the manufacturer of the standard volume model but disastrous for Jaguar's exclusive image. A volume car maker might also be tempted to rationalise the Jaguar sales network by selling the luxury car alongside its own standard models – fine for the sales of the volume cars but it would do nothing for Jaguar's sales. Then there is the question of research and development. A large motor corporation might be tempted to rationalise that, too, perhaps by instructing Jaguar executives to use the parent company's engine rather than develop a new one of their own. On the face of it a sensible commercial decision, but potentially disastrous for Jaguar because the whole Jaguar image is premised on the concept of a Jaguar car driven by a Jaguar engine.

As the expiry of the golden share draws closer Jaguar's biggest problem is that of profitability. By the mid 1980s Egan had succeeded in turning Jaguar into a more efficient old-fashioned company. Twenty-year-old machinery was still being used to make twenty-year-old models but at least productivity had been trebled. To turn Jaguar into a modern company Egan invested in new equipment and new products and Jaguar looked set to become a world-class car company, but then the problems began to appear. In 1987 – despite record production, record sales and record turnover – profits dropped from over £120 million to under £100 million, partly because research and development was now taking a larger slice of company income, partly because new equipment led to rising depreciation costs and also because the strengthening pound was adversely affecting profits from the US. But the City of London tends to judge a company on its short-term perform-ance, rather than its long-term plans. The fact that Jaguar had absorbed these extra costs and continued to grow was in Egan's view a major management achievement. That was not how it was perceived in the City of London and even at Browns Lane there was a recognition that the company would need to do something if it was to match its rivals. Michael Beasley explains that 'While the turnaround of Jaguar had been successful in UK terms . . . the truth was we were starting to show signs of plateauing. Certainly progress was getting more and more difficult. So you either wait for the plateau to arrive or you say, "We must act now."' Jaguar decided to act. It set up a select group of determined managers in their early thirties who, in the words of Beasley, 'had the guts to stand up and say to the board of directors, "You've got it wrong. You've got to change."'

Dr William Edwards Deming is an 89-year-old business guru who is regarded in Japan as something of a prophet; in his home country, the United States, he is less well known and his ideas are nowhere near so widely practised or understood. It is Deming who is largely credited with the transformation of the Japanese economy in the years following the Second World War from being based on low quality and mass production to reliance on high quality and low prices. His theory is essentially a very simple one: he believes that senior managers should develop and improve their company's management systems, leaving more junior managers to solve the day-to-day problems that arise in the course of running the business. Specifically, he urges senior managers to strive for *continuous* improvements within their business, to eliminate slogans and production quotas, to work closely with suppliers and to train and educate everyone who works for the company. His philosophy is called Total Quality Management and following the turnaround of Jaguar under Sir John Egan, it has played an important part at the company.

According to Egan, part of Jaguar's problem is that it is British. It operates in the British economy and 'The UK is not a world-class economy.' He sees three types of international economy. The socialist model, which he clearly rejects; the capitalist model, in which the market manages the economy and in which important industries are sometimes allowed to fail; and finally what he describes as 'the world-class economies'. He believes only three countries have really attained the status of world-class economies: the USA, Germany and Japan. The US economy is one in which incentives play a great part and which is especially good at encouraging start-up businesses: as older industries die out there is a steady stream of new industries ready to take up the slack. By contrast the German economy is based on quality engineering and an educational and training infrastructure second to none. It may not be as big as the American economy but it is just as efficient, thanks to discipline, training and organisation. The Japanese have developed managerial systems that encourage individuals to support corporate goals in a manner and with a degree of enthusiasm unheard-of elsewhere. What all three have in common is the development of sophisticated and interventionist managerial systems. Instead of allowing an unfettered market to manage change in industry and commerce, the world-class economies protect and support essential productive industries.

Egan believes that in Britain people have not paid enough attention to the manufacturing companies, that they have not been given the kind of support they would have received in other countries. He believes such companies are the power house of the economy and says, 'You can't run a world-class economy without them.' If Jaguar is threatened with a takeover bid it will trigger a national debate about the future of British industry and the kind of economy the British people want. If and when a takeover bid materialises, Egan's message to Jaguar shareholders and, by extension, to other businesses, will be a simple one. 'The company that takes you over doesn't do it for your benefit, it does it for its own.'

After a decade of Thatcherism, Egan believes that the British economy 'can't do the wide range of competent things that world-class economies can do . . . most things that the Japanese, the Germans or the United States set out to do they can do and they can do well. There are some things in this country which are almost impossible to do.' Of the three world-class alternatives, Egan believes it is Japan that offers the best role model for Britain. 'When it comes to designing behaviourally. sound managerial processes the Japanese have done a very, very good job. I think their ideas represent the kind of ideas that are probably necessary for industries like the motor industry. It was quite clear to me that the Japanese were streets ahead of everybody else in terms of their behaviourial approach to managing things and indeed their performance was so incredible that it was obvious that other people were not going to be able to compete . . . We then discovered that the culture was transferable when we saw what was going on at Washington [northeast England] with Nissan. All of the ancient problems of the car industry were being addressed.'

Egan's admiration for Japanese management techniques and his discovery that they could be adopted in Britain happened to coincide with a steady fall in Jaguar's profits. The company that had been on the edge of extinction in 1980, rescued, revitalised and then privatised in 1984, was suddenly looking vulnerable again. By 1987 Jaguar was simply not making the same kind of continuous improvements in productivity, quality and profitability that it had been making in the early 1980s.

A group of young executives at Jaguar were given the challenging task of discovering where the company was going wrong. Under the direction of the manufacturing quality manager, Kes Lodge, they travelled all over the world, seeking wisdom from a wide range of business

brains before coming to the conclusion that while Jaguar had introduced many innovative ideas, from quality circles to just-in-time
supplies delivery, each new idea had been introduced in isolation. As
Egan puts it: 'They gave us "A" for effort but clearly there was no
philosophy gathering this all together. And they said, "There is a
philosophy. It's called Total Quality Management. You've done many
of the bits and pieces of it but you should be doing all of it now." ' The
young executives recommended that Jaguar travel Deming's road and
Egan concurred. He was impressed, in part, by the fact that Ford in
America had adopted similar methods to tackle management problems
there: 'I took the view that these managerial methods seemed to be
appropriate for us and probably a life-line.'

Jaguar arranged a weekend seminar for its senior executives with
Myron Tribus, an engineer, academic and one of Deming's foremost
advocates. It was held in Toronto, the most convenient place for the
busy Tribus to meet the senior Coventry directors, and in the summer
of 1988 Jaguar began to implement the Deming philosophy, assimilat-
ing it first at board level and then gradually moving down into middle
management. Michael Beasley took charge of the programme. 'Un-
doing some of the things we had been born and bred with was quite
painful . . . for the senior managers. The more senior the more painful,'
he says.

A central theme of Deming's philosophy is that to be successful a
company needs to overcome the fear that is endemic in so much of
middle management. Pressurised from above by senior management
and froɪn below by the workforce, middle managers operate in a
climate of constant fear and tension. Deming insisted it was counter-
productive and encouraged some people to give senior managers the
sort of messages they want to hear rather than the truth, exaggerating
what is achieved and what can be achieved. Egan now acknowledges
that he has not always been given a true picture of what was being
achieved by his quality circles. 'There was seemingly more being done
than actually was being done,' he admits. Instructions would be sent
down to Jaguar's 600 middle managers, 'and they know that half these
things will create enormous damage. The trouble is they don't know
which half. So they send a lot of our instructions back saying "Yes, it's
done" when it hasn't been . . . and in many cases thank God they do,

otherwise the damage would have been even greater.' As Michael Beasley admits, 'It is true to say that I have – and I know John Egan has – shot the messenger on more than one occasion. That's not helpful because it's absolutely vital that you know what the truth is, otherwise you react to the wrong things and plan on the wrong basis.'

In its public relations and in the building of its image, the Jaguar Car Company leans heavily on the name and standing of its founder, Sir William Lyons. Every Jaguar model is supposed to have the feline 'Lyons lines': without them, it is not a Jaguar.

When Jaguar unveiled its XJ-220 sports car at the 1988 Birmingham International Motor Show the intention was simply to grab the headlines. The car was presented as the road-going version of the company's racing car, a mid-engined two-seater designed to accelerate from rest to 100 mph in just 8 seconds, powered by a 6-litre, 48-valve V12 engine with a top speed of over 200 mph. The car did not have a price tag, though informed opinion suggested that potential purchasers would need at least £250,000. But the XJ-220 was not a *real* car, at least it was not a real car in the sense that most people understand cars to be real. Jaguar did not intend that this extravagant model should be driven on the road at all, still less that the company should actually produce it in any numbers. In the argot of the motor industry it was a *concept* car, its purpose to generate publicity rather than to be a means of transport. Yet the response to Jaguar's new model was quite astonishing. Despite the company's refusal to say how much it would cost, a number of people sent Jaguar blank cheques, insisting that whatever the price they wanted to buy one.

The Jaguar super-car had begun life early in 1985 as nothing more than a design exercise for a team of Jaguar engineers working under Jim Randle. As the enterprise progressed it seemed to gather a momentum of its own, with Jaguar staff lovingly devoting their spare time to the project and company suppliers offering parts and design assistance. By early 1987 the company had spotted the design's headline-grabbing potential and decided to develop it as a concept car for the 1988 Motor Show. When the car was unveiled it dominated press coverage and, now recognising its full potential, Jaguar decided to hand the design over to Jaguar Sport Ltd, the joint venture company half-owned by Jaguar and half-owned by Tom Walkinshaw, in order to assess its commercial viability. It now seems that the super-car may go into limited production in the early 1990s.

The XJ-220 was a perfect example of a motor manufacturer 'stealing the show' with a well-timed public relations exercise, but anyone who thought the car was intended to play a major part in Jaguar's future would have been sorely mistaken. Ironically, the engineers who were working on the high-profile XJ-220 were also working on the product that *would* very largely determine Jaguar's future, but this second product was being developed in conditions of commercial secrecy unparalleled in the British motor industry. It was nothing less than a replacement for the best-known car the company had ever built: the E-type Jaguar.

A luxury sports car is the one element currently missing from the Jaguar product mix. The company builds a range of saloons – from the standard XJ-6 to the Daimler limousine as well as the XJ-S grand tourer – but it has no true sports car, and that leaves the company at a distinct disadvantage when competing for sales against companies like Porsche.

The new sports car project was codenamed 'XJ41' but is commonly referred to within the motor industry as the 'F-type' It represents, for Jaguar, the next piece in the corporate jigsaw puzzle. Over the last few years Jaguar has achieved substantial success in motor racing and that has undoubtedly helped sales, but without a sports car in its range no company can capitalise fully on its racing success. The hope is that the new XJ41 will allow Jaguar to make full use of the cachet that comes from its racing programme.

The man with responsibility for developing the XJ41 is Jim Randle. 'When I first put the ideas together for the car it was going to be a simple, high-performance, low-specification car . . . very much in the E-type image. Since that time various needs and requirements have been placed on it and as a result it has become much more highly "spec'd" and therefore much more powerful. It needed four-wheel drive and it has now become an extremely sophisticated car. So it will have all the performance – and I hope, all the charisma – of the E-type, but it will be a quite refined motor car.'

Like the rest of the Jaguar range, the new sports car will be a direct descendent of earlier models, a car with a modern look but also with the feline shape Sir William Lyons would have incorporated. When it is unveiled in the early 1990s Jaguar plans to have a basic three-car range – saloon, grand tourer and sports car – with the intention of replacing one of the three every third year, thus giving each product a life-span of about nine years.

The F-type is currently being developed at Jaguar's new engineering centre at Whitley in Coventry. Behind the high-security fences staff move from one section of the complex to another by using a computer-ised card to pass through security doors. Each card is personalised and grants the holder access to those areas he or she needs to visit; if someone tries to enter a section for which they have no authorisation, a computer notes the fact. Whitley was opened in 1988 as a purpose-built research and development facility on a 155-acre site Jaguar bought from Peugeot Talbot in 1985 for just over £4 million. Three years and £55 million of investment later, Jaguar had the most advanced auto-mobile design facility in Britain. So highly regarded is it that executives from even Mercedes-Benz have journeyed over to inspect the plant.

It is all a far cry from the almost makeshift days of 1922. Sir William Lyons has practically been canonised by his admirers yet it is easy to forget that in many ways he laid the foundations of Jaguar's slide into near-bankruptcy. He failed to introduce modern management systems, he failed to invest adequately and when he did invest it was often in poor, second-hand machinery. Given the importance that Jaguar attaches to the Lyons heritage it would be understandable if Sir John Egan were unable to acknowledge the negative side of Sir William's 50-year rule. Nothing could be further from the truth. Sir John offers no excuses: 'There was a general meanness in terms of payment to people and in terms of investment . . . They often skimped on things they really shouldn't have done . . . The cars themselves were never out-standingly reliable. On the other hand they got by – I don't think they were ever far away from the industry average.'

Inevitably comparisons are drawn between Lyons and Egan. In fact the two men are poles apart. Egan is a manager who would never dream of trying to design a car. Lyons may have been a good designer but he was an atrocious manager. Perhaps the only thing the two men had in common was a timely intuition of what the public wanted to buy. In Lyons's case it was cheap good looks, in Egan's case quality and reliability.

[207]

On Lyons's abilities as a businessman, Egan is ambivalent: 'I don't think he ever lost money when he ran the company. He was able to grow and prosper and it was an outstanding personal achievement. Some people, however, turned such outstanding personal achievements into much bigger, more balanced businesses . . . There was no reason why it shouldn't have been a much bigger company today, if there had been the willingness to allow the company to grow behind those brilliant products with a professional management.' While conceding that Lyons 'did a better job than BL' in running the company, Egan's view is that he nonetheless made some fundamental mistakes, like diversifying too widely. 'He would have been better off fully exploiting the world position that he personally was in because I think he probably was the leading designer of luxury cars in the 1950s and 1960s. I think he actually knew more about it than anybody else did. It was a pity that that wasn't exploited in creating a more solidly based company. Sir William had an unsung hero working for him called Bill Heynes, who was a good engineer with an outstanding group of two or three geniuses around him who could deliver very big packages of refinement, road-holding and power. It was a giddy mixture based upon the product. *It was never a professionally run company.* It was as though there were three or four meteors and everybody was grabbing on to the tail of each one.'

The company has changed, the market has changed. Whereas Jaguars used to be sold to one kind of buyer, whether snob or *Sweeney*, today there is no such thing as an average Jaguar owner. Each Jaguar market attracts a different type of buyer, a different mentality. Roger Putnam, Jaguar's marketing director, explains: 'We sell in Britain to the "hired guns" of large bureaucratic companies who are into the boardroom and club atmosphere. The car is very much allied to that sort of atmosphere but in Germany or the States we are dealing with something totally different. There you are looking at a man who is self-indulgent, who is making a statement about himself and what he would like other people to think about his lifestyle . . . to him Jaguar represents a style which is akin to craftsmanship – like an English shotgun – the best in the world. He is buying something that goes way beyond just a means of transport . . . He would love people to think that because he has bought a Jaguar he has acquired style and taste.'

The one thing all Jaguar buyers do have in common is that they are rich, and as the post-war baby boomers reach the peak of their careers and of their personal earning capacity it is a matter of some satisfaction to Jaguar that demographic trends mean there are now more rich people around and that the market for luxury cars is growing. But complacency would be a mistake. The car industry is in a state of constant flux and it is a highly cyclical business. Jaguar is certainly not complacent. Investment is a key priority, training is a major commitment, modern management theory is practised and statistical process control has replaced intuitive guesswork.

For almost 70 years Jaguar has symbolised the British economy. It began in a spirit of energetic enterprise and in the years leading up to the Second World War the company grew because Britain was the workshop of the world. In the years after the war it grew because Britain was going through a boom. In the 1970s Jaguar stumbled as Britain stumbled, thanks to poor industrial relations, pitiable management and lack of investment. The decade of the 1980s brought with it Mrs Thatcher and North Sea oil and Jaguar recovered as Britain recovered – but is the recovery sustainable?

The biggest change that Jaguar faces is that associated with the implementation of the single European market in 1992. That market is now as important to Jaguar as the US market. Reduction in the plethora of national technical standards and emission control regulations will be generally beneficial for the company as will VAT harmonisation across the European community, but other changes may present substantial challenges. It seems likely that 1992 will offer improved access for Japanese car companies with a European base and the fast-growing European luxury car sector is a certain target for them. On top of that, the increased competition that will inevitably follow from the single European market will lead to a downward pressure on luxury car prices. All in all, Jaguar is a company facing unpredictable trading conditions when its own future is uncertain.

The announcement by the American Ford Motor Company in September 1989 that it proposed to acquire 15 per cent of Jaguar's shares was widely construed as the prelude to a hostile takeover bid. Ford said it could help Jaguar with cash, marketing assistance and technical know-how. Jaguar said it did not need Ford's help and would seek to preserve its continued independence, planning to persuade another foreign car maker to take a large – but minority – stake in the company, thereby blocking Ford and allowing the Coventry management team to stay in control. But with or without Sir John Egan's blessing, a large slice of Jaguar's equity will now pass into foreign hands. In the argot of the City of London, Ford put Jaguar 'into play' and the battle for the company's future was on.

As Jaguar and Britain face the 1990s they must answer some difficult questions. How do a manufacturing company and a market economy live with fluctuating exchange rates? How can British industry re-double its efforts to achieve the competitive edge that German and Japanese companies have achieved? Can successful independent companies remain successful and independent, or is every British company fair game in the age of takeover terrorism? If Jaguar proves unable to solve these fundamental problems the implications both for the company and for Britain are chilling indeed.